CATE

NOMAD

George A. Custer in *Turf, Field and Farm*

NUMBER THREE

The John Fielding and Lois Lasater Maher Series

NOMAD

GEORGE A. CUSTER
IN
Turf, Field and Farm

Edited by Brian W. Dippie

University of Texas Press, Austin and London

FRONTISPIECE: Custer with the "King of the Forest," Yellow-
stone Expedition, September 1873. (Photograph by William R.
Pywell; courtesy of the Custer Battlefield Collection, National
Park Service, Department of the Interior)

Requests for permission to reproduce material
from this work should be sent to Permissions,
University of Texas Press, Box 7819,
Austin, Texas 78712.

LIBRARY OF CONGRESS CATALOGING IN PUBLICATION DATA

Custer, George Armstrong, 1839–1876.
  Nomad.
  Includes bibliographical references and index.
  1. Custer, George Armstrong, 1839–1876. 2. Indians of North
America—Great Plains—Wars—1866–1895—Sources. 3. Great
Plains—Social life and customs—Sources. 4. United States.
Army—Military life—Sources. 5. Outdoor recreation—The West—
History—Sources. 6. Generals—United States—Correspondence.
7. United States. Army—Biography. I. Dippie, Brian W. II. Turf,
field and farm. II. Title.
E467.C99A34 1980   973.8'1'0924 [B]   80-11809
ISBN 0-292-75519-8

FOR SCOTT BRIAN DIPPIE
Our Littlest Nomad

CONTENTS

ILLUSTRATIONS

INTRODUCTION

WHOM SHOULD WE BELIEVE, Robert Utley has asked, John Ford or Arthur Penn? *She Wore a Yellow Ribbon* or *Little Big Man*? Were the United States cavalry and infantry officers who served in the West in the nineteenth century stern-but-just representatives of advancing civilization, men who fought the Indians out of a sense of duty and patriotism, never personal animosity, and who, far from hating their red-skinned foes, sympathized with them in what they knew was a lost cause? Or were they bloodthirsty 'squaw-killers,' men devoid of conscience who relished action against the Indians because slaughter would pave the path to promotion and a post back "in the States" and who despised the enemy as human vermin to be exterminated for the betterment of mankind? These are the antipodal stereotypes that have come down to us through the years: the gallant, humane officer-gentleman and the callous, glory-hunting military murderer.[1]

What is most striking in reading the memoirs of the men who served in the West is how little Indian fighting they actually did. They spent most of their time at the post, absorbed in the details of military routine; expeditions or patrols into hostile country encountered few Indians and fought even fewer. Despite the impression of constant, pounding action, dramatic rescues, thrilling bugle calls, and desperate charges, on the whole campaigning was as frustrating as it was tiring, and there was more dust than glory to be had chasing after Indians for Uncle Sam. Not action, then, but monotony was the keynote of frontier duty. The post was a small town—often isolated, rife with gossip and jealousy—and there was a pressing need for diversion. Consequently, officers and enlisted men alike exercised their ingenuity in devising ways to entertain themselves. Baseball, gardening, band concerts, amateur theatricals, dances, picnics, horse races, foot races, and, invariably, the bottle all provided escapes. But for the officers in particular, field sports were the supreme pastime. When they were not writing to their superiors requesting leaves of absence, they were writing to friends, male and female (unmarried young women were assured a surfeit of attention from the corps of eligible bachelors), inviting them for a holiday at the army post. Among the enticements held out to the men, the promise of excellent hunting always topped the list. The West offered no Broadway theaters, no Delmonico's, no elegant casinos, but it did offer the antelope, the deer, and the mighty buffalo, and these were inducements that could bring a New Yorker thousands of miles eager for the chance to rough it and collect some trophies in the bargain. Whatever its other drawbacks, in short, the West was a sportsmen's paradise.[2]

Many officers were such ardent hunters and fishermen that their journals, memoirs, and articles on Indian campaigning sometimes read as though they were intended for the sportsmen's papers of the day. Their enthusiasm for a favorite fishing hole or the pleasure they took in recounting a particularly memorable hunt serve to remind us that theirs was a very natural out-of-doors lifestyle. Moreover, field sports were sanctified by tradition, especially when hounds and horses were added to the picture; they were fitting recreation for the members of an officers' corps that was then still an elite body bound by a strict code of behavior honoring the chivalric ideal. Students of nineteenth-century Southern character often speak of a cult of chivalry that flourished among the antebellum planters. It was manifested by a courtly devotion to women, a penchant for things martial (firearms, the "code duello" as a means of redressing grievances between gentlemen), a love of horses, and a fondness for the hunt, preferably to the hounds in pursuit of fox or deer. The Southerner's passion for horse racing was consistent with the cult, since "chivalry," as a historian of romanticism in the Old South has pointed out, derives from the French word *cheval*, or horse; "cavalry," it need only be added, shares a similar origin, and the cavalry officer was in his and the public's mind a legitimate nineteenth-century cavalier.[3] His profession and his pleasures mingled on the hunt. Hunting was training—in horsemanship, in marksmanship, in physical conditioning. It was a demanding pastime that honed the martial skills while providing a welcome relief from the "tiresome bill of fare" that was otherwise the soldier's lot.[4]

To the portraits of officers captured on-screen by John Ford and Arthur Penn we should add a third, then, one the officers themselves would have recognized approvingly, that of the well-bred sportsman. One thinks of Captain Frederick William Benteen of the Seventh Cavalry, a chronic grumbler by all accounts, but a man who could wax enthusiastic over the fishing he enjoyed on an Indian campaign and who might be said to have preferred catfish to trout, and trout to most people and all his fellow officers.⁵ Or of General George Crook, the despair of some of his contemporaries in 1876, who accused him of spending more time stalking bear, mountain sheep, and elk and mastering the intricacies of casting for trout than he spent stalking and mastering the Sioux.⁶ Or of George Armstrong Custer, the most celebrated and reviled of them all, frozen in a dozen photographs in his buckskin hunting outfit, with parties of dignitaries out West for a buffalo hunt, pensive in his study surrounded by the trophies he had mounted, proud beside a dead elk or behind a dead grizzly or with his ever-present hounds—ghostly shadows in most of the pictures as they gave vent to a restless vitality that they could not suppress long enough to permit a sharp exposure unless they were lolling on the ground, fatigued after an exhausting chase and still as stones. It is worth noting that Custer, who has filled both roles in the drama of America's westward expansion—gallant, humane officer-gentleman and callous, glory-hunting military murderer—favored no guise more than the one represented in these photographs, that of the experienced hunter.

The basic facts of Custer's life can be set forth without controversy, though not much else about him can be. George Armstrong Custer was born on December 5, 1839, in the small farming community of New Rumley, Ohio. He grew up in Monroe, Michigan, but was appointed from Ohio to the Military Academy at West Point in 1857. Four years later he graduated and was commissioned a second lieutenant in the Second Cavalry. By war's end he was a captain in the regular army, a brevet brigadier general and a major general in the United States volunteers; moreover, he was a popular hero, a *beau sabreur* in the always-romantic cavalry, known far and wide as the Boy General. Effective July 28, 1866, Custer was appointed lieutenant colonel of the newly formed Seventh United States Cavalry and awarded the brevet rank of major general; when he fell on the Little Big Horn a decade later, on June 25, 1876, he was still Lieutenant Colonel, Brevet Major General, George Armstrong Custer, Seventh Cavalry. Such a plain recitation of fact conceals more than it reveals, however. For besides being a spectacularly successful young officer in the Civil War, Custer was, and remains, an enormously controversial figure.

There are no easy routes to an understanding of his character. Estimations of Custer today usually turn on estimations of his performance at the Little Big Horn, and these have been as varied as the epithets applied to him—the Darling of the Gods, the Last of the Cavaliers, the Napoleon of the Plains, the Murat of the American Army, the Chief of Thieves, Glory-hunter. He has been called an Indian-hater and a butcher; he has also been called an empathetic student of the Indians whom circumstances forced him to fight. He has been depicted as a devoted son and husband, a faithful friend, a gentleman to the core, with a boisterous, fun-loving, prank-playing side that only made him the more likable. He has also been depicted as a driven, self-centered, unfeeling martinet surrounded by a clique of hand-picked sycophants who catered to his every whim, laughed at his jokes, marveled over his oft-told and well-embellished exploits, and joined his adoring wife in constantly propping up his elephantine ego. The portraits of Custer that result are so palpably one dimensional that the chore confronting every student of his life is one of constructing a believable man out of a cardboard cutout painted one side black, the other white.

The black-white images were, it should be stressed, partially fostered by Custer's own personality and his relations with his contemporaries and are thus to some extent inherent in the kinds of sources available to the student. In this respect, no event in the General's life was more significant than his marriage on February 6, 1864, to Elizabeth C. Bacon, a judge's daughter from Monroe. Elizabeth, or Libbie, Custer was the General's greatest booster, his constant companion in life and loyal defender in death. A sweet-faced young woman of twenty-one when she wed, she was a still-handsome, white-haired woman of great charm and dignity when she died a few days before her ninety-first birthday in 1933. During her long years as General Custer's widow, she filled the void left by his passing by writing three volumes of reminiscences of their life together in the West.[7] They permitted her to relive the past while earning an income and keeping the Custer name before the public as she wanted it remembered. Long before her death she had become the guardian of an American legend she had helped create. Criticism of Custer's tactics abounded in the press immediately after the battle and periodically resurfaced during Mrs. Custer's lifetime. But it was always muted by her presence, and because she outlived most of the General's would-be critics the field was hers and the Custer reputation secure. No student of Custer today can neglect the legacy left by Mrs. Custer's writings. She saw her husband as a perfect hero and, along with Custer's first biographer (and her virtual collaborator), Frederick Whittaker, shaped the image most Americans would accept for over half a century.[8]

But within a year of Elizabeth Custer's death the detractors took the field. In 1934 Frederic F. van de Water published a life of Custer that depicted him as an immature, obsessed, and shallow glory-hunter. Iconoclasm was the vogue in Depression America, and Van de Water's portrait won acceptance, becoming so entrenched in the public's mind that by 1970 the Custer of the movie *Little Big Man* was simply a cartoon villain without a trace of humanity, let alone heroism, remaining.[9] Such caricatures aside, the reversal in Custer's posthumous fortunes since the 1930's has not been entirely a matter of kicking the dead lion now that the lioness was gone as well. Documentary material published in the last quarter-century plays havoc with Custer's boy-gallant reputation, while research into neglected areas of his career has shed considerable light on a personality for too long examined principally in relationship to his final campaign. One cannot help feeling that somewhere between the Last of the Cavaliers and the Glory-hunter there is a man waiting to be discovered. But the disputatious nature of almost all writing on Custer continues to cast an obscuring shadow.

Even when the subject would seem to be the relatively innocuous one of Custer's activities as a sportsman, the problem of striking a balance remains. A newspaper correspondent who accompanied the Seventh Cavalry on its exploring expedition into the Black Hills in 1874 described General Custer as "a great man—a noble man" and, rarer still, "a soldier that neither drinks, smokes, nor swears. But what, some one will ask, are his vices? His soldiers will tell you he has none, unless an almost inordinate love for the higher brute creation may be called such, for General Custer has the best dogs and the best horses he can procure within the limits of search. His leash of hounds is probably as large and well-bred as any in the country, and his own and the horses of his regiment, the Seventh Cavalry, are famous all over the States, while he has the reputation of being the best sportsman and the most accurate shot in the army." [10]

In contrast, Luther North, an experienced plainsman who accompanied the same expedition in a scientific capacity, recalled Custer's fondness for relating his hunting exploits but saw little confirmatory evidence:

> Custer was quite sociable and did a good deal of talking. He was a very enthusiastic hunter, and was always telling of the good shooting he had done. He had along a pack of Scotch stag hounds, and nearly every day there would be a chase after jack rabbits or antelope, and though they frequently caught the jack rabbits, I never saw them catch an antelope. While General Custer was always telling of the great shots he made each day that he hunted, he didn't seem to care much about hearing of any one else doing good shooting.
>
> One day Mr. [George Bird] Grinnell and myself were hunting off to the right of the command. We were perhaps a mile away and up the side of a big hill, when three blacktail deer that were frightened by the command came running up the hill toward where we were. We got off our horses and when they ran past us about one hundred yards away, I killed them all with three shots.
>
> Mr. Grinnell thought it was quite wonderful shooting, and when we got to camp he took the saddle of one of the deer and carried it over to the general's tent. When he gave it to him he said, "Capt. North did some very good shooting, he killed three running deers with three shots."
>
> The general said, "Huh, I found two more horned toads today," and that was his only comment on the shooting. [11]

Even when the subject was hunting, Custer managed to divide his contemporaries. The result is two opposing images: noble sportsman versus petulant spoilsport.

Besides being an avid hunter, Custer was a writer, and he left behind a record in print of some of his most memorable days in the field after Indians and game. His only book, *My Life on the Plains; or, Personal Experiences with Indians* (1874), originally appeared in twelve successive numbers of *The Galaxy* magazine in 1872.[12] But it was not his first venture into writing for a general audience. Between 1867 and 1875, under the apt pseudonym "Nomad," he contributed fifteen letters to a New York–based sportsman's journal, *Turf, Field and Farm*.[13] Until recently, they were almost unknown. Custer's biographers have alluded to the Nomad letters, but the best of the lot, Jay Monaghan, was obviously unfamiliar with them when he wrote that they appeared "in *Turf*, in *Field and Farm*, and in *Forest and Stream*."[14] They first became readily accessible to serious researchers with the microfilming of the E. B. Custer Collection at the Custer Battlefield National Monument in 1971; seven years later John M. Carroll prepared a typescript edition, *Nomad: Custer in Turf, Field and Farm*, that brought them all together, belatedly redeeming a promise Custer had made at the end of *My Life on the Plains*:

Many of my friends have expressed surprise that I have not included in "Life on the Plains" some of the hunting scenes and adventures which have formed a part of my experience; but I feared the introduction of this new feature, although probably the pleasantest and in many respects most interesting of my recollections of border life, might prolong the series of articles far beyond the length originally assigned to them. I hope, however, at an early day to relate some of my experiences with the large game so abundant on the plains, and in this way fill up a blank in these articles which my friends who are lovers of sport have not failed to observe.[15]

The collected Nomad letters at last fill the blank, and while the resulting volume is undeniably a potpourri, it is unified by Custer's abiding love for hunting, horses, and hounds.

There is an important exception to this statement. When Custer began contributing to *Turf, Field and Farm* in 1867, he departed from sporting topics to devote three full letters (#3–#5) to the Indian expedition he had accompanied earlier that year. They anticipate several chapters of *My Life on the Plains*, but there are significant discrepancies between the two versions. I have taken particular notice of these in my annotations because I think they raise larger and more serious questions about the overall reliability of Custer's writings. While aware of its biases, historians have been too much inclined to cite *My Life on the Plains* uncritically. It was written close to the events described and thus is presumed to be accurate in its details. In fact, Custer's reminiscences—and, for that matter, Mrs. Custer's, too—*are* full of interest and *do* present a reasonably faithful picture of the incidents discussed. But they are also full of small factual lapses, for the most part unimportant, that sometimes add up to fundamental variations in emphasis or interpretation. This is particularly evident when one traces the evolution of a tale from its origin in one of General Custer's letters to his wife through its successive transformations in a Nomad letter and then in *My Life on the Plains* or in one of Elizabeth Custer's volumes of reminiscences.

The process is a perfectly natural one, but the historian is reminded that the warning *caveat emptor* is equally applicable when it comes to "buying" any one of the Custers' versions of events—and this can be asserted on no better authority than Elizabeth Custer herself. In the close confines of the garrison, where associations were limited and social life somewhat incestuous, she wrote, "We all had much patience in listening to what must necessarily be 'twice-told tales,' for it would take the author of 'The Arabian Nights' to supply fresh anecdotes for people who had been so many years together. These stories usually varied somewhat from time to time, and the more Munchausen-like they became the more attentive was the audience." Added to this was the West itself, where people "live an intense, exaggerated sort of existence, and nothing tame attracts them. In order to compel a listener, I myself fell into the habit of adding a cipher or two to stories that had been first told in the States with moderate numbers." [16]

This disarming bit of candor should forewarn the reader that occasionally the truth must be stretched for the sake of the story. If, in his Nomad letters and elsewhere, Custer claimed a more unerring eye than he actually possessed, if he remembered the hits and forgot the misses and added a few yards to the distance traveled by a well-aimed shot, if he thought his horses were the fastest, his hounds the most perseverant, his hunting tallies the largest and most varied, his firearms the best, surely these are pardonable faults in the realm of the sportsman where fishermen live by the one that got away, hunters create epic sagas out of a brace of mallards or a slain deer, and honorable tradition permits an extra "cipher or two." Custer's letters to *Turf, Field and Farm* were not holy gospel, but they were well received by a like-minded readership who could only relish Nomad's challenge to equal his score after a summer's hunting and who would be happy, in stating their cases, to "hold up their right hands" as he asked them to.

The element of invention in Custer's writings brings up another point that needs stressing: they were *literary* works, meant to entertain, that employed such devices as hyperbole, punning, drollery, extended conceits, conversational interludes, sarcasm, and rhetorical questions. They were also freely spiced with literary quotations and allusions, suggesting a man who was, as a contemporary said, a "great reader." Custer was aware that his education was in some respects deficient and "betrayed the keenest desire for knowledge and cultivation." [17] He disliked most popular fiction and "rarely read novels," according to his wife. [18] He did, however, clearly read the periodicals of the day, including the sportsmen's journals. He was fond of works of history and, judging from a partial list of the volumes in his library and the many passages he quoted, had a real love for poetry.[19] The Nomad letters reflect his tastes, and in my notes I have made an effort to trace Custer's literary allusions where possible as an indication of his range of reading and an insight into a neglected aspect of his character. It also seems to me that Custer's literary pretensions help account for some of the exaggerations and departures from fact that led Captain Benteen to dub his book "My Lie on the Plains" and repeatedly advise that it be taken "cum granum sales," for even Benteen conceded that it was "readable enough, but to one who was along through the whole series of years which it covers, the falsity of much of it is as glaring as the sun at noonday."[20] Perhaps had Custer been a less ambitious author, his prose would have been less ornate and more factually precise.

Viewing his work in terms of its literary qualities—and intentions—a final question arises: Why did Custer write? One answer seems obvious. For him, as for many other frontier officers, writing was an escape from boredom. A few were creative writers—poets and novelists; more were historians, scientists, field correspondents for newspapers, and dedicated controversialists. They contributed technical articles to the military journals, wrote essays and books on topics of current interest (a favorite was the Indian Question), and recorded their Western experiences for posterity. Custer may not have been a sterling student at West Point, but he had never stopped trying to improve. While other officers killed the tedium of garrison life by peering at the world through the bottom of a bottle, the abstemious Custer filled in idle periods busily studying and scribbling away at his desk. (Even here controversy intrudes, though the Custers were mostly amused by it: rumor had it that Elizabeth Custer actually authored the articles that appeared above his name.)[21] Custer wrote, then, to avoid the temptations that beset—and destroyed—so many fellow officers on the frontier and to make productive what would otherwise be wasted time. He wrote to preserve his version of events and to point out his role in them, to supplement his income once he learned *The Galaxy* would compensate him for his contributions,[22] to keep his name before the public, and to associate himself with the world of arts that he venerated. On his frequent trips East, the Boy General spent much of his time with actors and actresses, poets and journalists, sculptors and painters. He liked their company, admired their talents, and no doubt fit in nicely as a considerable celebrity in his own right who, out of his familiar element, shone all the brighter. Each time *The Galaxy* carried one of his articles or Nomad made an appearance in *Turf, Field and Farm*, Custer's reputation appreciated accordingly. He was not only a distinguished soldier, he was also a man of letters, and this much is certain: onerous as he found writing to be, and pressing as the deadlines were, for him the rewards always outweighed the drawbacks. His wife gave him constant encouragement, and even after a long day's ride on his last campaign he could be found holed up in his tent at night, notes in hand, laboring over the next installment of his Civil War memoirs for *The Galaxy*.[23]

Fourteen years after Custer died, Silas Farmer's compendious *History of Detroit and Wayne County and Early Michigan* listed him as a "visiting author" because *My Life on the Plains* "entitles him to an author's place."[24] It was a simple tribute but one he would have savored.

In preparing this edition of the Nomad letters I have used the John Carroll typescript, carefully checked against the originals in his collection for accuracy. The texts offered here are exact with two exceptions: obvious typographical errors have been corrected (period spellings like "pappoose," capitalization, personal quirks in diction and punctuation have not); and the letters have been paragraphed, something done haphazardly, when at all, in their original publication.

John Carroll initiated the Nomad project with the University of Texas Press and has remained involved in it throughout. He is responsible for procuring the book's illustrations, including the drawings by Ernest Lisle Reedstrom, and has offered an extensive commentary on my notes. I am also grateful to Archer H. Mayor, formerly of the University of Texas Press, and Donald Davis, who provided me with information on Kirkland C. Barker. The staff of the Interlibrary Loan Service at the University of Victoria were as efficient as always, and I wish to thank them as well as the many scholars whose works, cited in my notes, have made my own work possible, especially the members of the Little Big Horn Associates, whose *Research Review* proves increasingly indispensable. My greatest debt is to my friends and colleagues in Victoria, my wife, Donna, and our two children, Blake and Scott, who put up with me while I followed Nomad on his wanderings.

NOMAD

George A. Custer in *Turf, Field and Farm*

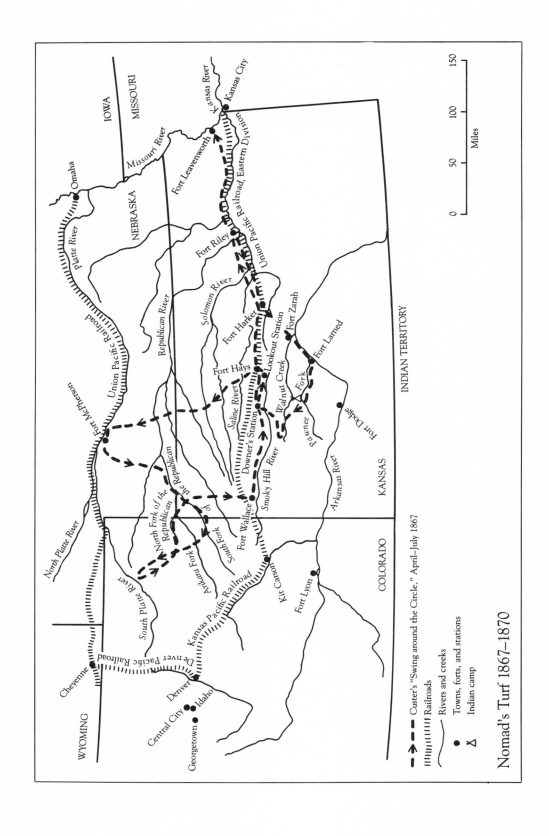

Nomad's Turf 1867–1870

Custer's "Swing around the Circle," April–July 1867
Railroads
Rivers and creeks
Towns, forts, and stations
Indian camp

Miles
0   50   100   150

WYOMING
Cheyenne
NEBRASKA
IOWA
MISSOURI
Omaha
Platte River
Missouri River
Union Pacific Railroad
North Platte River
North Fork of the Republican
Republican River
Solomon River
Fort McPherson
Fort Riley
Fort Leavenworth
Kansas River
Kansas City
Union Pacific Railroad, Eastern Division
Fort Harker
Fort Hays
Saline River
Downer's Station
Smoky Hill River
Fort Wallace
South Fork
Arikara Fork
the Republican
South Platte River
Kansas Pacific Railroad
Denver Pacific Railroad
Denver
Central City
Georgetown
Idaho
COLORADO
Kit Carson
Fort Lyon
Arkansas River
Fort Dodge
Fort Larned
Pawnee Fork
Walnut Creek
Fort Zarah
Lookout Station
KANSAS
INDIAN TERRITORY

I

KANSAS, 1867

"This life is new to most of us" [1]

GEORGE A. CUSTER began writing his Nomad letters to *Turf, Field and Farm* under peculiarly trying circumstances and with a hefty ax to grind. A popular hero in the Civil War, with a spectacular record and a rank to match, the Boy General had to face a comedown when he was returned from his rank of major general in the volunteers to his regular army rank of captain on January 31, 1866. But he landed on his feet, everything considered, and joined the newly formed Seventh Cavalry at Fort Riley, Kansas, in October 1866 as its lieutenant colonel and second in command of the regiment. Custer had been stationed in Texas on postwar Reconstruction duty for six months but now would have his first taste of Indian compaigning in the West. It came in March 1867, when he had the "fortune or misfortune (?)" of leading the Seventh on General Winfield Scott Hancock's 1,400-man expedition to cow the southern plains tribes and reduce them to docility. [2]

Throughout the winter of 1866–67 Westerners had been clamoring for some decisive action on the part of the government to stop the incessant Indian raiding and, more ominous, the massive outbreak predicted for the spring. The papers were full of rumors of an impending Indian war. Though a writer for the *Nation* in mid-January dismissed "as apocryphal the story of 'twelve tribes' coalescing for the winter's campaign," he did "credit a somewhat general rising among the Sioux and Cheyennes." The Western press never aspired to such equanimity where Indians were concerned, and newspapers from Montana to Kansas filled their columns with unconfirmed reports of grisly massacres and desperate sieges. [3] Scenting the whiff of hysteria off the plains, and faced with the need to protect the stage routes and the railroads then stretching westward against scattered depredations, the army decided to take the initiative. But its brass found themselves constrained by the divided jurisdiction over Indian affairs created in 1849 when the Indian Bureau was transferred from the War Department to the new Department of the Interior. This "deprives us of a legal right to control them and prevents our adopting preventive measures," William T. Sherman, commander of the Military Division of the Missouri, advised his department commander Hancock on March 14, 1867.[4] Moreover, Western fears aside, the national mood in 1867 was set against war, and Congress was inclined to try negotiating a peace with the restive tribes as the more honorable and less expensive solution to the Indian problem on the plains. Consequently, Hancock's expedition became a show of force intended to overawe the warriors rather than to punish them, as the generals recommended.

With its objectives somewhat muddled at the outset, the expedition's success was never very likely. One officer in the Seventh Cavalry professed himself baffled as to the purpose of the whole operation, though he had a few suspicions of his own: "I have no idea where we are going! . . . For my part, I am unable to arrive at any fair conclusion as to the real object of the expedition, and am half inclined to believe that General Hancock wishes to go on a reconnoissance through his Department, visit the Indian tribes, and the Rocky Mountains, and hunt buffalo, on a big scale, and so has hit upon this plan of doing it!"[5] Hancock went on the record many times as to what he hoped to accomplish, but none of his formal statements was clearer than what he said in an informal letter he wrote on March 10 inviting artist-reporter Theodore R. Davis to accompany the expedition:

I propose going in the direction of the Arkansas and Smoky Hill, with 1,200 men—possibly a few hundred more. I had intended to redress some outrages but the late action of Congress has been such that I shall now go for the purpose simply of displaying some *sufficient* force. To show the Indians that we are now ready for peace or war.—Leaving to the Indian Bureau the duty of investigating the facts and indicating the course to be pursued in reference to outrages of past date. Our visit may prevent an outbreak. If one is intended, it may precipitate it. The Indians threaten to stop travel over the Overland and Pacific R.R. We *will* demand peaceful dispositions and also will punish aggressions or hostile acts coming under our notice. . . . I expect to be absent six weeks.[6]

Grandiose in conception and intention, Hancock's expedition raised grandiose expectations to match. When it succeeded principally in stirring up Indian anger without inflicting much of anything in the way of punishment, bitter denunciations followed and the search for a scapegoat was on. Critics charged—wildly—that the expedition had wasted $150,000 for each day it was out. Far more serious, it had precipitated what might prove to be a general, and infinitely more costly, war on the plains. Who should shoulder the blame for what most everyone agreed had been a disappointing performance by the army?

Custer, new to the business of Indian campaigning in 1867, had much to learn and found his first spring and summer in Kansas a hard schooling. With a command plagued by supply problems and depleted by desertions, he rode across hundreds of barren miles over a four-month period, wore his men and his horses down to a nub chasing after an elusive foe, endured countless frustrations and the personal deprivation of being separated from a wife he adored, never really fought any Indians, and ended up, on July 21, in arrest at Fort Harker, Kansas. There is no doubt that he had spent much of his time in the field that spring and summer fretting over his wife's safety and consumed by the desire to be with her. Lonely and depressed, on May 2 he wrote to her, "I almost feel tempted to desert and fly to you."[7] His longing had not eased as the summer wore on, and on July 15, with an escort of four officers and seventy-two men, Custer had left his command at Fort Wallace, the westernmost in the string of posts along the Smoky Hill road in Kansas, and set off at a punishing pace to effect, as events proved, a reunion with his wife at Fort Riley, some 275 miles to the east. Though Custer justified his unwise foray on military grounds, he was charged by his superior, Colonel Andrew J. Smith, with absence without leave from his command and conduct prejudicial to good order and military discipline. The specifications under the second charge were that he had employed soldiers, horses, and, for part of the trip, government ambulances and mules on unauthorized private business and that furthermore, in his hurry, he had not bothered to pursue a party of hostile warriors or recover the bodies of the two troopers from his detachment they were presumed to have killed. A disgruntled officer in the Seventh filed additional charges stemming from an incident during the campaigning earlier in July when Custer, incensed by a spate of desertions, had ordered a group of troopers who were making off in broad daylight ridden down and shot. Three of the thirteen deserters were wounded, one fatally, and Custer made a public display of denying them medical aid when they were brought back to the command.[8]

For the twenty-seven–year–old Boy General, used to adulation and success in the far grander theater of the Civil War, these charges marked an ignominious end to an inauspicious introduction to Indian fighting. Three weeks after Custer's arrest General Hancock, asked during an official inquiry whether the cavalry had "stood the fatigue well" on his expedition and subsequently, blandly responded, "Not well, but it is owning to improper use." Then, without naming names, he fingered Custer for the blame: "The animals were driven to death without any purpose and without sufficient forage. I have known officers to travel 150 miles in fifty-four hours with 75 horses [a reference to the last stage of Custer's push to Fort Hays en route to his wife at Fort Riley].

An officer now makes charges for many such abuses of cavalry horses."[9] Already stung and humiliated by his arrest, Custer, who persisted in seeing Hancock rather than Smith as the agent behind his "misfortune," was not about to sit back quietly and be made the scapegoat for what he deemed his superior's failures.

Six days before his court-martial convened at Fort Leavenworth on September 15, Custer penned his first letter to *Turf, Field and Farm*. On October 11 the court issued its findings—Custer was found guilty on all specifications, with no criminality attached to the most serious. Up until then Custer had dwelt on buffalo hunting in his Nomad letters; now, taking advantage of the forum offered him by *Turf*, he dipped his pen in vitriol and between October 26 and December 15 composed three letters relating his version of the first phase of the spring expedition and placing the blame for provoking an unnecessary Indian war squarely on Hancock's shoulders. In the Nomad letters he would contribute to *Turf* over the next eight years Custer scrupulously avoided discussing his Indian campaigns, limiting himself to matters of interest to the journal's readership—horse races, race horses, hunts, hounds, and the like—and reserving his military adventure for the broader audience—and the handsome fees—that *The Galaxy* magazine offered him. In the series of articles he published in *Galaxy* in 1872 as "My Life on the Plains," he retraced the events described in the Nomad letters in much greater detail. But his later version of the 1867 expedition is not simply an enlargement of the earlier one; rather, it entails numerous factual changes, some quite major, as well as a dramatic, 180° reversal in Custer's position on Hancock's culpability in inciting an Indian war. Perhaps in five years, and remembering the criticism in the Eastern press of his own victory over the Cheyennes at the Washita in 1868, Custer had come to believe along with most of his brother officers that civilian management of Indian affairs and not the army was entirely to blame for the Indian problem. Thus, when he wrote his memoirs in 1872 he simply shifted responsibility for the Hancock expedition's failure from the army onto the Indian Bureau and, in the process, directly rebutted the charge *he himself had made in 1867* that General Hancock through inexperience and arrogance had plunged the country into a needless and expensive Indian war.

In my notes to the first five letters, particularly letters #3–#5, I have taken pains to compare the version of events that Custer offered in 1867 with the version he offered five years later in an autobiography that has become the standard source for his "life on the plains." The variations pointed out will, I think, prove instructive.

1. "On the Plains"

SEPTEMBER 9, 1867 *published September 21, 1867*

A constant reader of, as well as subscriber to, the *Turf, Field and Farm*, I have often wondered why, among your many correspondents, writing as they do from almost every country and clime, none as yet have deemed this section of Uncle Sam's domain as possessing sufficient interest to induce upon their part a visit and an account thereof. I am well aware that a trip to or across the Plains involves, in some respects, no little sacrifice upon the part of the visitor. This is particularly true where the happiness of the individual depends upon the comforts, or, more properly speaking, the luxuries of civilization. For example, he whose breakfast is unpalatable until after the perusal of the morning papers, fresh from the press, would undoubtedly be compelled to forego this acknowledged indulgence; likewise he whose evenings would be miserable if denied the opportunity of dropping in at Niblo's, and there witnessing, for the three hundred and ——th time, the Black Crook, a predominant feature of which seems to

be a display of a universal absence of wardrobe.[1]

To such person or persons my advice would be, avoid the Plains; and yet I may be writing hastily, for surely we can boast of having the Black Crook served up in the most delectable style, and as to being brought out for the three hundred and ——th time, to us this number appears insignificant. The troupe to which I refer has been before the public constantly since a period beyond which the memory of man goeth not. For fear some of your rural readers may not have heard of this celebrated company, I will state that it is known under the general title of "Lo, the poor Indian,"[2] sometimes particularized by the names of different members of the troupe, such as Sioux, Cheyenne or Comanches. This combination is purely, and in every sense of the word, a travelling one, seldom exhibiting long in one place, and then only to the most *select* audiences. The last point at which they are advertised to appear is at or near Fort Laramie; and in such high estimation are they held by the Government, which, in a legitimate way, desires to encourage and promote histrionic talent wherever found, that Lieutenant-General Sherman, General Harney, Senator Henderson, and an unlimited number of favored ones have been designated and authorized to proceed to Fort Laramie at the expense of Uncle Sam, and there, by their presence and Uncle Sam's *presents*, give eclat to the opening performance of the season.[3] The next point at which this troupe is advertised to appear is Fort Larned, Kansas, where, under the auspices of the General Government, and before the same select audience, the original play of the Black Crook will be performed; and I might add, that the preconceived opinion of most of the knowing ones is, that this, like most performances on the stage, will end with a *farce*.[4] The strongest recommendation I can give in favor of this aboriginal troupe is, that in absence or disregard of costumes, the company at Niblo's could not, to use a common expression, hold a candle to them; here we see them in the most primitive style, and in the fullest meaning of the term *au naturel*.

Without desiring to be understood as being disregardful of, or indifferent to, the tempting enjoyments and luxuries of civilized life, I cannot but believe that the pleasure in these would be greatly heightened if varied by an occasional sojourn among these prolific wilds. To the sportsman is this particularly true. Here he may find employment and gratification, let his desires be ever so boundless, and as to the list of game there is no gun but that here may find a target worthy of its calibre.

It was my fortune or misfortune (?) whichever way it is viewed, to have accompanied the Indian expedition, which early in the Spring set out from Fort Riley, Kansas, and made the circuit from that point to the Arkansas River, striking the latter near Fort Larned, Kansas; thence north to the Smoky Hill River, leaving it near Fort Hays; thence nearly due north to the Platte River, striking it thirty miles east of Fort Mc-Pherson. At the latter post a brief halt was made, during which General Sherman visited the command. After replenishing our store of supplies we moved southwest to the Republican, whose course we followed up for two days, then struck northwest to the Platte, this time reaching it upward of two hundred miles west of the point at which we first saw it. After a halt of but one day we set out upon our return to the Smoky Hill River, intending to reach it at or near Fort Wallace, which march of two hundred and eight miles was accomplished in seven days. In this "swing around the circle" I met with enough incidents to fill a small volume.[5]

To attempt to give anything like an accurate or full account of the game we encountered would be impossible. You may rest assured we were not restricted to Hobson's choice.[6] Our table fairly groaned under the load of choice game daily heaped upon it. From a buffalo steak to a broiled quail we indulged *ad libitum*. Beginning at buffalo as the largest, we had buffalo, elk, black-tail deer, antelope, turkey, geese, duck, quail and several variety of snipe. When we added to this list wolves—of at least three varieties, and with which the market was overstocked—beaver which was to be found upon almost every stream we crossed, with here and there a wild-cat or panther, it will be seen that he must have been a sportsman of most fastidious taste who failed here to find abundant and choice sport.

On one occasion, one of the party having shot a fine fat beaver just as we were going into camp, I determined to test the merits of what by many frontier epicures is pronounced a most savory dish, a broiled beaver tail, but, whether owing to a vitiated taste or lack of familiarity with such a delicacy, I failed after one fair and impartial trial to pronounce it the dainty morsel it had been represented. There was a fatty, lamp-oil taste connected with it which to my mind would be agreeable only to a Laplander, or perhaps to one of our fellow citizens residing in our newly acquired possessions, several degrees north of this latitude. [7]

If I failed, however, to become an advocate of beaver diet, I was more successful in regard to another and undoubtedly more unpopular article. If there are any of your readers who do not feel disposed to believe what I am about to relate, I can only say they have my permission to discredit it, as I certainly should do had some unknown endeavored to palm off the same story upon your humble correspondent one year ago. I had often been urged by my friend, Major-General A. J. Smith, [8] to eat or taste a broiled rattlesnake, of which there are unlimited numbers to be found daily—not broiled, of course. At first I regarded the invitation as a joke, one too, which if attempted to be carried into execution, might be fraught with serious results. But it is said we can accustom ourselves to anything. In time the idea became less repulsive; it certainly possessed the charm of rareness. I concluded to cast my prejudices and fears aside and venture upon the gastronomic experiment. Procuring, therefore, a rattlesnake, one, too, of the largest kind, I consigned him to the individual who officiated as chief of the culinary department, with directions how to prepare it for breakfast the following morning. Had I, instead, given him a deadly amount of prussic acid, with directions to prepare it for my tea, he could not have looked more horror-stricken. Thinking, no doubt, I had made some mistake in handing him the snake, and desiring to test my sincerity, he remonstrated by saying: "It is a rattlesnake!" to which I briefly replied: "I know it!" It was plain to be seen in what estimation I was then held by my friend of the kitchen. Regarding me with a look full of pity, he departed for the mess-fire, evidently regretting the misfortune which had so suddenly deprived his employer of reason. Faithful, however, to my directions, his snakeship was duly prepared for my breakfast. Impressed with the responsibility of my position, and casting all partiality aside, I set down at the table, resolved, "without fear, favor, or affection," to decide the case before me according to the evidence. As I was about to *carve* or dissect the specimen before me, I happened to cast my eyes toward the opening of my tent; there stood the cook peering at me from the outside. He watched me until satisfied by his own eyes that I had actually eaten a portion of the snake. He waited no longer, but, as if no longer doubting my insanity, left me "alone in my glory." Now for the verdict. The flesh of the rattlesnake, when cooked, is as white and delicate as that of a young quail; it readily separates from the bones, of which there are not many. The flavor to an impartial taste is most delicious—in fine, a broiled or stewed rattlesnake is a dish, which, if called by another name, would find favor in the opinion of all epicures. [9]

I have hunted foxes in Ohio, deer and turkey in Michigan, as well as in

Texas, and alligators in the bayous along Red River, but never until the past season have I enjoyed an opportunity of hunting and killing buffalo. As my later experience has proved more successful and gratifying, let me relate my first encounter with a buffalo. We had broken camp on the head waters of Walnut Creek, in the western part of Kansas, and were moving westward, wishing to have a little sport.[10] I left the column, and galloped in advance for a few miles, taking with me but one attendant, indifferently mounted. I was mounted on a fine, thorough-bred. I took with me half a dozen hounds, among them two young dogs, a present from that liberal and high-minded gentleman, Honorable K. C. Barker, of Detroit, Mich., whom I am proud to number among my warmest friends.[11] The dogs soon struck an antelope trail, and were not long in raising their game; but, after a chase of a few miles, during which I had followed the dogs so closely as to leave my attendant far behind, I called off the dogs, deeming it imprudent, on account of the Indians, to be so far from support.[12]

Just as I was turning to rejoin the column, now miles in rear, I espied on the bluffs, some two miles in advance, what seemed to me must be a buffalo. As yet I had never seen one. Giving the unknown object the benefit of a doubt, I acted precisely as if it was a buffalo, and turned my horse's head in that direction. As yet I was undiscovered or unnoticed. My horse being much blown from his recent chase, I permitted him to take a slower gait, reserving his powers for the final trial. Being hidden by a ravine, I continued to approach within less than half a mile of the buffalo, for such it proved to be, before he took the alarm. As soon as he dis-

covered me, however, he started at full run, if run it can be called. I put spurs to my steed and the race began. Whatever name is given to the gait at which a buffalo travels, it certainly requires a good horse to overhaul a buffalo at full speed, and with a half mile to "gamble upon."

Among my dogs were two grayhounds; these I encouraged in the chase, and by placing themselves in front of the buffalo managed to check him some little. A rapid pursuit of three miles brought me so close that I almost lapped my game. Drawing my pistol, a revolver of the Savage pattern, I prepared to bring down the buffalo after the most approved style, viz., a shot in the centre of the body, just in the rear of the shoulder blade. I was now neck and neck, a blanket would almost have covered buffalo, horse, and rider. I was already thinking of the triumph with which I would enter camp, carrying with me the choicest portions of *my* buffalo, for I already considered him mine; and the triumph would not be small, for this was the first buffalo of the season, and in the command there were hunters of unlimited experience, among them some half-civilized Delaware Indians, employed as guides, etc. Would I not have cause for pride to eclipse and outrival all these, and that too at their favorite sport. With these thoughts flying through my excited mind, I decreed the death of my friend with the robe. He was a splendid specimen, of the largest kind, being as tall as the horse I rode, and much heavier. I almost regretted the necessity (?) which I believed I was under to render me the cause of his death; but as the sequel will show, it would have been better to have reserved my pity for another object.

Holding my revolver at arm's length, I directed my aim at what I believed the fatal spot, my finger already pressed the trigger, another moment and the victory would be mine; "but man proposes," etc.[13] The buffalo now for the first time seemed to regard the battle as begun, and requiring something further on his part than mere running. Acting upon this thought, he determined to assume the offensive, which he did by a turn toward me so threatening as to frighten my horse from his course, and cause him to turn short to the left. So sudden was the change in direction I was almost unseated. In bringing up my pistol hand to the assistance of the bridle hand, I accidently pressed the trigger of my revolver, and discharged the bullet into my horse's neck, the ball entering about six inches in rear of the ears, and evidently penetrating the brain, and the noble animal fell dead from the leap he was then taking.[14]

It may now be asked what became of the rider, the late proprietor, in his own estimation, of the buffalo. I will answer. Describing something between a parabola and a circle, he reached mother earth by passing over the horse's head and striking ground fully ten feet from where the horse had fallen. Without attempting to analyze my thoughts at that moment, I will merely say that *buffalo* was uppermost in my mind. I expected the next moment to be gored and trampled to death. The buffalo was now within a pace or two of me; in fact in being thrown from the horse I had fallen directly in front of the buffalo. How changed were our relative positions now compared with what they were but a moment before. I was too much stunned to endeavor to rise, and yet I realized my situation. Whether the buffalo was dumbfounded by the changed aspect of affairs, and looked upon the lofty tumbling he had just wit-

nessed as a new and dangerous kind of tactics, with which he would do well not to trifle, or considered my condition then and there as being sufficiently helpless and humiliating, I know not. This I do know, and seeing it at the time, gave me inexpressible pleasure: taking one look at me, the buffalo contented himself with one threatening, scornful shake of the head, and departed, looking neither to the right or the left, leaving me in possession of the field, but in all other respects *sorely* defeated.

As hostile Indians were supposed to be in that vicinity, it may be imagined my stay on the prairie—alone, and with not a living creature in sight, except my dogs—was made as brief as possible. I had some doubt as to my location with reference to the rest of the command. I knew I had ridden several miles alone; as near as I could determine, I must have made a half circle across the route the column would take, passing from left to right. Taking my direction accordingly, I set out on foot, abandoning, of course, my saddle, bridle, etc. I had the pleasant satisfaction of knowing that if I failed to strike the command, I would be at least one hundred miles from any other civilized beings, and would have nothing before me but the almost certain prospect of being picked up by some one or other of the many bands of hostile Indians infesting that region. This consideration undoubtedly did not check my speed. After a walk of over two miles, I saw the dust of the cavalry moving toward me. Sitting down, I passed the time, until their arrival, in considering the uncertainty of all human calculations.[15]

A brief explanation followed the surprise of my friends at finding me dismounted and alone in the prairie. A party was sent after my horse-equipments, which they succeeded in finding. Mounted upon a fresh horse, I proceeded with the column until coming in sight of a considerable herd of buffalo. Several of the party proposed to "try their luck," and, notwithstanding the complete evidence I had just received regarding my own, I could not resist the temptation of another trial. This time I was successful, and killed my game. But as my letter has been unwittingly drawn to an unreasonable length, I will not weary your readers by the recital, at this time, of this, nor of many subsequent successful hunts.

2. "On the Plains"

SEPTEMBER 29, 1867 *published October 12, 1867*

In my letter of the 9th instant I gave you a description of my first effort at buffalo-hunting. Since that most unsuccessful chase I have participated in many others, all more or less gratifying, from the fact, no doubt, that, unlike the first instance, I generally came off winner. From the many grand rides I have taken in pursuit of this noble game, I am somewhat at a loss to determine what shall be the subject of this letter. I am not one of that class, who, in order to praise a particular kind of sport, find it necessary to deride all others. On the contrary, there is no legitimate species of hunting common to our country in which I have not participated, and in which I have not derived unbounded sport. Each and all have their claims to favor, and each is justly entitled to its advocates. I will admit there is something inspiring in being well mounted, and riding after a well-toned pack in pursuit of the wily, but fleet-footed Reynard. Particularly is this true when, to be "in at the death," involves the taking, *en route*, of a few formidable fences or ditches. Further than this, I will confess that the music of a well-arranged pack, when earnestly settled to their work, possesses far more enticing charms to my ear than those claimed for the latest opera. Deer-hunting, in all its various modes, has its attractions; coon-hunting, with its pleasant attendants, its merry jokes, its rich, roasting ears, confiscated probably from a neighboring field; and, last but not least, the struggle itself between the game and the dogs furnishes sport not to be scorned. I might go on adding indefinitely to this list; but to no purpose. I claim that in the way of true, manly sport, buffalo-hunting, *par excellence*, stands at the head of the list. To be a successful buffalo-hunter, there is required a combination of all the attributes necessary in other modes of hunting. First, is horsemanship; second, courage; third, skill in the use of firearms.[1]

The obstacles most to be dreaded by the horseman are the innumerable prairie-dog holes, or dens, by which the surface of the prairies is sometimes cut up for miles in extent. When it is considered that these holes, or entrances, are to be found every few yards, that their depth is from one to three feet, and the aperture is about the size of a horse's hoof, it will readily be seen that a headlong chase over such *terra incognita* would likely be attended with some danger. To steer boldly, and at the same time swiftly, in pursuit of his game, requires, under the above circumstances, both skill and courage; a deficiency of the latter quality will induce the hunter to check his speed, and, perhaps, pick his steps more carefully. This, while being the more prudent course, will certainly not place him within range of his game. He must, as it were, take his life in his hands, and, trusting to the sure feet of his steed, cast fear behind him. Again, when he has wounded and brought the buffalo to bay, his courage may again be called into requisition, for I have scarcely, if ever, encountered a more dangerous enemy than a wounded and infuriated buffalo bull, who, seeing escape fruitless, determines "to fight it out on that line." At such times neither man nor beast seems to possess any terrors for him. Of your many readers not a few, perhaps, have shared in the reckless excitement of a cavalry charge. Most, if not all, have read glowing descriptions of such exhilarating scenes. To such, I would say that, after having participated in charges of cavalry against masses of infantry, squadrons of cavalry and batteries of artillery— sometimes, too, carrying everything before us—I can compare the wild, maddening, glorious excitement of such scenes to nothing else so nearly as that to be experienced in riding boldly into a herd of buffalo, singling out,

and, after a fine run of one, two, or more miles, bringing your game to bay and despatching him.[2] It was no stranger to such emotions as I have described who first said, in speaking of his horse,

With a glancing eye and curving mane,
He neighs and champs on the bridle-rein;
One spring, and his saddled back I press,
And ours is a common happiness.
'Tis the rapture of motion! a hurrying cloud,
When the loosening winds are breathing loud—
A shaft from the painted Indian's bow—
A bird—in the pride of speed we go.
Dark thoughts that haunt me,
    where are you now?
While the cleft air gratefully cools my brow,
And the dizzy earth seems reeling by,
And nought is at rest but the arching sky;
And the tramp of my steed, so swift and strong,
Is dearer than fame and sweeter than song.
There is life in the breeze as we hasten on,
With each bound some care of earth has gone;
And the languid pulse begins to play,
And the night of my soul is turned to day.
Bound proudly, my steed,
    nor bound proudly in vain,
Since thy Master is now himself again.

But I must return to my story. In the latter part of April last we were encamped for a time upon a small tributary of the Smoky Hill River, and not far from Fort Hays.[3] Buffalo at that season had not made their appearance in that vicinity in any considerable numbers. No large herds had been seen, and parties of half a dozen or more hunters had with difficulty been able to kill half their number of buffalo in one day's hunting. Gradually a spirit of rivalry sprung up between the different officers, and it was determined this vexed question, as to who could kill the most buffalo in a single day, should be decided; whereupon the officers, numbering some eighteen or twenty, were divided into two parties, each under its chosen leader. It was agreed that one side should hunt on a certain day, the opposite party to hunt on the day following; the party killing the fewest buffalo was to provide a champagne supper for the winning side. To verify the number of buffalo killed it was required that the tongue of the animal killed must be produced. While enlisted men were permitted to accompany each party as attendants, etc., it was forbidden that they should take part in the hunt or assist in bringing down the game. My lot was cast with the party which was to hunt on the first day.[4]

Early upon the morning of that day we assembled at the rendezvous, preparatory for the start. Each member of the party present provided himself with a brace of revolvers, and some had added to these a Spencer carbine. Most of us were well mounted. Accompanying the party was a wagon and ambulance, the latter carrying our refreshments, the former intended to transport our game, or such portions of it as we chose, back to camp. Unfortunately several members of our party were prevented from attending, duties or sickness keeping them away, so that when we had mustered our entire strength there were but seven hunters, all told. This was rather disheartening to commence with, but we endeavored to console ourselves with the old saying that "a bad beginning makes a good ending." The proposed hunting ground was about fifteen miles from camp. Thither we proceeded, passing on the way numerous antelope and other smaller game. Upon nearing the desired point, we beheld in the distance what all conceded to be a small herd of buffalo. Instantly we were on the alert. Each looked to the condition of his pistols, tightened his girths, and pre-pared for the chase. By means of a field glass we could determine that the herd consisted of seven buffalo, just the number of our party. We interpreted this coincidence in our favor. "There is one for each of us," was the remark of more than one of the party. It was the unanimous opinion that it was our duty, as it was our interest, to see that not a single buffalo of those in sight should escape, and by way of rendering this conclusion more emphatic, it was added that we deserved defeat if each member of the party did not secure his buffalo. To insure success, the preliminaries were as carefully arranged as if we were about to attack a battery. To save ammunition and prevent confusion, it was decided that upon the first charge each of us, commencing with the one who rode on the extreme left, should select the buffalo which should be the object of his attack, and having made this selection, no interference by other members of the party would be received. It was an easy matter to lay down the rules by which we were to be governed, just as, prior to a great battle, are the plans perfected which are to win the victory. But, as in the latter case, it so rarely happens that a battle is fought as first planned, owing to the incidents which occur during the contest, so did we find that it is less difficult to plan than to execute. Knowing something of the peculiarities of the buffalo from first experience, we were enabled to approach to within five hundred yards of the herd before they took the alarm. The buffalo when alarmed, always runs against the wind. I never knew an exception to this rule, neither have I ever heard any reason or cause assigned. My own impression, which seems a rational explanation is, that it is a necessity. The head of the buffalo, particularly that of a bull, is covered with a dense tangled mass of hair and wool, several inches in length, and almost completely covering or hiding the eyes, the latter being quite small in proportion to the size of the buffalo. Under ordinary circumstances, the vision of the buffalo must be very much obstructed, or blinded, by his eyes being covered, but when running against the wind, the hair or wool, is blown back from his face and he is enabled to see his way without let or hinderance.[5] As soon as our game took the alarm, nothing was to be gained by delay, consequently the entire party clapped spurs to their horses and "away."

After a chase which would have done credit to steeds of better blood and condition than that of some we rode, we found ourselves within long range of the nearest of the herd. Bidding a truce to all our rules and prohibitions, we opened a regular *feu de joie* upon our fast-retiring game. In the excitement of the moment all order was forgotten, and each and every one seemed intent on securing that which was nearest, whether it conflicted with the rights of others or not. One or two of the party were now riding after buffalo for the first time in their lives. Their nerve, none of the steadiest, was now under excitement wild. It would sometimes happen that a hunter would find a buffalo between himself and some other member of the party, but acting under the rule that all shots which missed the buffalo were not to be counted, it was difficult to tell at times who was in the most danger of being shot, the buffalo or one of his pursuers. Fortunately, and through no credit or care of their own, none of the party received a shot, though many narrow escapes

were made. After a skirmish which, for rapidity of firing, would have compared favorably with the fusillade of a stampeded picked reserve, we found ourselves in possession of five of the seven buffaloes which originally constituted the herd. Two had made their escape, no doubt attributable to a faulty disposition of our forces; but, everything considered, we had cause to congratulate ourselves. We had made but one charge: it was still early in the day, and we could boast of five buffalo tongues, which in reality were the *coupons* we were to present to the umpire, and would, if sufficiently large in numbers, return us interest in the shape of a bountiful supply of champagne with the usual *et ceteras*.

After securing these evidences of our success, and giving our horses a brief rest, we proceeded to the crest of a slight eminence near by, from which our eyes were gladdened by the sight of a more extensive herd grazing upon a slope not two miles distant. We took our course accordingly with the utmost circumspection: it behooved us to husband the strength of our horses; the day was an extremely hot one, and no water within ten miles of where we then were. Our first chase had more than taken the edge off of our horses. Unfortunately the game took the alarm before we had approached within a thousand yards of it. This necessitated a long chase. The buffalo were fresh, our animals were somewhat jaded, but yet they entered into the spirit of the pursuit with all the zest imaginable. The herd became separated into smaller herds as soon as the foremost of our party overhauled it. In this way each separated from the rest, and acted independently of each other. I, to my sorrow, was mounted on what might have passed for a first-class farm-horse, but I soon discovered that buffalo-hunting was not his *forte*; the spirit was willing, but the flesh was weak. Encourage him as I might, by voice and spur, I was not long in discovering that the buffalo could outfoot him. I then adopted new tactics, remembering that the battle is not always to the strong, nor the race to the swift. I hoped, by keeping in sight of the buffalo, and occasionally crowding him, to tire him down.

This plan I adopted, and followed until it had led me some four or five miles from the point of starting. My horse already showed evident signs of distress, but his competitor in the race seemed to have no advantage in this respect. His tongue—that coveted object—was protruding several inches from his mouth. Seeing that the result of the chase hung in the balance, and that both parties were laboring under serious difficulties, the thought suggested itself to me that a compromise might readily be effected by which the contest would be ended, which was as follows: The buffalo seemed to have a greater allowance of tongue than he could well dispose of; for the transfer of this superfluity to my possession, I would gladly have withdrawn from the race, and relinquished my claims to my opponent. On we went, with heavy odds on the buffalo. I believe my plan would have resulted favorably to me had no obstructions been found on the track. As it was, we came to one of those abrupt ravines, or gullies, which was almost impassable. The buffalo rolled down one bank, and waddled or climbed up the other. In doing so, however, I was able to get within pistol range, and delivered two or three shots as he rose the opposite bank, the only

effect of which seemed to be to accelerate his speed. After all, must I lose my buffalo tongue, to say nothing of its present owner? So it seemed. I determined to make one more desperate effort, believing the buffalo was on his last legs. To this end I endeavored to take my horse over the ravine. Here he failed, and in endeavoring to regain his lost footing suffered a severe sprain in the loins, which completely disabled him from all further participation in the hunt.[6]

My attendant soon after joining me, I procured another horse and set out to rejoin the rest of the party, some of whom were still in pursuit of their game. The herd was now very much broken. I met two very fine bulls as I was returning, and being mounted on an experienced hunter I gave chase, and was soon alongside.[7] My horse, anticipating what was required of him, needed but little attention from me. I concluded to discard the use of my revolvers and trust to my Spencer carbine. Letting the reins fall on my horse's neck, I used both hands in taking as deliberate aim as could be taken going at that breakneck speed. Two well-directed shots had been fired, already the speed of the buffalo was diminishing, and the blood rushing from his mouth and nose told me my aim had reached a vital part. Further pursuit was unnecessary. Checking my horse, I soon had the satisfaction of seeing the bull halt, then reel and stagger to the ground. Knowing the danger of approaching too hastily, I waited until assured he was harmless, when I dismounted and secured the tongue, leaving to the wolves or Indians the lion's share.

Rejoining the party, it was found that we had added six tongues to the five already procured. Our spirits rose proportionally, and we agreed to a cessation of hostilities until we had refreshed the inner man and baited our horses. This being concluded to our satisfaction, it was decided to make one more run, then strike for camp, now some twenty miles distant. Our wishes were soon gratified; a small herd was soon discovered and the entire party gave chase. Our combined efforts soon added another tongue to our list, making twelve. With the exception of one partriarchal-looking bull, the remainder of the herd made good their escape. This one, however, seemed determined either to sneer at our attack or to sacrifice himself to insure the safety of his followers. Be this as it may, our undivided attention was turned toward him. Seven to one was certainly heavy odds, but our adversary seemed confident as he awaited our approach. The first person to arrive within range delivered a shot from his revolver, which, striking the buffalo in the flank, produced no other effect than to cause the latter to give a violent kick as if stung by an ordinary fly. Others of the party, riding up, fired, with little deliberation in their aim, feeling assured that the odds would win. Talk about your Spanish bull fights. If the Spanish bull is more terrible or bold than an enraged buffalo bull, I can say, "from the crafts and assaults" of all such, "deliver us." Manfully did the old hero struggle for the mastery. Time after time did he charge his foes, each time to drive one before him; but, unfortunately for him, the other six improved this opportunity to get near enough to empty their pistols in his side. A pistol shot fired against the tough hide of a buffalo, will, nine times out of ten, produce no other effect than to infuriate him, and

woe unto the luckless horse or hunter who allows himself to be overtaken in one of these mad charges. The victory seemed decidedly in favor of the buffalo, until in one of his desperate attacks, and when assaulted by all but one of his opponents, the Doctor, who was one of our party, cried out in his excited manner—"Shoot him with a carbine," "shoot him with a carbine."[8] Acting upon this wise suggestion, a well-directed shot from one of the party ended the contest in our favor, and added one more tongue to our trophies, making in all thirteen tongues, or nearly two to each of the party.[9]

We felt satisfied with the result. It now remained to keep it a secret from the opposing side until their return from their hunt, otherwise they would know exactly how many they required to win, and might be stimulated to greater exertion than they otherwise would. They were likely to muster a stronger force than we had been able to turn out: this might make an important difference. We reached camp about sundown, and were at once besieged with questions from the opposite party. To all these we returned evasive replies, and endeavored to appear somewhat disappointed. One of our attendants gave out the impression that we had obtained *nine* tongues. The story was swallowed as true, and ten was decided to be the number which would secure the victory.[10]

At sunrise on the following morning, our opponents numbered nine in all, and provided with extra horses, set out for the hunting ground.[11] During those seasons of the year when the plains are covered with buffalo, and when the latter are so fat as to be unable to run fast, it is an easy matter to ride into a herd and bring down or disable an unlimited number, but at the time of which I write, it was different. The game was extremely scarce, and that to be found was in its best condition for running.[12] Of the incidents of the second day's hunt, I know nothing. The party returned to camp in detachments of two and three, the last not reaching camp until midnight. When all were assembled, the two parties, accompanied by the umpire, proceeded to the tent where the tongues were to be formally presented and counted. The tones and manners of our opponents were extremely confident, and without waiting for official announcement of the result of the first day's hunt, we were informed that *eleven* tongues had been brought back in against our *nine*. But when the umpire announced that the party of the first day had thirteen tongues to oppose to eleven claimed by their opponents, there was an elongation of the countenances of the defeated nine, which contrasted strongly with the confident manner of a few moments previous.

All were satisfied. A caterer was sent to St. Louis who returned with the wines, fruit and confectionary, which added to our varied supply of game, not excepting the twenty-four tongues, the result of the hunt, furnished as bountiful and inviting an entertainment as has probably ever been served up west of St. Louis. Toasts were proposed, speeches made, songs sung, and stories told, until the small hours of the morning warned us to seek repose in the arms of Morpheus.[13]

3. "On the Plains"

OCTOBER 26, 1867 *published November 9, 1867*

A perusal of the daily journals, containing correspondents accompanying the Indian Peace Commission, vividly recalls to my mind some of the scenes and incidents which are now being discussed by the Peace Commissioners and the Indian chiefs as subjects for settlement between the Government and Indian tribes of the Plains. The incidents to which I refer—some of them, at least —are of quite recent occurrence. It was in the early months of last Spring that an expedition of considerable magnitude was fitted out at Forts Leavenworth, Riley, and Harker, under the personal command of Major-General Winfield Scott Hancock, whose ability and prowess, as exhibited during "the late unpleasantness," needs no word of commendation from me; but, however successful this distinguished officer may have proven himself when combatting a civilized foe, his experience the past year on the Plains has shown him that in order to outwit or circumvent the wily red man he has much to learn.[1]

This remark is not made in disparagement of any officer, but is intended to prove that the Indian warfare is a distinct and separate species of hostilities, requiring different talent, different *materiel*, as well as *personnel*, and different rules of conduct. I do not propose, however, to discuss our Indian difficulties, nor the best manner of disposing of them. What I proposed doing, when commencing this letter, was, to relate some of the events connected with this much-vexed question, and which fell under my personal observation.

The object of the expedition referred to was to effect some understanding with the tribes roaming between the Platte and Arkansas rivers, in regard to their attitude toward the Government. Many depredations had been recently committed along the overland routes of travel leading through this section of country. It was to ascertain who the depredators were, inflict upon them deserved punishment, and prevent the recurrence of any future outbreak that this marshalling of Uncle Sam's forces was deemed necessary. All this involved a council with the prominent chiefs. The principal tribes were the Comanches, Sioux, Kiowas, Apaches and Cheyennes. Runners were sent to the Indian villages, inviting these tribes to assemble near Fort Larned, on the Arkansas, and there discuss the point at issue. Agreeably to this invitation, the Sioux and Cheyennes assembled at Pawnee Fork, about twenty miles from Fort Larned. The Comanches and Kiowas were unwilling to move their families and lodges so far from their Winter homes, owing to the inclemency of the season and the poor condition of their ponies. They, therefore, halted near Fort Dodge, about fifty miles west of Fort Larned, and there awaited the coming of the expedition.

Most of your readers have probably heard of the Chivington massacre, which occurred in Colorado a few years ago. The Cheyennes were the victims in this instance, and, as it is claimed, the Indians who were massacred had been assembled under promises of good treatment, peaceful intentions, and protection against violence. A suspicion still lurked in the minds of all the tribes that perhaps the same purpose actuated the whites in this instance, and that after being collected, under pretence of forming a treaty, they were to meet the fate of the Chivington victims, and be slaughtered by the troops composing the expedition.[2] So strong was this feeling of distrust that the prominent chiefs of the Sioux and Cheyennes, with a view to prevent, as far as possible, any such action on the part of General Hancock's forces, came to meet the latter at a point several miles from their village, which was then located on Pawnee Fork. The

chiefs hoped to hold the council at the point of meeting, evidently with the intention of gaining time to secure the removal of their women and children, with their lodges, in case our intentions should prove hostile.

I believe it was on the morning of the 16th of April last that the expedition, consisting of artillery, cavalry, and infantry, left its camp above Fort Larned, and set out for the Indian village, the exact whereabouts of which had not been determined.[3] Imagine our surprise, after marching but a few miles, at coming in view of about five hundred chiefs and warriors, formed in line of battle upon the open plain, about one mile in our advance. At that time nothing was known of the intentions or motives of the Indians. This display was wholly unexpected, and might betoken war or peace. To ascertain what these were, and at the same time be prepared for any emergency or stratagem, our line was formed confronting that of the Indians. The latter were formed with much more precision and regularity than one would expect. Some were on foot, but most of them were mounted upon ponies, while not a few bestrode fine American horses— the latter, most probably, captured from Uncle Sam, as they bore the distinguished mark of U.S.[4]

Soon a white flag was seen flying on the left of their line, about which some thirty or forty chiefs were assembled. The bearer of the flag, accompanied by, perhaps, half a dozen chiefs, rode to a point opposite the centre, and midway between the two lines. Halting there, he signified his desire to hold a parley with us. In response to this invitation, General Hancock, accompanied by Major-General A. J. Smith and half a dozen other of his principal officers, rode forward to hold the desired interview.[5] As the Indians could only converse in their own tongue, it was necessary to employ an interpreter, who, on this occasion, was a half-breed.[6] The trouble was soon made apparent. The Indians desired to hold the council then and there, thus preventing our troops from approaching their village, and frightening their squaws and pappooses, who, as the chiefs stated, feared another massacre. To this request General Hancock would not listen, he desired particularly that as many Indians as possible should witness our numbers, and thus be impressed with the power of the Government to punish refractory subjects.[7] This he deemed essential as the Indians had imbibed the notion that no troops could be spared from guarding the frontier posts. As the village was reported as being some ten miles further up the Pawnee Fork, no time was to be lost if we desired to reach it in season to select our camp for the night.

Very reluctantly the Indians faced toward their village, and set out in advance of us to return to it. To prove how rapid is their motion, there were, as I have stated, about five hundred Indians in sight. When both parties set out for the village, the Indians were not more than a quarter of a mile in advance: the country was open prairie, yet, notwithstanding that the cavalry marched at its most rapid pace, there was not an Indian to be seen after marching five miles.[8] They had all, both foot and mounted, so far outmarched us that we had lost sight of them; this, too, in a country where the eye could sweep the horizon for several miles. The anxiety of the Indians to reach their village in advance of us, had impelled them at such a rapid gait.

About the middle of the afternoon we came in sight of their encampment. The spot chosen was most lovely, being located upon the banks of Pawnee Fork, and in a bend of the latter, while a small tributary flowing upon the other side formed, with the main stream, an admirable barrier to the approach of an enemy. At a distance the Indian lodges closely resemble the Sibley tent, so common in our Army. In fact, it was the Indian lodge which first gave Sibley the idea of the tent bearing his name. The lodge is composed of buffalo hides, dressed on both sides, that is, tanned; and when thus prepared the buffalo hide is in all respects like the ordinary buckskin, except much heavier. In the village there were three hundred lodges, each lodge was made of from ten to twelve buffalo hides. It is generally estimated that to every lodge there are about eleven persons, warriors, squaws and pappooses. According to this estimate, which was, no doubt correct, there were over three thousand Indians in the village. Our camp was selected and pitched about a mile below that of the Indians; it was not deemed advisable to locate nearer to them, in order to prevent disturbances between the soldiers and Indians. As soon as our tents were up a few of the leading chiefs, whose names I see mentioned prominently in connection with the treaty now being formed, came to headquarters with a view to holding the council that night. This did not accord with General Hancock's ideas of display, he desired the council postponed until the following day, intending at the same time to place his large command in such a position as to be seen by all the Indians. This was with a view to intimidate them. Of this they had enough: what were mere conjectures at first, now changed to positive convictions. The white man, according to their opinion, could mean nothing but treachery. This delay and parade of large forces could only be intended to effect their annihilation. The chiefs returned to their village about dark, promising to attend the council on the morrow.[9]

In a few hours after their departure from our camp one of the interpreters who had been visiting the village returned to General Hancock with the information that the entire population of the village was leaving as rapidly as possible. In other words, they were, according to their opinions, "fleeing from the wrath to come." They certainly intended to avoid a second massacre. The commander of Uncle Sam's forces was enraged at this intelligence. Was his favorite plan to be thus thwarted? Were the laurels he was to reap from his Indian policy to prove a crown of thorns? For nearly two hours he could not believe the intelligence given him to be true. Convinced, finally, of its correctness, he assembled some of his principal subordinates to consult as to the proper course to pursue. He finally decided that the cavalry should surround the village and detain by force, all Indians who had not taken their departure. The order was given. No time to be lost; and every precaution adopted to prevent giving alarm.[10]

The cavalry, with the exception of their commander, were sleeping soundly in their tents, little dreaming of the task planned for their execution. The usual mode of assembling must be ignored, no bugle notes should carry through the air a warning of our intentions. All order and commands of preparation must be given "by word of mouth." Accordingly, the officer commanding the cavalry, having already received his instructions from General Hancock, and being mounted, rode to the tent of each of his subordinates, quietly aroused the occupants, and in a few words briefly and quietly imparted to him his orders. These were simply "mount your men as rapidly and as silently as possible; see that each man is supplied with one hundred rounds of ammunition, and take your place in column, following the ———— squadron." To those not familiar with troops, it would have been surprising to note the rapidity with which a cavalry command could thus be aroused from a sound slumber, and mounted in their saddles. The tents were left standing, in charge of a small guard. Not one of the command knew ought concerning the cause of this sudden movement, although every one at once surmised the Indians were in some way connected with it. It was now bright moonlight, and the long column of mounted men could be seen, its entire length, as it slowly defiled across the plain, in the direction of the village. A funeral procession could not have been more silent; not a sound was heard, except the tramp of the horses. That the movement was attended with no little danger all were aware, for whatever our intentions might be, our conduct would certainly justify a much less suspicious nature than that of an Indian in supposing we intended them no good.

That we should be able to surround the Indian village, and maintain control over its inmates without a fight could not be expected. The scene verged closely upon the romantic; the night, as I have stated, was bright moonlight. In the distance behind us we could still see our campfires, while at headquarters the light in the commanding general's tent burned brightly, and, by agreement, served as a guiding point in case the moon became overclouded and we should lose our bearings. In front of us, and a little to our left lay the Indian village, partly concealed by the large cottonwood trees which lined the banks of the stream. The white lodges could be plainly seen, while here and there we could catch a glimpse through the openings of the lodge-fire inside.[11]

We approached to within half a mile of the village, but failed to discover any signs of animal life which would lead us to suppose its occupants were still there, except the occasional barking and howling of the Indian-dogs, of which there seemed an abundant supply. Fearing some stratagem, the column was moved in such a manner as to describe a circle about the village as centre, with a radius of about half a mile. An officer near the rear of the column halting the rear files at every short interval, and facing them toward the centre. In this manner a complete cordon was established around the village, effectually enclosing its inmates, and preventing any escape upon their part without our knowledge. So far, so good. The excitement was becoming intense, the ominous silence which reigned undisturbed, was interpreted as indicating some wily stratagem upon the part of the red man, intended to decoy us on, and to result in our massacre. For, be it remembered, the idea of a few hundred cavalrymen surrounding over three thousand Indians, was but an enlarged instance of the Irishman who in some prominent battle marched a dozen of the enemy, as prisoners, up to his commanding officer's tent. Upon being interrogated as to how he had effected their capture, he replied, "faith, I jist sooroundid 'em."[12]

Now if the Indians were willing to be surrounded, well and good, no trouble would be occasioned by so doing. If they had objections, and would support these objections with their bows and arrows, and their breech-loading firearms, it might be a debatable question as to which party was most likely to be surrounded. As for myself I will confess to experiencing no little anxiety as to who should come off best. As to the ability of the Indians to keep us beyond rifle range of the village I have not a doubt. The ground, intersected as it was by ravines, and thickly studded with large trees, afforded an admirable place for Indian defence. The dead, unbroken silence which now reigned was becoming painful and unbearable. I really think the war-whoop of a few hundred red devils and the whiz of a few arrows, would have been a grateful relief. We waited patiently a few moments, hoping some of our tawny friends would make their appearance, and an understanding be effected. We were doomed to disappointment. But if the mountain would not go to Mohammed, Mohammed could go to the mountain.

Accordingly a party of half a dozen, including an interpreter and your correspondent, determined to reconnoitre the village more closely. We approached, mounted, slowly and cautiously. Nothing was to be seen indicating the presence of Indians except the white lodges which now stood out more plainly as we approached nearer to the village. Almost before being aware of it we had reached the border of the village. Silence reigned supreme. We were now alongside one of the lodges, a low fire could be seen within. One of the party dismounted. Is it safe to enter? was the query from all. The interpreter was directed to call in loud tones, and in the Indian tongue, to the supposed inmates of the lodges, assuring them of our peaceful intentions, and such other injunctions as would insure us a friendly reception. No response. Was ever anything so provoking? Finally, the party which had dismounted stooped down and crawled through the opening of the nearest lodge. Those of us outside were then prepared to hear mingled the cry of murder from our friends and the warwhoop of the savage. We were pleasantly disappointed; no such alarming tones fell upon our anxious ears. The first words that greeted us from the inside of the lodge were "Gone, by Jupiter." We "smelt a mice." The Indians, not so deliberate as the Arab who "folded his tent and silently stole away," had not stood upon the order of his going, but had departed, abandoning his lodges and nearly all his stock of household furniture, if such it could be called.[13]

I will not add to this already extended letter by enumerating the various articles of Indian handiwork discovered by us. There were enough trophies and curiosities to have filled all the museums and private cabinets of such articles in the country. In the way of dressed skins, there were samples of all kinds and species, from the ornamented buffalo hide to a mole skin, not excepting several human scalps, finely dressed, and tastefully (?) ornamented with beads. So great was their haste in leaving that in some lodges the kettle still hung over the fire containing the material for the evening meal. Of course, our party at once resolved itself into individual plundering committees. So quietly had the Indians stolen away that their dogs were left asleep in the lodges. Toma-

hawks, pipes, knives, bows and arrows, and, in fact, everything which constitutes an Indian's equipment, were found in abundance. Our doctor—a Philadelphian, by the way—was of our party. He being of a very inquisitive, as well as acquisitive turn of mind, rushed from one lodge to another in search of curiosities. In one lodge, which he and the half-breed interpreter entered, the camp kettle was found suspended over a good fire, while in the kettle was an abundant quantity of fresh meat, evidently being prepared for the late occupants of the tent. "How fortunate," remarked the doctor; "just the opportunity I have been longing for. I have often heard of the Indian style of cooking, but never before had an opportunity to test it." The lodge was but dimly lighted, but the Doctor was not prevented thereby from finding his way into the kettle, and from the latter to his mouth. "What a treat," as he helped himself, minus knife and fork, to the rich juicy meats before him. "Splendid," as another huge morsel disappeared before his ravenous appetite. "I wonder what kind of game this is? antelope, perhaps," addressing this remark to the half-breed. The latter helped himself, and, after tasting it with evident satisfaction, replied: "Why, Doctor, it's *dog*." Imagine the abruptness with which the doctor concluded his repast. The joke was too good to keep; it passed from mouth to mouth until all had enjoyed a hearty laugh at the unfortunate experience of the disciple of Esculapius.[14]

To close my story rather abruptly, I will add that Gen. Hancock's rage at finding himself baffled and outwitted by the Indians was so great that he ordered all the lodges and other Indian property to be collected and burned, to replace which it would require upon the part of the Indians years of hunting and labor. Some of his subordinate officers advised against this severe measure, but to no avail. With the exception of a few lodges and other trophies, selected by officers as mementoes, the entire village was burned; and this act of burning, it is claimed by the Indians and their friends, was the cause of the Indian war which has been carried on the past Summer, and which the Peace Commissioners, with General Sherman at its head, is trying to close by effecting a treaty with the tribes engaged. The Government proposes to give the Indians one hundred thousand dollars for the lodges destroyed; and this amount is but a drop in the bucket compared with the total expenses incurred by an Indian war. As most of your readers are tax-payers, they may be interested in knowing where a large proportion of this revenue is expended.[15]

4. "On the Plains"

In closing my last letter I was left in the vicinity of the deserted Indian village. The late occupants of the latter had shown themselves totally averse to trusting their families as well as themselves in the power of the white man, and as an evidence of the sincerity of this distrust they had abandoned their entire store of household goods, lodges, lodge-poles, etc., rather than encounter the supposed treachery of their hereditary enemy. To the Indian the abandonment of the lodge-poles alone was a serious and almost irreparable loss. This may seem like exaggeration to those residing in well-timbered sections of the country, where the acquiring of a few poles would be but the labor of a few moments, but "on the plains" it is different. Here one may travel for days, and in marches of hundreds of miles fail to catch sight of a bush or shrub, much less a tree; and even when timber is found, as it sometimes is, on the borders of some stream of water, it consists of low, scrubby cottonwood, or a similar species, totally unfit for any domestic purpose. The Indian requires for his lodge-poles the best material. It must combine lightness with strength; sufficiently light to be borne or transported by his pony, strong enough to support his lodge against the most violent hurricane. Most, if not all, the lodge-poles belonging to the deserted village were obtained from the base of the Rocky Mountains, hundreds of miles away, and could only be replaced, probably, by a long and tiresome journey.

As soon as the departure of the Indians was officially learned at headquarters it was determined that the cavalry should be sent in pursuit and the Indians compelled to await the arrival of the remainder of the expedition, in this manner compelling them to hold a council with us, however much their wishes or fears should incline them against such a course. It was near one o'clock in the morning when this determination was arrived at. As the pursuit might continue several days it was necessary to carry additional supplies for both man and beast, particularly for the latter, as it was too early in the season to rely entirely upon grazing. Besides, as it was impossible to follow the trail of the Indians until daylight, we had given us, by necessity, three or four hours for preparation. We found the time none too long: almost before we were aware of it the dim but increasing light in the east warned us that day was breaking, and we must away. We were ordered to carry our supplies in *wagons*, to encumber ourselves with a long train.[1]

I am of the opinion, and my opinion is justified by experience, that no cavalry in the world, marching, even in the lightest manner possible, unencumbered with baggage or supply trains, can overtake or outmarch the Western Indian, when the latter is disposed to prevent it. The white man, in addition to his own weight, must add to the burden borne by his horse, several days' rations for himself, and not unfrequently for the latter also, unless the grazing is sufficient. Besides, his clothing, blankets, and equipment far outweigh that of the red man, who in case of flight travels in the lightest marching order. The Indian, born and bred to his prairie home, accustomed to look to it for his subsistence as well as his shelter, is never at a loss for either, let him be where he may. The buffalo supplies him with food; no bread is required; his pony, like himself, a stranger to the luxuries of civilization, seeks no better food than the wild prairie grass. The white man's horse, notwithstanding his triumphs upon the turf or the road, must yield to this insignificant specimen of the equine species, when competing with him upon the broad, un-

broken prairie. Taken from his regular feed of grain, and compelled to subsist on grazing alone, he soon gives way in strength; and after a few weeks of rapid marching, a halt is rendered imperative, and it is found necessary to go to some post, where, with grain and other facilities for recuperating his lost condition, he may be restored.[2]

In a pursuit of Indians, much time is necessarily lost in following the trail. Unlike in civilized warfare, if the solecism may be allowed, there are no roads to follow, no inhabitants to question by the wayside, no "intelligent contraband" to give "reliable information" as to the whereabouts and intentions of the enemy. On the contrary there are no data to govern a pursuing party except to follow the trail as the hound follows his game, and here again the white man is compelled to acknowledge the superiority of the Indian. Trailing is peculiarly and undeniably an Indian accomplishment. This is proven by the fact that all expeditions against hostile Indians, are provided with a sufficient number of friendly Indians from half-civilized tribes who are employed exclusively as trailers. I have met many frontiersmen who claimed to possess this faculty in an equal degree with the Indian; but I have had opportunities of comparing the relative merits of the two in this respect, and am forced to give my decision in favor of the red man.

On the occasion of which I write several Delaware Indians accompanied the cavalry. Before setting out the entire pursuing force assembled near the village. As soon as the Delawares joined they were told to take the trail of the absconding tribes. As yet nothing was known or determined as to the direction taken. A half dozen of the Delawares, under the lead of a chief, at once set out to execute the order. A hunter would have been delighted to witness the business manner in which they began "their work."[3] The usual stratagems had been resorted to by the Indians to conceal their route, well knowing, perhaps, that pursuit would be made. Instead of moving off in a body, thereby leaving a plain and perceptible trail, they had evidently left in small detachments, each detachment selecting an independent route. We knew the entire body would unite at some point, but where or in what direction we did not know. Now came in play the skill and knowledge of the Delawares. Separating and acting singly, each began circling like a well-trained fox hound thrown off the scent. The trail was now almost twelve hours old; the dew had fallen since it was made. Until the direction of the flight of the Indians could be determined, the command was held in rest near the village, ready to start when desired. As hunting parties from the village had probably passed out and returned daily, it was necessary to distinguish the trail of such parties from the one sought after. After a brief delay, the Delawares announced that they had struck the proper trail, and the pursuit commenced.

The pursuers could only follow during hours of daylight; the pursued could travel during all hours. This advantage added to the twelve hours' start taken by the latter, implied a long, and, most probably, unsuccessful chase. I could not but be struck with the ease and facility with which our Indian guides followed the trail. Often I would ride at their side, and to me there were no visible signs of any living creature having preceded us; no trail was perceptible, not even a track of a pony, or moc-

casined foot could I detect. I was in doubt. Could we be on the trail? To my expressions of doubt the guides replied with confidence, and pointed out the "signs," as they termed the trail, sometimes consisting of a bent stem of grass, a crushed plant, or the slightest indentation of the earth, all of which would have been totally invisible to my unpracticed eye. To silence my oft-repeated fears that we might be following the trail of a small party of warriors, while the main body, with the women and children, had gone in another direction, the Delaware chief assured me that at the first stream we should cross, he would convince me of the correctness of his words. True enough, so long as we kept to the table lands, where the earth was hard and dry, but little impression was left by man or beast in travelling over it; when we descended into the valley and approached the banks of a stream, the ground beneath our feet was soft and pliable, readily receiving and retaining any impression given it. The truth of the Indian's remark was now made evident. However easily a trail might be concealed on the prairie highlands, here it was different, and no animal, let alone a pony with an Indian family mounted upon it, could cross the valley and stream without leaving a plain trail.

In moving from one hunting ground or encampment to another, the lodgepoles are transported by arranging them in two bundles, a half dozen in each, the bundles are then strapped together at one end by a lariat, or thong, some three or four feet long; this thong is then laid across the back of a pony, the tied ends of each bundle resting near the fore shoulder of the pony, the two bundles hanging like the shafts of a carriage, the untied ends resting upon the ground a few feet in rear of the pony. It is the ends that drag which produce the plainest trail, much plainer even that that produced by the feet of the ponies. In addition to transporting the lodge-poles, which one would imagine to constitute a sufficient load, there is not unfrequently added a squaw, and from one to three pappooses, depending entirely upon the extent of the family and the wealth of the paternal head, the latter being most usually estimated by the numbers of his ponies or buffalo robes. That a small, half-starved pony, supporting such an immense load, should outmarch a large American horse with a lighter burden seems improbable, yet such is the case.

Being assured that we were on the true course, the pursuit began in earnest; our horses were urged to quicken their pace; instead of marching in one long column, which is always more exhausting to the rear portion of the command, the column was subdivided into half a dozen smaller detachments, the head of each detachment being abreast of the others, and from one to five hundred yards to the right or left of its next neighbor. This mode was practicable in a country where fences and other civilized contrivances were not found to bar the progress in any direction. Unlike an ordinary march of cavalry, when halts are made almost hourly, to rest the men and horses, we were required to push on, only halting occasionally for brief intervals to allow the men to rearrange their saddles or blankets. Neither man nor beast was given any nourishment during the entire day. We hoped, if successful at all, to accomplish the object of our expedition within the first three days. In other words, to use the parlance of the turf, we determined to force the running

from the word go, well knowing that the proverbial wind and bottom of our competitors must win in a long race.

Early in the day we reached the point on the banks of a small stream, where the Indians had halted and prepared their breakfasts. This was encouraging, as from indubitable signs observed by our Delaware trailers the Indians had not left this point longer than four or five hours ago—a most decided gain on our part, considering that the former had almost twelve hours the start. Here was over half the race won, and with ease, but here we encountered a brief delay: although short it disheartened us not a little. The stream just referred to ran between high and abrupt banks on each side; the cavalry, as the Indians had done before them, could cross with ease at almost any point; not so the wagons. Nearly an hour was spent in discovering a practicable crossing for the train, and then the teams required doubling to haul each wagon up the opposite bank.

While searching for a crossing the Delawares had effected the capture of two Indian ponies, which were found tied to a tree some two hundred rods above our point of crossing. Why the ponies had been left, and when, and who were their owners, were matters of conjecture only. One of them was apparently the property of a chief or warrior of distinction, as attached to the saddle were found some articles of Indian finery, consisting of ornaments, feathers, a scalping or war jacket, trimmed with dressed scalps, and other articles of a similar nature. The Delawares insisted that the owner could be no other than the noted Cheyenne chief "Roman Nose," recognizing, as they claimed, the captured property as his. Of the correctness of their opinions I could not determine. Various reasons were assigned, accounting for the ponies being left as they were. Their late riders could not have been gone many minutes, as the ponies were still warm and somewhat blown. The most plausible explanation seemed to be that the owners had probably been loitering behind, had reached the point where their tribe had breakfasted, after the latter had gone, and had tied their ponies to a tree while they should proceed up the stream in search of some game, on which to make their breakfast, and we had appeared on the scene at such a time and place as prevented their regaining possession of their animals. Whatever may have been the true causes, we were encouraged in our pursuit, and interpreted the occurrence as but the probable beginning of larger, and perhaps more important captures. As the hound, from scenting a single drop of blood from the frightened and wounded deer, is spurred forward to increased energy in the pursuit, so we were in our chase, incited by this little incident to redouble our efforts and increase our speed.

With the Delawares in advance, away we went, scanning the horizon closely at each step; relying entirely upon the Delawares to keep the trail, nothing was left us to do but to follow. Our reliance upon the Delawares was not from necessity, as accompanying the expedition were several frontiersmen who had been accustomed for years to Indian warfare. Among these was the famous Wild Bill, of no little notoriety "on the plains." The opening chapter of *Harper's Monthly*, some time in the Fall of 1866, was devoted to an account of the various exploits and hair-breadth escapes of this character,

but neither he, nor any of the frontiersmen, could compete with the Delawares in taking and following a trail.[4]

As we moved along over the open prairie, no object escaped our attention; here and there in the distance were to be seen small moving bodies, which to our unpracticed vision, might or might not be Indians. Our Delaware friends, however, were not so easily deceived, and assured us that what we saw from time to time were buffalo, or sometimes wild horses. Of the latter, we saw considerable numbers, in most instances, however, at a safe distance. Upon one occasion our guides succeeded in getting close enough to bring one down by a shot from his carbine, it was an exceedingly handsome roan stallion, five or six years old and well formed, his mane and tail being both long and heavy. I could not but regret the fall of so noble an animal.

It was about sundown when we reached the headwaters of a small stream up whose course we had been marching for some hours. Our guides informed us that after leaving this stream we could not find water again for twenty miles, neither could they follow the trail after dark. Under these circumstances nothing was left to us but to encamp for the night. A halt was ordered, the horses unsaddled and picketted out to graze, accompanied by the proper guard, while bright, cheerful fires, made of "buffalo chips," were soon blazing throughout the camp, around which the soldiers were busily engaged preparing their evening meal. For the safety of the camp, pickets were posted upon all the commanding points in the vicinity. As a further precaution, the Delawares reconnoitered the country well in every direction, and pronounced the coast clear.

It might be well to remark here, as a distinguishing feature of Indian warfare, that the Indians of the plains never make a night attack. I know of no instance on record in which they ever made their attack between dark and daylight. Their favorite hour is just at dark, or at the break of day. They rely upon the first dash for success, in other words they hope to effect a surprise. If they attack at dark, it is for the reason that if unsuccessful, their enemies cannot pursue them, if they attack at daybreak, it is with the impression that, at that early hour, their adversary, either sleeping or just waking from a sound slumber, may be found off his guard, and may be easily overpowered.

That night we lay down hopeful and reliant. We had undoubtedly reduced the distance between ourselves and the object of our pursuit; it was still early in the Spring, our horses were in fine condition, had been prepared for this work, and promised to hold out for several days longer. The Indians had been forced to move a month earlier than they desired or were prepared for; their ponies were yet in a half famished condition, the result of a Winter of starvation, and the Spring grass was still too limited in quantity to have enabled them to get in proper condition. Again, we were not pursuing a war party, but two entire tribes, burdened with their families and worldly goods. In this race the odds were certainly as favorable to us as we could hope for. But I am warned by the length of this letter not to trespass upon the already taxed forbearance of your readers. In a future number I hope to continue the story of our march.

5. "On the Plains"

DECEMBER 15, 1867 *published January 4, 1868*

Contrary to my expectations when closing my last communication, weeks have been permitted to come and go, and the continuation of "the story of our march" is still unwritten. If the suspense of your readers in the meanwhile is at all commensurate with the *suspension* under which your correspondent now writes, their condition may not be an enviable one. But to imagine for one moment that such an extended effect had been produced by so slight a cause, would be acknowledging the possession of a greater amount of egotism than is consistent with the claims of modesty.[1]

To return to our camp, where my last letter left us. An hour before daylight found us astir, busily engaged in preparing for the succeeding march. Our first attentions, as in duty bound, were devoted to the proper care of our horses. While the latter were being groomed and grazed, the company and officers' mess cooks were busily engaged preparing breakfast over scores of small,

cheerful fires which burned here and there, and which were made entirely of well-seasoned "buffalo chips," the only fuel to be obtained in many portions of the Plains. There is something enlivening, if not inspiring, in witnessing the jolly, rollicking manner with which a body of cavalrymen go through the various steps of preparation for a march. First we will witness the "stables"—not that it is proposed to accommodate each horse with fifteen feet of rope, one end of which is attached to his halter, the other to an iron pin eight inches in length, driven firmly into the ground, and then dignifying these precautions against estraying and Indian stampedes by the name of "stables." On the contrary, the term in cavalry, as many of your readers no doubt are aware, applies to the feeding and grooming of the horses, rather than to the sheltering of them. Let us go to the "stables," then.

It is scarcely dawn, but all is life and bustle. The men of each company are

[33]

busy with currycomb and brush, the officers superintending this important duty here and there, seeing that idlers properly perform their work, and that all employ their time well. Occasionally they will collect in small groups for a few moments, and discuss the incidents past and prospective of their march, and not unfrequently engage in friendly banter regarding the merit or demerit of their respective companies, or, perhaps, to discuss the relative speed of their favorite horses. Usually but little conversation is permitted between the men at this hour, but the strict rules governing garrison life are sometimes ignored while on the march and greater degree of "freedom of speech" allowed. Each company has at least one character or eccentric. Of course, it would be impossible, even if desirable, to describe the peculiarities of each of these. As the work of grooming proceeds many a laughable joke is told, many a hair-breadth escape related.

Sometimes a little removed from the main body, and on the spot where the grass grows greener or more luxuriantly than others, or to give the privilege of seclusion, will be seen a soldier devoting unusual but voluntary attention to his horse. This is a case where the relation of man and horse is reversed: the former has become from his own free will the servant of the latter or, at least the condition of servitude is mutual and one by which the horse is no loser. I have met many of these characters, and the service would be the gainer if there were more such. Let the march be ever so long and tiresome, no matter the lateness of the hour at which the camp is reached, the comfort of his horse is his first study and labor. Supper for himself will not be thought of until his companion, for he is more of a companion than servant, is provided with the best that can be had. Of one thing the horse is confident—he will receive a thorough grooming even if he is compelled to lie down hungry, as the necessary implements are always at hand. As to forage, his ever-mindful attendant will see that he at least has an equal share with the others, and however honest such a man may be in other respects, he deems it no dishonesty if, to insure his faithful friend a full feed of oats, he slyly abstracts from the portion of others the desired measure of grain. It is both beautiful and interesting to witness the degree of intimacy as well as the perfect understanding which under these circumstances spring up between man and beast, and as a consequence each seems more ready and willing to gratify the wants of the other. It would be a difficult matter to convince some cavalrymen that their horses cannot comprehend the meaning of almost every common word in the English language; it is no uncommon occurrence to hear a quite extended but one-sided conversation carried on between the two, and frequently the remarks of the rider do not seem to fall wholly unheeded upon the ears of the horse.[2]

"Stables" being attended to, breakfast comes next in order, and here we find our ears confused by sounds which would not prove an indifferent parody on Babel. Almost every language has its representatives, and when each tongue becomes diluted, strengthened, or as the case may be, by a slight admixture of Anglo-Saxon, and each voice is raised at the same instant, the effect may be imagined. As it is considered the province of mankind in general, and of soldiers in particular, to grumble, the subject of diet furnishes unlimited but not unimproved material for the exercise of that prerogative. Each man appoints himself an indignation committee of one, whose duty it is considered to be to report, whenever a listener can be found, a not very difficult undertaking where so much unanimity of feeling exists. But without this feeling of fault-finding the soldier's meals are not divested of mirth and hilarity. Many a good story is told and many a mirth-provoking joke related, and if all the original "good things" said by soldiers during mess hours were collected, they would fill "Harpers' Drawer" for all time to come. There would be lacking however, in this collection, the bright sayings of that precocious child "our little three-year old" who to my certain knowledge has remained at that infantile age for upward of thirty years.[3]

A hurried breakfast is scarcely disposed of when "boots and saddles" is sounded, and a few moments suffice to complete the saddlery and mounting, the last being done after the signal "to horse" is blown. Immediately after rings out clear on the bright morning air the cheerful notes of the "advance" and away we go as the column slowly lengthens out and assumes a brisk walking pace of four and a half miles per hour. Again the Delawares are in advance, but we do not follow the trail with the same ease as of yesterday. The rapidity of our pursuit had warned the fleeing tribes to break into small bands and separate, thereby distracting our attentions and diminishing the plainness of the trail. So closely did we push our game, that the freshness of the earth disturbed by their ponies' hoofs and by their lodge poles could not be distinguished from our own trail, while the number of ponies abandoned on account of exhaustion showed that our

competitors in the race were not disposed to give us many odds, but what speed and bottom would not do for them, natural sagacity would.[4] We could outfoot them: this they soon learned. We could not break our force into as many small detachments as they: self-preservation required that we should keep together. In this way the Indian derived an advantage over the white men and insured his escape. Of course, before breaking up into small bands, a point of rendezvous had been appointed to which all parties finally directed their course. When in the end it was seen that the pursuit had become fruitless, we found ourselves much nearer the line of military posts located along what is known as the Smoky Hill Route to Denver City, than to the line of posts situated on the Arkansas, and from which we had set out, consequently it was determined to strike for that line nearly due north, expecting to reach it at or near Downer's Station.

At the close of a night march, we found ourselves on the banks of the Smoky Hill River. Fortunately we discovered a ford almost free from quick-sands, the latter so prevalent in the western streams, and before daylight were all safely on the north bank within four miles of the overland stage route. An officer, and twenty men as escort, were at once sent to the nearest station, eight miles distant, to learn the news, particularly to ascertain whether the Indians had broken out along the route and if any considerable bodies of them had passed north. The remainder of the command was immediately ordered to unsaddle, pickets posted, horses grazed, and a tired, sleepy band of cavalrymen threw themselves upon the ground to steal a few hours' sleep. While they are wrapped in slumber let us accompany the small party which was sent off in search of Indian news.

Although, like all his comrades, exhausted and sleepy, the young officer in charge felt the responsibility of his position, and, with commendable zeal, determined to do his work promptly and well. The hour was still an early one; the sun had not risen sufficiently high to drive away the heavy, impending mist of the river, with no guide but his compass, our hero for the nonce set out at a high gait for the stage route, which was known to follow the general course of the river. The difficulties to be encountered in running a course on the open prairie in this remote section of the country are far greater than could be imagined by one who has never undertaken the task. It must be remembered there are no landmarks to serve as guiding points, no "lone tree" or standing rock, nor even a hillock, to use as points of reference. The compass alone could be consulted; if this should belie itself, or be misread, then all reckoning must go for nought.

A person standing near the headquarters of the camp might have seen our little party as it moved northward, gradually growing smaller and smaller to the eye, until at the distance of a mile or more it entirely disappeared behind the misty horizon. So far all went well; we had seen them well off. Why not imitate the example of the many, and endeavor to refresh ourselves with a brief nap? How long we slept, and how pleasantly we dreamed, we will not state; it will suffice to say that in the midst of both we felt ourselves grasped by the shoulder, and heard a tremulous voice repeat the word "Indians!" Nothing more was required to

thoroughly awaken us. As we had not disrobed preparatory to lying down, no time was lost in making our toilet. Rubbing our eyes, and casting them in the indicated direction, which, by the way, was the one opposite to that taken by the little party referred to, we beheld, sure enough, the object of alarm. Of course, they were Indians, was our first expression. The fog and mist had been dispelled by the rays of the sun, but our vision was none the less obstructed notwithstanding. Instead of these impediments we now had to contend against the *mirage*, infinitely more deceptive. Sufficient could be seen, however, to show to us that a force of no inconsiderable magnitude was advancing upon us, with hostile intent, and in most approved military style. Evidently it was a war party, as occasionally we could see the reflection of the sun on their weapons and firearms. Then, too, the order under which they moved showed plainly that our camp was the object of their proposed attack. First came a line of skirmishers; following these the main body. However frequently we had been deceived by mistaking a herd of buffalo for Indians, this time there was no room for doubt. The regular disposition and determined advance convinced the most skeptical that a well-appointed war party were approaching us, evidently bent on mischief. We could now see both horses and riders, but, owing to the distorted effect of the *mirage*, the height of both was so magnified as to make them appear like giants, double or even treble their natural size.

As yet but a few of our officers had been awakened. These, with their field glasses levelled upon the disturbers of our morning nap, were closely scanning each movement made. The unanimous conclusion was that our Indian friends (?), knowing of our night march, and of our consequent exhausted condition, were stealing upon us with the intention of surprising our camp, killing its inmates, and capturing the stock. To them no stir was visible. Our first thought after comprehending the situation was one of gratitude that the little party sent off in the morning had not encountered this war party; the second was one of thankfulness that some one was awake to give the alarm. If we were to be forced to fight the sooner we prepared for it the better. Some writer has remarked to the effect that "when a woman hesitates she is lost." The same would apply in the affairs of war. To gain time, and prevent being charged in our camp, the guard, whose horses are kept saddled, were mounted and, under direction of the officer of the day, sallied out to arrest the progress of the attacking party while the occupants of camp could be aroused and gain time to saddle up and mount.

Although the distance between the two parties had now been reduced to an almost trifling one, the causes before mentioned still rendered it impossible to determine anything beyond the mere fact that a considerable body of horsemen were nearing our camp. If only the blinding effect of the *mirage* could be removed, what a beautiful ground and fine bracing morning for a fight. On they came, though still indistinctly seen; they were within carbine range of camp, no time was to be lost. "To arms! to arms!" was sounded from headquarters, and the thrilling notes had scarcely died away when a sudden commotion was plainly observable in the lines of our foes. They, too, had heard the signal, and seemed by their action to comprehend its meaning as thoroughly as those for whom it was intended. Rapidly their skirmishers were called in, and instead of galloping through our camp with demonical yells, as we anticipated they would, their ranks were closed and, by a movement very closely allied to those of cavalry, they gracefully wheeled off to the right at a slow trot, leaving us more mystified than ever.

Our blood was up, and we were not to be deprived of our "bowl of blood" so easily. The officer of the day, with his party, was directed to pursue at a gallop, engage with the disturbers of our peace, and delay them until our entire force could join in the attack. Our attention was then directed to preparation for the anticipated melee. Before we had completed them, imagine our surprise to see the officer of the day, with his entire guard, coming slowly back to camp. Mystery upon mystery. What could it mean?

We were not long in being enlightened. The officer of the day had overtaken the party he pursued and learned all. The young officer sent out in the morning had succeeded admirably as long as our camp was in sight and served to guide him. Once separated from view of it either his compass was defective or his knowledge of its proper use imperfect; at all events he lost his bearings, and, like most men under similar circumstances, he began moving in a circle instead of upon a direct line. After describing a semi-circle of some miles about our camp as a center, he caught a glimpse of the camp from the side opposite that from which he had started. The appearance was so altered, and its locality so removed, that he imagined us to be a large encampment of Indians. What strengthened this supposition was the appearance of a few Sibley tents that some of our men had erected after his departure, and which closely resembled the Indian lodges. He surmised that we could be no other than the tribes we had been pursuing, and the question arose in his mind whether to return to camp, and with the entire force return to the attack, or with his little detachment make a bold strike and reap all the glory to be derived from a brilliant charge upon an immensely superior force of Indians. With commendable but rather selfish gallantry, he preferred the latter, and determined to assume a bold front, trusting to his sabres to do the rest. It has been seen how this little plan of reaping laurels at our expense was thwarted. As he had previously professed no little knowledge of the Plains, the joke was never permitted to be forgotten, but often furnished material for many a hearty laugh.[5]

After a few hours the party returned to camp, having been successful in their second attempt. They reached Downer's Station, learned that several parties of Indians had been crossing northward for several days at various points of the road, that many of the stage stations, which are located at intervals of ten miles along the road, had been attacked, the stage stock driven off, and one station burned. To tell the truth it was evident that the people along the route had on a very "big Indian scare," and not wholly without cause. The command at once was put in motion, taking the route leading eastward, intending to reach Fort Hays, now Hays City, on the Union Pacific Railway.[6] On the march we passed the various stations, each containing from ten to twenty men who had collected together for mutual defence. All reported the presence of bands of hostile Indians in the vicinity.[7]

Fifteen miles from Fort Hays we reached "Lookout Station," the ruins of which were still smoking, having been burned by the Indians on their flight north. As none of the inmates of the station had escaped, no positive clue could be obtained as to what tribes or chiefs were the perpetrators of the outrage. There were three men who had belonged to the station. We found their bodies lying within a few feet of the smoldering ruins, covered by fragments of partly-burnt timber. As a heavy rain had just fallen it was probable that this was the cause of the timber being left undestroyed by the fire. As it was, however, the bodies of the men were no longer recognizable, except as human beings; their remains were completely charred, their clothing had been removed, while the wolves, as if in rivalry of their equally wild, but more ferocious and barbarous neighbors, the Indians, had removed much of the flesh, leaving but grim, unsightly skeletons. These we collected and gave a decent burial. It was all we had in our power to do. The tortures to which these men had been subjected by their devilish destroyers can only be imagined. They only added one brief chapter to the history of the barbarous and savage cruelties to which the western pioneer places himself liable when he leaves the haunts of civilization, and seeks his fortune "on the plains."

The massacre of the three station keepers, and the destruction of Lookout Station, were made by General Hancock, in his official report, the cause of the burning, by his order, of the Indian lodges on Walnut Creek, although the fact is, as was known at the time, that the burning of the station occurred before the Indians had deserted their village, and as the two were hundreds of miles apart, it was not possible that the occupants of the village could have been the perpetrators of the outrages at the station.[8]

II

KANSAS, 1869-1870

"The plains were dear to us . . ."

AFTER HIS LETTER of December 15, 1867, Custer did not write another to *Turf, Field and Farm* until September 24, 1869. He opened it with an image rich in meanings, likening himself to the Prodigal Son returned from his wanderings after a two-years absence. All Nomad wanted, he wrote, was "to be restored to his place in the columns of the *Turf, Field and Farm.*" But Custer was also the Prodigal Son who had returned from the disfavor of his court-martial to the warm paternal embrace of General Philip H. Sheridan, who gave his "son" a second chance and was amply rewarded for his trust.

Indeed, things had begun looking up for Custer as early as September 1867, when Sheridan replaced Hancock as commander of the Department of the Missouri. He could do nothing for Custer at the time, though he took some of the sting out of his suspension by allowing Custer, a favorite of his since the closing phase of the Civil War, use of his quarters at Fort Leavenworth over the winter. In March 1868, Sheridan took active command of his department and began his operations against the Indians. A peppery and impatient man, he wanted results but, like his predecessor, found that the warriors were defying—almost mocking—the army's efforts to control them. Consequently, Sheridan concluded that more-daring measures were in order, and he decided to mount an all-out winter campaign against the Indians to catch them in their camps when they were least mobile and most vulnerable.[1] This amounted to a tactical shift from the defensive to the offensive, and for these purposes Sheridan felt that he needed Custer's dash, energy, and persistence. If Custer had not displayed these qualities to the utmost in 1867, he would for his old commander, and on September 24, 1868, Sheridan sent him as flattering a message as he would ever receive: "Generals Sherman, Sully, and myself, and nearly all the officers of your regiment, have asked for you, and I hope the application will be successful. Can you come at once? Eleven companies of your regiment will move about the 1st of October against the hostile Indians, from Medicine Lodge creek toward the Wichita mountains." It was a jubilant Custer who telegraphed back from his "retirement" quarters in Monroe, Michigan, that he was on his way. In his memoirs he made Sheridan's request a moment to savor—a dispensation from on high, a perfect vindication of his past actions, and, as he saw it, a thorough repudiation of his enemies. A telling couplet introduced his account:

Comrades, leave me here a little, while as yet 'tis early morn;
Leave me here, and when you want me, sound upon the bugle horn.

Those who had sought to discredit him, after an extensive Indian campaign that had failed to produce "any material advantage," had been forced to bow to Sheridan's will and, caps in hand, beg his return.[2]

It was a once-in-a-lifetime opportunity, and Custer resolved to make the most of it. Through the remainder of the year and the following spring he was the vigorous, pressing cavalryman of old. And on November 27, on the Washita River in Indian Territory, he scored a signal victory by visiting destruction upon the Cheyenne village of Black Kettle. An attack at dawn caught the Indians by surprise, and though they resisted fiercely, they were driven from their camp with losses placed at 103 killed and another 53 women and children captured. The pony herd—875 head—was shot, and all the captured property—lodge skins, saddles, robes, weapons, and the like—was burned. Sheridan cheered the victory as decisive, and Custer returned triumphant despite the protest that Sheridan's winter campaign and the Washita battle had merely replicated the horrors of Sand Creek with its indiscriminate slaughter of combatants and noncombatants alike.[3]

But for Custer personally, the murmur of protests was lost in the swelling chorus of acclaim. He remained in the field through the spring of 1869, braced by constant evidences of Sheridan's esteem and the settling conviction that he was the supreme Indian-fighting army officer of his day. His first biographer, Frederick Whittaker, would insist in 1876 that Custer brought peace to the southern plains "alone and unassisted, *just because he was given his own way.*"[4] As a reward for his services, Sheridan on April 7 offered him a leave, adding "if you desire such, you can have as long as you please."[5] It was the army equivalent of a ring on his finger and a feast of fatted calf, but Custer chose to spend the late spring and summer in Kansas, where his renewed fame brought a benumbing succession of visitors to his headquarters in camp near Fort Hays—some two hundred between June 1 and October 16, by Mrs. Custer's estimate.[6]

They wanted to meet the General, eat with him or, best of all, hunt buffalo with him. Nomad contributed accounts of the two most memorable hunts to *Turf, Field and Farm*, but though the spring and summer of 1870 have been described as "merely a repetition of those of 1869, with more visitors," he ignored the hunts of that year and limited himself to a single letter recounting a special excursion he accompanied marking the completion of the Kansas Pacific Railroad to Denver.[7]

By this time [Whittaker observed], Custer's fame as a cavalry general was completely overshadowed by his more recent triumphs as an Indian fighter, and his still more recent exploits as a mighty hunter. His Scotch deerhounds had increased in number till he owned quite a large pack, his rifles were growing numerous, his sporting letters to the *Turf, Field and Farm* had made him a friend of every hunter in the United States, and the English noble and gentle tourists, out for a buffalo hunt, always stopped at Fort Hays and brought letters to General Custer, who was supposed to know everything about the plains and buffalo.[8]

It was a remarkable turnaround for the disillusioned and dispirited Boy General who three years before had ended his first faltering campaign on the unfamiliar plains in arrest awaiting court-martial. The Prodigal had returned to become master of the situation; and Mrs. Custer, in her reminiscences of the period after the Washita, remembered fondly that "the plains were dear to us because of the happy hours spent there."[9]

6. "On the Plains"

SEPTEMBER 12, 1869 *published September 24, 1869*

After wandering in strange lands among a wild and barbarous people, and after an absence from your columns of nearly two years, "Nomad," like the Prodigal Son, returns from his wanderings, and asks, not that you shall bring forth the best robes, and put a ring on his hand, and shoes on his feet, nor that you shall bring hither the fatted calf and kill it, as we are told was done, when the original Prodigal returned, but he simply craves to be restored to his place in the columns of the *Turf, Field and Farm*. To go back to the date and place when I so unceremoniously took my departure, and thus record, for the benefit of your readers, the succession of incidents—some of a personal, some of a sporting, and many of a purely historical character—would occupy too much of your valuable space, and might exhaust the patience of your readers. "Let the dead (past) bury the dead" shall be my motto in this instance, and I will proceed to truthfully chronicle the incidents, and some of the results, of a grand buffalo-hunt just concluded, and in which your *rambling* correspondent participated.[1]

Letters from Lieutenant General Sheridan and Major General Schofield,[2] received some two weeks in advance, informed us that two youthful scions of English nobility—two real Lords—proposed visiting us, who, to use the words of the distinguished Lieutenant General, were "chock full of buffalo-hunting," and we were requested to give them satisfaction, so far as the buffalo were concerned. When this intelligence first reached us, we began perfecting our arrangements for a hunt, which should be the grandest of the season. Our expectations of completely satisfying our distinguished visitors were not of the most positive character, for the reason that we had in times past been favored with the presence of small parties of foreign gentlemen eager to bring down the noble buffalo, and few of them had ever proved successful hunters.

As a small party of officers of the Seventh Cavalry had been out hunting but a few days before, and had succeeded in *bagging* forty-seven fine fat buffalo, and as thousands of the latter were known to be grazing within a few hours' ride of camp, we consoled ourselves with the thought that whether our expected guests should prove good hunters or not, we could have our sport at all events. On Tuesday last[3] the train from the East over the Kansas Pacific Railroad, brought us our English friends, accompanied by Colonel Gentry, of General Sheridan's staff.[4] It was deemed advisable to devote the remainder of Tuesday to rest, and also to enable the officers of the Seventh Cavalry and of the post of Fort Hays, near by, to become acquainted with the representatives of Britannia. While these introductions are being made, I will take the opportunity to introduce the distinguished foreigners to your readers.

Lord Waterpark occupies a country seat in Staffordshire, England. He is a young man, of perhaps two-and-thirty years, bearing the English cast of features, and, like most Englishmen, is passionately fond of the chase and its necessary attendants—good horses and dogs. Aside from his country seat in England he is the possessor of extensive estates in Ireland. His companion, Lord Paget, is perhaps a few years the junior of the two. While he may not be a more earnest lover of sport than Lord Waterpark, he is undoubtedly the most enthusiastic of the two. He evidently comes from a military stock, his grandfather having held high command under Wellington, at Waterloo, while an uncle rode second in command to Lord Cardigan in the memorable charge of the six hundred at Balaklava.[5] A sister of Lord Paget's married the late Marquis of Hastings, whose brief but dashing career on the turf must be familiar to most of your readers. From Lord Paget I learned many incidents connected with the sporting career of the Marquis, and learned many traits in the character of the latter which impressed me with the belief that the Marquis was more sinned against than sinning.[6] Both Lords Waterpark and Paget are extensive travelers, the former having *done* India in his journeyings. Since their arrival upon this continent in April last, they have as all true subjects of Her Majesty should, visited the British Provinces. During *the season* they have been sojourning at Newport, where they have been the recipients of no little attention. It was while at the latter resort that a fair friend, Mrs. M——, who when at home is usually found in a palatial mansion on Madison Avenue, and whose guest the writer upon more than one occasion has had the happy honor to be, remembering perhaps the ill luck which usually attended the hunting expeditions of foreigners upon the Plains, made a wager with Lord Waterpark that he would not kill even one buffalo. It was difficult to determine which my noble lord considered the greatest incentive, the actual killing of a buffalo or the winning of the wager.

Wednesday morning came, cool and bracing, just such a day as Lexington might have desired, when he made his four miles in 7:19-3/4.[7] To save returning to and from camp, from the immediate hunting ground, until the hunt was concluded, it was deemed best to take with us tents, bedding and mess arrangements, as well as the forage for our horses, while to aid in killing time in the evening after we had quit killing buffalo for the day, we took with us the band of the Seventh Cavalry. An early hour found us in the saddle, and heading southward, our party with its long line of wagons, its citizens, officers and soldiers, and last but not least its ladies, for several of the fair sex accompanied us, presented a motley appearance, while the band as we marched or rode out of camp struck up Garryowen,[8] making the occasion seem more like a war expedition than a simple hunting party, simply bent on sport.

Another Richard appeared upon the field,[9] and one so closely connected with our hunt that reference to it must be made. A large excursion party of citizens from Central Ohio, embracing citizens from Cleveland, Columbus and Cincinnati; the party numbered from one hundred and forty to two hundred, nearly half being ladies. The objects of the excursion were almost as numerous as the individuals composing the party, some, in fact the large majority came to take a view of Kansas, with a view to investing in land; others came from curiosity; some came because their friends did likewise, while a few came with no settled object or reason, except that being an excursion party, the fare was cheaper than usual, and like Toodles, they bought a ticket thinking it "might come handy in the family."[10] Many of the party being farmers it was not to be expected that they would have an eye to anything not embraced in the agricultural line. This party passed this point *en route* to Sheridan, the present terminus of the Kansas Pacific Road. The day previous to the arrival of the English noblemen, while stopping at the station near our camp, many of the officers rode to the depot to see the party. In this way the latter learned of the proposed buffalo hunt, and all were eager to participate.

Cordial invitations were given by the officers for the party to stop over one train on their return to the East, which would give them the opportunity to join in the proposed hunt. The invitation was accepted and arrangements at once made for meeting the excursionists at the depot, early Wednesday morning, with ambulances, spring wagons, and springless wagons, principally the latter, while for some few of the more venturesome horses were provided.[11]

When the entire hunting party, thus strengthened (?) was formed, it presented a sight worthy an artist. I can only compare it to some of the scenes described by Lever in connection with the Irish elections years ago, when each member mustered his corps of constituents or supporters, and marched to the hustings, every man armed with his favorite weapon, and mounted upon horseback or in wagons, no two of the latter resembling each other, all impressed with the principle that "might makes right," and "to the victors belong the spoils."[12] Perhaps our English friends were reminded of this resemblance as they cast their eyes back and surveyed the *hunters*.

Imagine from ten to fifteen huge government wagons packed with at least a dozen stalwart farmers, with here and there an editor, a doctor, a lawyer. So densely are they crowded in, owing to the limited number of wagons available that there is no possible chance to sit down, standing room being barely obtainable. Considering that it is at least fifteen miles to the hunting ground, a *standing* ride in a government wagon over thirty miles of prairie, is not the poetry of motion. Then place in the hands of each of our excursionists a firearm, and the picture is complete. To be sure there was great lack of uniformity in the style of weapon, about as much variety as was to be found in one of our regiments at the early part of the war. Here you would find a very short man with a very long, old-fashioned musket; his next neighbor, who most likely was a six-footer, was perhaps armed with a short, double-barreled shot gun, muzzle loading. He, no doubt, hoped to make up for a lack of range or deficiency in calibre by his own unnecessary length. Some carried smooth-bores, while others were fortunate enough in having the latest style breech-loading rifle. Some had their capacious pockets crammed with cartridges, while others in their excitement came off without a round of ammunition.

Nothing of interest occurred until we neared the valley of the Smoky Hill River, some dozen miles from the station, when a half dozen antelope leaped up before us in plain view of the dogs. The latter gave chase. A few of the officers as well as the English noblemen joined in the pursuit at full speed. There was no expectation of catching the antelope, but merely to give our guests an opportunity to judge of their great speed. While all were going at a rattling pace—antelope, dogs and horses—the horse of the Adjutant of the Seventh Cavalry made a misstep, and plunged his foot into a prairie-dog den, causing both horse and rider to tumble over and over. Fortunately nothing more serious than a bruised shoulder for the former, and a distressed frame of mind for the latter was the result. Why it is I cannot explain, but it always seems as if the officers of the line enjoyed a little mishap befalling one of the staff far more than if one of their own number was the unlucky

one, and this instance proved no exception to the rule.[13]

Arriving at our hunting campground—the site of the latter was selected, directions given for pitching tents, & c., and preparations made for taking a run after buffalo before dinner. A large herd, numbering several hundreds could be seen some three miles distant. Thither we directed our march. Accompanying the hunters were many ladies, most of them riding in ambulances. One young lady, Miss T——ge, of Columbus, Ohio, however, to borrow an honored phrase from military reports, "deserves special mention," for her dashing fearlessness and wonderful determination as an expert and graceful horsewoman.[14]

Upon nearing the buffalo herd advantage was taken of depressions in the ground to approach as closely we could unobserved. While so approaching we suddenly came in view of a large buffalo bull grazing quietly on our left. As we were still nearly a mile from the herd, and as the aforesaid masculine buffalo did not seem disturbed at our approach, several of the citizens riding in wagons considered this their best opportunity to get a shot at a buffalo. No sooner said than done; out jumped at least a dozen of them and gave chase on foot; the buffalo had about half a mile the start. Realizing his full danger (?) and not wishing to take undue advantage of strangers, he set off at a deliberate trot. Heavy odds were now offered on the buffalo and no takers. No one seemed to doubt his chances against the entire field. The main interest was as to the winner of second money, and for this there were about fifteen contestants. They discovered what most strangers do upon visiting this country, that distances are very deceptive, and the buffalo seemed disinclined to show any further favor. The pursurers started out as if intending to force the running, and so they did. "On Macduff, and d——d be he who first cries hold, enough." Away they go, a thousand blankets wouldn't have covered half of them; in fact they were too heavily blanketed already, and nearly all sweated themselves out of the race before reaching the first quarter. Those who were able continued the chase at diminished speed until the mounted hunters, fearing the old buffalo might carry the alarm to the herd towards which he was heading, send a half a dozen of their number to dispatch him, which was soon an accomplished fact. No sooner had the buffalo fallen than every wagon and ambulance containing excursionists, was driven so as to be in at the death. Scissors and knives were brought into requisition to clip locks of hair from a *real* buffalo, and these were to be carried to the Buckeye State and there exhibited as evidences of success.[15]

Leaving our dead, let us accompany the original hunting party, now rapidly nearing the unsuspecting herd. By previous understanding all the mounted hunters were to advance in even line until it was seen that the herd had taken the alarm, when, the word being given, the entire party was to charge pell mell into the herd and bring down his game—if he could. Unfortunately one of the party gave the alarm too soon, which forced us to take a longer run than usual, before overhauling the game; but away we galloped, "a fair field and no favor" sure enough. For nearly two miles we went almost at a two-minute gait. This brought us alongside the herd; then commenced the real sport. It is utterly useless to at-

tempt the description of a buffalo hunt —the enjoyable part of it must be seen, not read. One must find himself astride a good horse, with a trusty pistol or carbine in his hand, then after a hard gallop in pursuit of his buffalo, to get near enough to the latter to plant one or more well-directed shots just behind the foreshoulder, then see the immense animal come to bay and offer battle. This is when it behooves the hunter to have his wits about him; if not, he will find himself and horse suddenly caught upon a pair of powerful horns and lifted into the air.

This was the fate of three buffalo hunters within the past ten days, one of which your correspondent was so unfortunate to be. One horse and rider was caught upon the horns of an infuriated buffalo bull, and both lifted bodily from the ground. The rider escaped with nothing worse than a terrible fright, but the horse was gored to death by the maddened animal. Another horse was overtaken and both he and his rider lifted clean from the ground; fortunately both escaped with but little injury. Equally lucky was your correspondent when suddenly turned upon by a wounded bull; one horn struck the horse in the hindquarter, and, glancing, raised a welt several inches in length. The other horn struck the horse on the side, and would have penetrated the body had not the main force of the blow been received by a thick felt saddle-cloth.[16]

This alone saved the horse's life; as it was, he was lifted from the ground and thrown out of his course. Let no one imagine a tameness about buffalo hunting; on the contrary, I believe it is the most exciting of all American sports. At the close of the run, the commencement of which I attempted to describe, the hunters assembled and it was found that forty buffaloes had been brought down. As this was merely a preliminary attempt to the more extensive hunt of to-morrow, we after securing the tongues and a few choice parts, set out on our return to camp, where we arrived before 3 P. M., and where a bounteous dinner soon met our hungry gaze. Our ride and chase had whetted our appetites, and proved a most relishing sauce to every dish set before us. Every one was anxious to relate his or her adventures. The excursion party, those who had hunted in wagons and ambulances, returned to the railroad to take the Eastern train, about a dozen who had come on the excursion train remained by special invitation to participate in the following day's sport.

At daylight the entire camp was awakened by the band playing some lively air as a reveille. Breakfast was hurriedly prepared and as hurriedly eaten, so that seven o'clock found about forty hunters in the saddle, eager for the fray. A ride of five miles brought us close to a fine herd. The same precautions as of yesterday were adopted, this time with better success. A short race placed us alongside the herd. I have participated in many buffalo hunts during a three years' sojourn on the Plains, but this hunt, in fine running, glorious sport and numbers killed eclipsed all former ones. After horses and riders appeared satisfied, we rallied upon a central point, and by actual count it was determined that we had killed eighty-one buffaloes; Lord Waterpark killed four, Lord Paget killed five, your humble scribe brought down seven, the largest score he ever made in one run. This was surpassed by only one other hunter, who killed nine. Some killed none, while most of the party

killed at least one. Miss T——dge had the honor of bringing down two with a revolver, for which she received the congratulations and admiration of the entire party.[17] Our English cousins were jubilant with joy and enthusiasm. They could not find words to express their admiration for our greatest of all American sports. Such remarks as "To-day is the best spent in America," "I would gladly come all the way from England for such a day's sport," "It's not so tame as I imagined," and "Zounds, how that fellow of a bull charged me," were taken as indications of the appreciation of the hunt.

But few accidents had occurred to mar our success. The leader of the band had been thrown in the chase, and his shoulder dislocated. Mr. W——r, correspondent of the N. Y. *Times*, being mounted upon a well trained buffalo horse, found the latter a little too eager to join in the pursuit, and in attempting to clear a ditch the horse was as unfortunate as to make the leap without his rider. The latter, hearing something drop about that moment, found himself on the ground with little or no injury, but satisfied as Artemus Ward might say, that buffalo hunting was not his forte.[18] Mr. S——h, correspondent of the *Ohio State Journal*, got the impression that somebody had carelessly fired a shot through his horse's neck. Subsequent investigation developed the fact that he was right, but that somebody was the rider of the horse at the time the shot was fired. The direction of the ball being almost perpendicularly downward from the mane it was evident that either the rider of the horse or some man stationed in a balloon must have fired the shot. As there was no balloon visible at that time, it follows that the rider, who at that moment was no less a personage than Mr. S——h, must, in his pardonable excitement, have shot his own horse. I have reason to believe that such accidents do occur, as I remember having shot no less than three horses while hunting buffalo the first year of my experience on the Plains.[19]

The next morning we broke up our pleasant little camp, and set out for the camp of the 7th Cavalry, near Fort Hays. The two English gentlemen and myself made a detour to the right of the traveled road, hoping to come upon a small herd of buffalo. In this we were not disappointed—we found two fine herds, and succeeded in killing six. Our return to camp was unbroken by any accident worthy of note. I omitted to refer to a fine chase after what is known on the plains as a jack-rabbit, but which the Englishmen pronounce to be the real Scotch hare. It was the morning of the second day of the hunt, soon after leaving camp, that a fine one broke cover right in front of our horses. I had half a dozen stag hounds with me, most of them young dogs. With a tally-ho that might have done honor to an English fox chase, a dozen well-mounted gentlemen, including Lords Waterpark and Paget, started with the dogs. A beautiful chase was successfully terminated by Maida, my favorite, and the gift of my friend, K. C. B. of Detroit, picking up the hare, much to the surprise of many of the spectators, some of whom believed the hare the fleetest of all animals.[20] We reached camp in time to meet an engagement to dine with a few friends at the post. Nothing could exceed the exultation of our English friends at the success of their hunt.

The impression created by them upon our entire party could not have been more favorable. We all united in voting them to be a pair of jolly good fellows, and it was with inconceivable gratification that we received their promise to make us another visit at some future time. Lord Paget promised upon his return to Old England to send the writer a specimen of its pure stag hounds, selected from one of the best packs.[21] When I secure him, and obtain a cross between him and my present stock, let the owners of gray or stag hounds, look out for a challenge; and may you, dear TURF, be there to see.

Thursday morning last a small party of us accompanied our guests to the railway station, where they would take the Western train for Sheridan, thence by stage to Denver, from which point they propose taking a run to some of Colorado's beautiful Parks, testing the excitement of trout-fishing; then to Salt Lake City, stopping a day or two to pay their respects to Brigham and his harem;[22] after which by the great continental road, the Pacific, to San Francisco, making the Yosemite Valley the terminus of their western tour. They hope to return about the middle of next month *via* Omaha and Chicago. At the latter famed city Nomad hopes to meet them, and, if practicable, it is planned that our trio shall proceed to Detroit, muster our esteemed friend K. C. Barker into the service, and devote one day to duck-shooting, and, perhaps, be invited to a sail on the beautiful yacht "Coral," the champion of the Lakes. What says my friend K. C. B. to this arrangement?[23]

EDITORIAL NOTE
[by S. D. Bruce?]

"The Hunt on the Plains"

SEPTEMBER 24, 1869

Our readers, we are confident, will welcome the reappearance of Nomad in our columns. He writes us this week of a grand buffalo hunt on the Plains. And for the personal gratification of the editors he sent three photographic views of the hunt.

The first is a novelty, remembering that the picture was "taken on the spot." Out on the wild prairie a fierce bull has been brought to bay by a half dozen well directed shots. The hunters, all in the saddle, are drawn up around the enraged animal, Gen. Custer most prominently in the foreground, on his horse Dandy; the latter, by the way, is reputed the best buffalo horse on the Plains. He is a fine looking animal, and a great favorite with the General. A pack of hounds are in front of Dandy, the graceful creatures standing quietly as if afraid to mar the tableau by even the wag of a tail. The bull is a large one. He stands firmly, tail erect, and head lowered as if preparing to charge the hunters. The grass, growing wild and rank, seems to be about three feet high, and, ere the set of the sun that lights up the scene it will form the death couch of the central figure of the tableau. To have secured this picture the artist must have worked with great expedition.[1]

No. 2 is a view of the hunting camp, which Nomad describes in his letter. The spot seems to be a lovely one. The beautiful little valley is full of animation. The white tents, to the distant eye, look like snow flakes, lightly resting on the broad expanse of green; the army wagons are grouped in picturesque style, the horses are grazing among the rich herbage, the smoke of camp fires ascends heavenward in cloud-like coils, and human forms stand idly in front of tents, or recline carelessly upon the grass. The whole looks like a formidable outfit for a hunting party, but then our correspondent explains that they went prepared for comfort as well as sport.

No. 3 represents a group, taken in

[51]

front of the large tent, in the evening after the hunt. The sun appears to be going down, for the light seems lambent, the atmosphere hazy. There are eighteen human figures in the group, in addition to three dogs. On the extreme left is Gen. Custer, reclining on the grass at the feet of Miss Talmadge, of Columbus, Ohio. The General is clad in a buckskin hunting suit, and he holds in his hand a copy of the *Turf, Field And Farm*, which has just found its way to the camp so distant from the office of publication. It is not the same General Custer that we saw years ago on the balcony of the Louisville Hotel, bowing to the crowd that had gathered to welcome him. It was in the closing hours of the war, and the name of Custer was linked with deeds of heroism and daring. He was the *beau ideal* of a cavalry leader, and as he stood that night in front of the crowd that blocked up Main street, his long hair falling down his shoulders, his face bronzed but nearly beardless, his form tall but thin and sinewy, flags floating over his head, and lamps flaring and casting mystic shadows, he looked more youthful than he really was, looked a knight of bold adventure, a spirit of dash and courage. The General has grown stouter, more rugged since then, and, in the picture at least, his flowing beard robs his face of much of its old boyish look. At the time his reputation for public speaking was nearly as high as that of Gen. Grant. We wonder if time has changed him in this particular.[2] Miss Talmadge, who is chronicled as infusing so much life into the hunting party, wears a jaunty hat, and she looks archly down upon the demure General and the sleepy hound at her feet. Lord Waterpark is seated in a camp chair, the right leg carelessly thrown over the left. His is a full English face, with a self satisfied expression. Lord Paget is seated upon the ground, resting his back against the tent pole. He has wrapped himself in a long loose white coat, and is indolently puffing away at his cigar. Gen. Sturgis,[3] in undress uniform, bronzed and portly, occupies a camp chair, and next to him is a bright young face, hood drawn carelessly over the back part of the head, and eyes looking out into the gloaming. Two hounds are crouched at her feet, restrained by the firm hand of a young officer kneeling upon the grass. This fair young being is the wife of Gen. Custer. The other figures, that is a majority of them, are officers of the Seventh U. S. Cavalry.

The three views form an interesting series, and we are greatly indebted to our correspondent for them. They were photographed by Mr. W. J. Phillips, Preston, Mo., who accompanied the hunting expedition. We have an invitation from Gen Custer to join him in a grand hunt in the plains, but fear that we cannot accept, much as we should like so to do. But of course, our friend, Hon. K. C. Barker, of Detroit, will not decline the invitation extended to him.[4]

1. Custer (mounted, facing left, directly behind the buffalo) with a party of Seventh Cavalry officers and a few of his hounds, August 1869. (Photograph by W. J. Phillips; courtesy of the Custer Battlefield Collection, National Park Service, Department of the Interior)

2. The hunting camp near Fort Hays, Kansas, September 1869. The foreground figures may include the two English lords, Paget and Waterpark. (Photograph by W. J. Phillips; courtesy of the Custer Battlefield Collection, National Park Service, Department of the Interior)

[53]

3. Members of the hunting party. Those described in the editorial note are General Custer, lolling in the grass on the left perusing a copy of *Turf, Field and Farm*; Miss Talmadge seated behind him; the two English lords, Waterpark and Paget, the center of attention since no one stands behind them; Gen. Samuel D. Sturgis and, seated next to him, Elizabeth Custer. Others mentioned in Custer's letters or the notes are Frank Talmadge, standing behind his sister; Lt. Myles W. Moylan, leaning against the tent pole in the middle of the picture; Lt. William W. Cooke, in forage cap and Dundreary whiskers, behind General Sturgis; Lt. Thomas W. Custer, the General's brother, seated on the ground in front of Mrs. Custer. (Photograph by W. J. Phillips; courtesy of the Sternberg Memorial Museum, Fort Hays State University, Hays, Kansas)

7. "The Hunt on the Plains"

NOVEMBER 8, 1869 *published November 19, 1869*

The *Turf, Field And Farm* has long been aware that that Prince of sportsmen, Hon. K. C. Barker, of Michigan, had in contemplation a buffalo hunt on the plains. But while enabled each year to separate himself from the routine of business and enjoy a month of sport either in bagging duck in the marshes of Lake Erie, or in deer hunting among the forests of Northern Michigan, it was not until the present season that he has found time and opportunity to share in the excitement of a buffalo chase.

On the first of October a select party of nine ardent lovers of sport set out from Detroit, Michigan, on board one of Pullman's palace sleeping cars, their destination being the camp of your correspondent near Fort Hays, Kansas, on the line of the Kansas Pacific Railway. The party headed by Hon. K. C. Barker, consisted of Hon. W. G. Beckwith, the genial and popular President of the Michigan State Agricultural Society; General R. L. Howard, of Buf-

falo, who as being one of the division commanders of the New York State Guards, and one of the enterprising business men of New York, as well as a prominent promoter of the interests of the turf, and largely interested in the breeding of fine horses, needs no introduction from me; Mr. John B. Sutherland, of Detroit, the capable Superintendent of the Michigan Central Car Factory; Mr. Jefferson Wiley, who, although largely identified with the iron interests of Detroit, proved himself an admirer of fine horses (particularly sorrels); Mr. Samuel Lewis, of Detroit, a gentleman of leisure, fond of travel, sport and the ladies; Major Horace Gray, of Detroit, an old campaigner of the Western Army, who takes great pleasure in fighting his battles over again when surrounded by an appreciative audience. The Major had had an experience on the plains years ago, consequently the novelty to him was not so great. Mr. Charles H. Mack, of Detroit, who although the most youthful of the party, was also one of the most enthusiastic and tireless of sportsmen. Last, but by no means least, comes Mr. J. H. Morgan, of Amherstburg, Canada. Mr. Morgan's ancestry can be traced to the Green Isle, and like a true Irishman Mr. Morgan is ever ready to engage in anything that promises sport or amusement. He is always "at home" whether it be astride a good horse in the midst of a herd of buffalo, or seated in a lady's drawing room, exchanging the compliments of the season with a fair one. His merits are particularly noticeable as well as appreciable when reclining with a party of friends around a camp fire after a successful day's hunt, he keeps his listeners in a state of constant merriment by drawing from his inexhaustible fund of stories and adventures. In fact, to use an expression illustrating the point of one of his best stories, Mr. Morgan's "arrangements are perfect."

The Cavalry encamped near Fort Hays had received orders from Department Headquarters to break camp about the 1st of October and set out for Fort Leavenworth, three hundred miles Eastward, where they were to enter Winter quarters. While in preparations for the march a telegram was received from K. C. Barker stating that the hunting party would leave Detroit for the plains on the 1st of October. Here was a dilemma; it would not do to break camp and march from the hunting grounds before the arrival of K. C. B. and his party, and yet "orders must be obeyed" is the rule in the army. A telegram was at once sent to Major General Schofield, commanding the Department, stating the circumstances of the case and requesting authority to delay the march until after the hunt; back flashed the reply granting the au-

thority desired. Then began the preparation for the hunt; horses known to be good buffalo horses were selected; revolvers and carbines were thoroughly cleaned; tents, wagons and ambulances provided, and last but not the least important, the mess-kit was overhauled, vacancies supplied, and stores replenished; for if there is one thing above another calculated to give one a ravenous appetite it is a good slashing run after buffalo, involving a ride of from fifteen to thirty miles across the country. Then after returning to camp there is no more welcome sight than a well-supplied table, or, as the old woman once said to her guests, "Plenty of it, such as it is, and very good what's of it."

In due time, or rather in undue time, as some delay was experienced on the route, the party reached Hays, where being met at the cars by Nomad, with conveyances, was soon transported to the camp of the Seventh Cavalry.[1] It being desirable to reach the vicinity of our hunting ground, some twelve miles distant, the same day, a lunch was speedily disposed of, hunting habiliments donned, while horses ready saddled were led up for the use of those who preferred that mode of locomotion to the tamer and less exhilarating ride in ambulances. Nearly all the officers of the Seventh Cavalry joined in the hunt, making with the men who accompanied us a party of about seventy-five. As we rode out of camp, the band, also of the party and mounted on white horses, struck up a lively march, which with the prancing high-mettled steeds, the glistening arms, the well-bred pack of stag-hounds, formed a cavalcade and occasion long to be treasured in the memory of the beholder. One of the gentlemen remarked that the scene reminded him of events described as belonging to the feudal ages, when marshaling his retainers some ancient Baron marched forth to battle or the chase. This was before the discovery of gunpowder had marked, as is said, the downfall of true chivalry. The effect of the scene was too powerful upon those of our friends who had started in ambulances. Inspired by the martial strains and imbibing the exhilaration enjoyed by their mounted companions, they soon exchanged their places in the ambulances for seats in military saddles, and all were soon galloping across the plains, eager for the fray.

We hoped only to locate our camp and be prepared for real work by dawn of the following day. Our camping ground was reached just as night began to take the place of day. A large camp fire was soon blazing, by whose light we pitched our tents and spread our blankets. By unanimous vote the camp was named Camp K. C. Barker. After a cup of tea it was decided to retire early in order to be fully refreshed for the morning's labors. Some of the party realizing the novelty and excitement of the occasion, found sleep a difficult problem until the "wee sma' hours" of the morning began to arrive. It may not be amiss to state that our camp was located but a few hundred yards from the ground we had occupied but a month before when showing the two English noblemen, Lords Waterpark and Paget, something of "life on the plains."

Long before the first peep of dawn the band sounded our reveille. Scarcely had the first notes floated forth clear and strong like the notes of a shepherd's horn before our entire party, like the followers of Roderick Dhu, rose almost instantaneously, and as if by magic.[2]

Toilets were hastily arranged and spurs buckled on, while breakfast, the most important prelude to a day's sport, was soon prepared and as speedily disposed of. Then we were ready to hear the words "Mount your horses" given. Now began a little delicate management, or, more properly speaking, handicapping. It is no easy matter to select a dozen horses, each of which can be relied upon to carry their riders alongside a buffalo, particularly if the aforesaid riders have never ridden after buffalo before. But this difficulty becomes magnified when the weight of the members of the party varies from one hundred and twenty-five to two hundred and thirty pounds. The principal anxiety was in reference to K. C. B. and Mr. Beckwith, the former weighing not far from two hundred and thirty, the latter being slightly below him in weight.[3] Everything had been arranged beforehand seemingly, but by some misunderstanding one of the scouts sent out at daylight to discover the exact whereabouts of the buffalo, had taken the most powerful of our buffalo horses, which happened to be the one intended for K. C. B. The scout had so blown the horse that the latter was unfit for further use that day. A different, and as the sequel proved, a very inferior horse, was substituted for the use of our friend of the heavy weights. An ugly cut on one of his knees, followed by two or three awkward attempts to stumble, destroyed all confidence which might have been placed in him. How well this lack of confidence was deserved let the result determine.

After a due amount of canvassing, each man found himself assigned to his steed, or *vice versa*. At the word all the "riders were up," stirrups and curb-chains adjusted, when placing ourselves under the guidance of our scout who had discovered the whereabouts of the herd, we proceeded at leisurely gait to the scene of action. But why attempt to describe a buffalo hunt. It must be shared in to be fully appreciated. An idea suggests itself; instead of describing the hunt, why not substitute a portion of the description furnished by Mr. Wiley, one of the party, to the Detroit *Post*. As far as language goes, Mr. W. has been most successful in his terms. I will let Mr. W. tell his story from the time we first left camp, near the railroad:

And now, off with city, and on with hunting gear, for we have eighteen miles to go, and at best cannot reach our destination till dark. Soon the camp becomes the scene of bustling activity and hurried preparation; for we are to hunt in no ordinary style. We are to be accompanied by a detail from the several companies of General Custer's command. Very many of the officers also are to accompany the party. Eight wagons, containing tents, supplies and camping paraphernalia, and horses to mount fifty hunters, and three ambulances, for the accommodation of those who might not wish to mount a horse; all these are to go with us. Finally all is ready. As we passed down the long line of tents, our line of march stretching out for half a mile, the band which accompanied us striking up a stirring tune, the effect was grand. One of our number, in his enthusiasm, solemnly assured us he should never go hunting again without a band of music. We soon left behind us the camp, the selection of whose site would have done credit to an Indian's taste, and struck out on the open plains. All this was pure enjoyment. Words were useless, and we could only reiterate "splendid!" "Grand!" The clear sky, bracing air, the broad expanse of prairie, the constant and increasing signs of buffalo as we proceeded, the quick, sharp bark of prairie dogs, huddled together in their crowded villages, diving into their holes as we approached with a defiant shake of their tails, the horses fretting at their slow pace, the superb riding of the officers, all these conspired to attract and

absorb our attention as we continued on our march.

But hear that ringing cry on the right! And what rider is that in the advance, followed by many others? "That is General Custer." How his voice rings out in the clear prairie air! and at what a terrific speed he dashes on! Hurry up, hounds! but give that rabbit a moment's time, and he will find safety in the first prairie dog hole he reaches. And now, rabbit, hounds and riders disappear down the ravine, and we know not the end till General Custer rides quietly up and throws a large hare into our ambulance.

The shadows lengthen, the sun sets, twilight fades and darkness comes before we reach our camping place on Big Timber Creek (Camp Barker). But soon the camp fires dispel the darkness; the tents are up, and with a chat over our hot coffee about to-morrow's hunt, we turn in for the night. To sleep? Not all of us, that to-morrow is to see our first charge on buffalo, and the novelty of the day's experience furnished excitement enough for some of the party, at least, to keep their unwilling eyes open till the small hours of the morning. A reveille from the band starts us out of our slumbers long before the dawn of day. A hearty breakfast, and preparations are made at once for a start.

General Custer has already sent out scouts in different directions in search of buffalo, and we await their return with impatience and suspense. Here is one returning over the brow of the hill. "General, I find buffalo about a mile and a half from camp, to the South," he reports.

This puts us in our saddles at once; and out we go, each of the party carrying two revolvers, soldiers following with carbines; wagons accompanying to bring back buffalo meat, and two ambulances ominously suggestive of danger ahead. A fine sight, these fifty horsemen, armed and eager for the fray! We travel on, one, two, three, four miles before a herd of buffalo are descried on a hillside, about a mile distant, looking like so many black spots upon the grass. The whole cavalcade ride, well together, slowly toward the herd. We pass down a slope, along the hollow, up the opposite height, and again the buffalo appear. Now we can descry their forms. Down the long slope we go, and as we begin the next ascent, and think that in passing the summit we shall change our slow pace to the horses' full speed, as we make the grand charge, I think all the party were conscious of a very rapid increase of pulse, and a decidedly new sensation.

But here we are! the summit is reached, and there are the buffalo about thirty in number, a quarter of a mile distant, quietly grazing. But what immense fellows they are! Are they to fall at the fire of the insignificant pistols, that lay still in their holsters at our side? And now as we are going slowly down the incline, with hardly a word spoken, but our nerves strung up to their highest tension, they discover our approach, give us one look, point their heads to the South, and start off on a long rolling gallop, with the grace of an elephant and the beauty of a hippopotamus! seemingly at so slow a pace that there will be no difficulty in coming up with them. And now, charge! and off dash the whole company. The horses, trained to the business, start at a speed that, but for our excitement, would seem too dangerous to be enjoyable. But, keep a firm seat; your horse is bound to be in at the sport, and, *nolens volens,* you must go. On rushed the troop pell mell. A run that seemed short, but we know not how long, brings the fleetest horses into the herd. In they rush, other riders soon following, and the buffalo, bewildered, begin to scatter. And now the party are well up, and the sharp report of a pistol is heard here and there. The herd has disappeared like a dissolving view, and in place of it, one, two or three buffaloes are galloping off in this or that direction, and one, two or three horsemen in full pursuit. Now the work begins. Gallop on! Let the buffalo run. He will lead you down the next slope, and perhaps the next after that. Don't get excited. Keep your pistols in their holsters. Now press him hard as he ascends again. He can run down hill at a breakneck pace; but he is yours on the rise. Now you overhaul him. Look at the uncouth, immense fellow, laboring heavily along, his head down, his tongue lolling from his open mouth. Ride up to him; give the spur to your reluctant horse; out with your pistol. You are near enough at fifteen feet; one shot just behind the foreshoulder. Look out, if he is wounded he will make for you. Give him another shot; turn your horse quick—give him the spur; the old fellow is almost on you. Now turn again—the buffalo is your! His tail is up—sure signal of distress. The blood begins to drop from his mouth and nostrils; unfailing symptom of a mortal wound. Dispatch him at your leisure, he will soon come to bay; and, at length, pawing the ground in impotent rage, he will stretch himself upon the plain, and the contest is ended.

All this is what the old hunters did, killing buffalo with as much nonchalance as if going to their dinners. But our party, many of them, were far from showing such self-possession. Was it not too much to ask?

"How did you burn that hole in your sleeve, M.?"

"I don't know anything about it."

"What has happened to your hand, S.?"

"Pistol went off some way, and filled my hand with powder—don't know where the ball went. Jove! how it smarts."

"What are you firing off your pistol in the air for, W.?"

"Oh, I had my hand on the trigger—didn't mean to pull it."

And so we rush on, soon far apart pursuing our several buffalo. At the end of our hunt, a circle of three miles shows twenty-four dead buffalo within its limits. The hunters began to assemble, and give their accounts of the chase. Here comes Mr. L with Major G. "A narrow escape, Major, to have your horse pushed into the creek. Nothing but your old army experience saved you."

Here comes a soldier, his horse sadly gored in the thigh, and another, escaping by a miracle—his horse showing a long furrow in the hair upon the side—escaping with not even a flesh wound. Another horse comes in, shot in the hoof. But we are all safe. No, we have got to hear from General Custer, Mr. B. and party. Their chase has taken them too far. We shall find them in camp. Now the wagons roll up. The best part of the buffalo, the tongue, the hump, the hind-quarter perhaps, are transferred to the wagons, and we are off to the camp. Horses pretty well used up—riders ditto, but feeling triumphant, enthusiastic, and satisfied.

It is four P. M. before we reach Camp Barker. "Very sorry to hear about Mr. B.," is the first intimation we have of any accident to General Custer's company, who had soon been lost to sight after the first charge in pursuit of a grand old bull. Thrown from his horse—unconscious, and saved from the attacks of the buffalo by General Custer and party, who diverted his attention to themselves.

At length the missing party arrive, Mr. B. wearing the appearance of a prize-fighter, as to his left eye, after a champion contest—but insisting he will be in riding trim in the morning. Evening finds us seated around the camp fires, fighting our battle over again, till by tacit consent we withdraw to our tents. To some of the party, too tired to enjoy the refreshment of sleep, there was a malicious satisfaction in hearing the groans and ejaculations of the others, as they sought to change the position of their aching limbs.

This was one day's experience, succeeded by another, and another, till all were satisfied with their success, and willing to stay the slaughter of the innocents.

The accident to Mr. Barker came very near proving a most serious one. Mr. Barker, mounted upon an animal that had justly excited his suspicions from the first, singled out his buffalo on the first charge, and after separating him from the main herd began emptying his revolver into the sides of the buffalo, horse, rider and buffalo going at a break-neck pace. It was with no little anxiety that the writer witnessed the contest then transpiring. He must be a bold rider, who, mounted upon a strange horse, is willing to strike out at full speed over a country known to be infested with prairie dog holes, wolf dens and quicksands. The risk of a fall is always sufficiently great, but to a man of K. C. B.'s weight it is fearful. The horse proved unsteady under fire. Barker concluded to cross from the left to the right side of the buffalo; in doing so he passed close to the haunches of the latter. The buffalo at this moment concluded to give battle, and turned to intercept the horse. "Look out for him, Barker," was the warning cry of a friend, but Barker's eyes were directed to the front. Again is the warning repeated. This time 'tis heard, and Barker glances toward the buffalo, but too late. Already the horns and head of the buffalo are partly concealed by the long flowing tail of the horse, while the lat-

ter feeling the points of the enraged animal's horns pressing his flanks, leaps with affrighted vigor to elude the coming blow, but in doing so unsettles his rider's seat. For a moment Barker is seen attempting to recover himself, but as to the horse, now unmanageable from fear, plunges madly forward, the rider gradually loses his balance, and the next instant goes headlong to the ground. What I did or what any of the half dozen friends who fortunately were following close in rear, did at the time, cannot be clearly stated. That we all realized the full extent of the danger which surrounded our comrade was certain, but how to relieve him.

As if by intuition, and without uttering a word, all headed their horses toward the buffalo, who, finding himself the object of so much undivided attention, allowed himself to be diverted from continuing his attack on Barker, now lying perfectly helpless and insensible within three bounds of the buffalo. The latter again chose to confide in the swiftness of his legs rather than the strength of his horns, a decision which spared to Detroit one of her most estimable citizens, and to the sporting world one of its brightest ornaments. Seeing the buffalo well under way our attention was next directed to ascertaining the extent of the injuries received by our friend. He was still lying insensible, breathing as if partly suffocated. By means of restoratives and fresh air—of the latter there being an abundance—we soon had him on his feet, and upon "time being called," in the course of a quarter of an hour he announced himself ready to mount his horse. This time a change of horses was affected, by which, although placed astride of a lighter animal, it was with the assurance that he was "sure-footed and not afraid of buffalo." If timidity had been one of Mr. Barker's characteristics, he would have been content to call it "quits" with the buffalo; but no, his dander was up, and he surprised his hearers by announcing that his late narrow escape from a possible death was *"just the thing."* To use his own expressions: "I know now just how to take them and how to ride," and as for the blackened eye and bruised cheek, he declared that "no money would buy them."

While Barker is fully recovering from his fall and anxiously looking for the next herd, let us follow our equally portly friend Mr. Beckwith, who, mounted on a mettlesome charger is punishing in *deadly* earnest a huge buffalo bull. What would some of our Michigan farmers say, who, "for seven long years," have only known Mr. B. as the affable and dignified President of their State Agricultural Society, if, instead of his usual quiet, undemonstrative manner, they could now behold him as he goes at full speed over the apparently even but treacherous surface of the plains both bridle reins in left hand and revolver in right hand. It is plainly evident that the head and front of the Agricultural Society is on the rampage, but it is soon seen that there is method in his madness, for coming within easy pistol range of the huge animal, which is straining every muscle and nerve to escape, he begins a deliberate fire from his revolver, steadying his horse as he prepares to fire. Shot after shot is fired into the sides of the huge monster, who still keeps up his speed, as if proof against powder and ball. The chances seem to be in favor of escape of the buffalo. The revolver is nearly empty—one shot yet remains—if this one fails to strike a vital part the contest ends, and the buffalo escapes. Again the pistol arm is extended and poised an instant, as if to catch the motion of the horse. For the last time, glancing along the little slender barrel, the finger presses the trigger, and away speeds the bullet to its destined mark, this time with success, as the blood is seen to spurt from the nostrils of the buffalo, clearly indicating that his race is run. Soon he slackens his speed, makes an effort to charge upon his pursuers, stops, totters, and falls, to rise no more. Mr. Beckwith announced himself satisfied, "having accomplished the objects of the expedition."

Turning our faces toward camp we had not proceeded far before we discovered a fine herd off to our right. Mr. Barker expressed his determination to bring down his buffalo out of this herd. Approaching as near as possible, without giving the alarm, a very fine start was effected. K. C. B. singled out his buffalo, which proved to be a fine bull about five years old, and very fleet. It required a good run to bring pursuer and pursued within pistol range of each other, but once accomplished Mr. B. began making his presence known, by deliberately emptying his large Colt's revolver, directing his shots immediately in rear of the foreshoulder and below the middle of the body. Barrel after barrel was discharged until the revolver was empty, and still the speed seemed unslackened. Replacing this revolver in its holster and drawing another, the firing was continued. The last shot of the second revolver had been fired, making twelve in all, and still the race went on with no signs of distress. An attendant handed Barker a third revolver. This, in turn, was emptied into the buffalo, and all apparently to no purpose. A fourth revolver is supplied, from which four shots are fired, when the buffalo's never-failing signal of defeat—bleeding at the nose—is perceptible. Slowly decreasing his speed, the buffalo soon comes to a halt, the next instant he is down on his side, and before his heart ceases to beat or he to struggle, Barker is out of the saddle, and, with hat in hand, leaps upon the buffalo and gives three hearty cheers, in which he is joined by all of the party, who are within hearing. The head of the buffalo is soon recovered from the carcass and conveyed with the party to camp, from which point it was expressed the same day to Detroit, there, to be placed in the hands of the taxidermist for preservation. By this time I presume it is mounted in the rooms of the Audubon Club, of which K. C. B. is the worthy President.

The following day was the Sabbath, and although hundreds of miles from church or chapel, it was nevertheless determined to "Remember the Sabbath day to keep it holy," a resolution which gave no little pleasure. At sunset the band played "Old hundred," the effect of which upon most of our little party was more powerful than if sung by a well organized choir with all the accompaniments of church and congregation.

Monday morning we set out for our farewell hunt. I was anxious to see Gen. Howard bring down his buffalo, an event he was prevented from accomplishing on the first day by the accident which happened to Mr. Barker. Gen. H. was well mounted, his horse was trained to buffalo, and was good for a five-mile run over most any country. A splendid herd was soon found and an admirable start obtained. The General having on the first day discovered the staying qualities of his horse, determined to trail his game until the pace began to tell, then force the running. This plan worked to perfection, but not so the revolver carried by the General. After discharging one or two chambers it would not remain cocked, a fact which nearly cost the life of both horse and rider. Fortunately, one of Remington's heavy breech-loaders was at hand for which the worthless Colt was exchanged. This put a new phase upon the matter, but a most unfortunate one for the buffalo. After a spirited race of nearly three miles over all sorts of country, the General had the satisfaction of bringing down a very fine buffalo. Mr. Beckwith also succeeded in killing another, making his second. It would be impossible to give the result of each separate chase; suffice it to say each member of the party killed at least one buffalo, and Mr. Morgan, of Canada, proved himself the champion hunter of the party, bringing down, unaided, no less than seven buffaloes. He narrowly escaped a serious accident, a revolver ball passing through his sleeve, fortunately without serious injury to his person. Our hunt here terminated, and it was found that fifty-three buffaloes had been killed. A ride of a few hours brought us to the cavalry camp near the railroad station.[4]

This letter, already drawn to a great length, cannot be completed without a brief reference to an incident of the hunt, which, although unforeseen and unpremeditated, cast a gloom over our entire party, and went far to disturb the otherwise uninterrupted pleasure of the hunt. To give our visitors an opportunity to witness the great speed of the antelope and American hare, or, as it is best known on the plains, the buck rabbit, I took with me from camp about half a dozen fine staghounds, including two lately sent from Michigan by K. C. B. Foremost among all these was Maida, my favorite dog, the companion of my long and terrible marches of last Winter. She who by day trotted at my stirrup, at night shared with me my camp couch. In the first run after buffalo, the dogs, contrary to their usual custom, became separated from me and accompanied others of the party. They soon singled out a buffalo and readily brought it to bay. With little forethought or prudence several of the hunters opened fire upon the buffalo while the latter was contending with the dogs. Maida had seized hold of the buffalo, and while clinging to its throat was instantly killed by a carbine ball fired by some one of the awkward soldiers who accompanied the party. Words fail to express the grief occasioned by the untimely death of so faithful a companion.

Poor Maida, in life the firmest friend,
The first to welcome, foremost to defend;
Whose honest heart is still your master's own,
Who labors, fights, lives, breathes for him
    alone.
But who with me shall hold thy former place,
Thine image what new friendship can efface.
    Best of thy kind adieu!
The frantic deed which laid thee low
    This heart shall ever rue.

8. "On the Plains"

SEPTEMBER 24, 1870 *published October 7, 1870*

With material for half a dozen interesting letters, I will skim over the surface, and offer you what will probably prove but indifferent matter to the readers of the *Turf*. About the middle of last month I was gratified to receive an invitation from Mr. Perry, the President of the Kansas Pacific Railway, to become one of the grand excursion party which was to signalize the completion of the Kansas Pacific Railway from the Missouri River to Denver, Col., by a trip over the new route. The invitation was accepted.[1]

The excursion party was, as the letter of invitation expressed, composed of the officers of the connecting lines of Eastern railroads and the representatives of the principal papers throughout the United States. The party, numbering about one hundred and twenty-five, started from St. Louis on August 30. The train used on this occasion was the most magnificent and costly collection of cars ever put together. Such was the assertion of Mr. A. B. Pullman, General Superintendent of the Pullman Palace Car Company, who ought to be good authority. The aggregate value of the cars was two hundred thousand dollars, there being eleven of Pullman's finest specimens, among which were three hotel cars, amply supplied with every luxury and delicacy in the way of eatables and the accompaniments that money and foresight could obtain. In the party were representatives from every section of the country, the East, the West, the North and the South. The cabinet was represented, well represented I might say, by the Hon. J. A. J. Creswell, Postmaster General, and his genial assistant, Hon. Giles A. Smith. The White House had its representative in the person of Col. J. T. Ely, private secretary to the President. To enumerate the Presidents, Superintendents, and other officials of the various railroads represented, would be to call attention to many of our old and well established lines of travel East of the Missouri. The telegraph was most happily, and at the same time usefully represented by Gen. Anson Stager, General Superintendent Western Union Telegraph Company, and his assistant Col. R. C. Clowry. Through the kindness and courtesy of these two gentlemen, members of the excursion party were granted the free use of the wires, and were thereby enabled to send social and business messages back to their friends from all points of their line of travel. Then there were representatives, and worthy ones too, of the press of New York, Boston, Philadelphia, Washington, Baltimore, Chicago, Cincinnati, St. Louis, Mobile, Nashville and Springfield, Ill. England had three representatives; Congress was represented by Hon. Erastus Wells, member from St. Louis, Mo. *Harper's* and *Leslie's Weeklies* had each their respective artists. The names of many more of the party might well be given. Suffice to say the party was most happily formed, not an uncongenial spirit in all. Politics, by silent consent, was most appropriately tabooed, and all went merry as a marriage bell.

The first halt for any length of time after leaving St. Louis, was made at Leavenworth, Kansas. Carriages were here provided by the citizens, and a ride through the city and out to the fort was enjoyed by all who chose to participate. Leaving Leavenworth the party proceeded Westward, stopping at Lawrence and Topeka long enough to take a hasty glance at the towns, and at the latter place to view the new and handsome Capitol now approaching completion. Traveling leisurely along, halting at the various towns springing up on the line of the road, among the most important of which is Abilene, now the greatest cattle mart in the West, next to Chicago, the party finally arrived at Brookville, where a halt was made until morning. This was to give the excursionists an opportunity to see as much of the road and country by daylight as was practicable. Early the following morning, before any of the party had left their comfortable Pullman couches, the train was again in motion towards the mountains, which were still five hundred miles distant. Just as the party was being seated to breakfast, Fort Harker appeared in the distance. The speed of the train was slackened sufficiently to enable a hasty glance to be had of the fort, and to catch a few of the enlivening notes from the Fifth Infantry band, which was drawn up near the station.

Bidding adieu to Fort Harker and the little border town of Ellsworth, we now strike boldly out "across the Plains," and enter what many of us learned from the school atlas is the "Great American Desert." A ride of seventy miles brings us to Hays City, with Fort Hays and the camp of a portion of the Seventh Cavalry in the distance. Here we are greeted by the sight of a squadron of Seventh Cavalry troopers drawn up, under command of Col. Cook;[2] while a party of traveling minstrels, vulgarly termed on the Plains "Kauffman's wind-jammers," who has just arrived from the East on a little pleasure tour, very kindly consent to play two entire airs.[3] At this point the party was increased by the addition of several officers and ladies from the garrison and camp, most of whom, however, returned upon the Eastward-bound train, which was met about eighty miles West of Hays.[4]

As we glided along, scarcely perceiving the rapidity of our motion, our attention from time to time is attracted to herds of buffalo or antelope, quietly grazing within rifle range of the road. Many of the party came provided with breech-loaders, and at every opportunity open fire from the car windows, with but indifferent effect. To guard against accident, a pilot engine is constantly kept about one mile in advance of the train. Some of the party took station on this for a short time, among them Gen. Creswell, the Postmaster General. He is reported to have brought down a huge bull by a shot from his rifle when the engine was moving at great speed.[5]

Gliding along swiftly but most pleasantly, we reached Kit Carson at 9 P. M., where we are to halt until morning. Here we have an opportunity to see a border town in all its glory (?). Every house except the railroad depot is either a liquor saloon or dance and gambling house. It is fair to presume that aside from the employees of the railroad, express and telegraph companies, there is not a resident of the place but is cheating either the penitentiary or gallows of a most deserving victim. The excursionists took a stroll through the town the following morning, before the departure of the train. It was then long after sunrise, yet the games begun the previous evening were still kept up at several of the tables in one of the establishments which we had the temerity to enter.

Casting our eyes around the room, we saw several sleepers, some on benches and chairs, others on tables, and some on the floor. We inquired of the proprietor if such sights were customary, to which he replied that that was the dullest time for *business* of the twenty-four hours. Observing a few musical instruments and a platform for musicians, we inquired whether he kept a band in attendance every evening.

"Oh yes, or how could we dance?" This led to the further interrogatory as to where the women came from.

"Oh," responded our willing informant, "there are plenty of them. I can show you twelve girls in those back rooms," pointing to the door at the rear end of the hall. Out of mutual regard for the twelve girls (which in this case bore no resemblance to the "Twelve Temptations"), and for ourselves, we declined the offer.

"Do you never have trouble with your patrons?" we asked.

"Yes; in fact we kill a man every night or two. There (pointing to a bullet hole through the window) is a shot that killed one of my best friends night before last."

"Who fired it?"

"Sergeant Shreve shot at another man, but missed his mark and killed my friend; but the man Shreve shot at fired three balls into Shreve, killing him instantly, so that makes it all right," and as if to verify the statement he had been making, he pointed us to blotches of fresh blood on the floor and walls, and even on his clothing.[6]

It was with not a little relief that we heard the conductor call out "all aboard!" and we shook the dust of Kit Carson from our feet as we again turned our faces towards Denver. From Carson to First View, a water station, nothing occurs—no incident or scenery to break the monotony of our ride. At First View, as the name partly indicates, the traveler making his way towards the West, catches the "first view" of the mountains, still some eighty miles distant. Pike's Peak, once the mecca of so many fortune hunters from the States, is the first point perceivable. A couple of hours' ride brings us within view of the entire range, from Pike's Peak in the Southwest to Long's Peak in the Northeast, embracing a distance of one hundred and fifty miles. A person unaccustomed to mountain scenery might well mistake the first view obtained of the range for that of a low, long line of distant clouds, the outlines between the crest and the sky being scarcely perceptible in places, while the general and changing color of the mountains as we approach them, closely resembles that of the clouds.

For the gratification of the excursionists two flat cars had been prepared with awnings and seats, and were in waiting at Kiowa Station, twenty miles from Denver, to be placed on the road in front of the engine of our train, to enable the party to enjoy an undisturbed view of the mountains as we approached them, and to give us the additional and rare enjoyment of a view of sunset in the mountains, the time of our advance having been regulated for this object. For the thoughtfulness in arranging the cars in this manner we were indebted to Gen. Palmer, the director of construction of the road, under whose personal supervision the principal part of the road had been built.[7] Admitting that "the pen is mightier than the sword," we are forced to confess that in our hands we find it not sufficiently "mighty" to attempt even a description of the gorgeous grandeur, the sublime magnificence of the scenery as we beheld it. It is well worth a trip "across the continent" to experience at least once in one's life the grand emotions which a view of the mountains, after crossing the level, unbroken plain, inspires.

As we approach Denver, which is twelve miles from the base of the range, we behold the immense fields of snow covering the crests, while in strange contrast the valleys between us and the mountains are clothed in their greenest verdure. We reach Denver at 10 P. M., too late to determine anything as to its appearance. A large concourse of citizens were in waiting at the depot to bid the representatives of the East welcome to the Garden City of the mountains. The Mayor and other city officials were foremost in thus tendering a most cordial and free welcome. Carriages were in waiting to drive those of the party who desired it to the city, an opportunity which was most generally taken advantage of.

From Denver to Cheyenne is a branch railroad, connecting Denver with the Pacific Road from Omaha to San Francisco. This branch road was built by the Kansas Pacific Road virtually, and is run in connection with the latter road. We presume it will not be long until it becomes in name, as it is in fact, a part of the Kansas Pacific Road.[8] It was the programme for us to proceed to Cheyenne the following morning, spend an hour or two at Cheyenne, and return to Denver by 10 P. M. Midway between these two points we saw the village of Greeley, named in honor of the philosopher of the N. Y. *Tribune.*[9] Four months ago there was not a single house on the site where now resides, in comfortable dwellings, over six hundred inhabitants. The soil has, even in this brief time, proved highly productive. Vegetables of six weeks' growth were exhibited to us which would astonish some of our eastern gardeners. It is proposed, and the plan is perfectly feasible, to irrigate this entire country by constructing ditches from the mountain streams. This will in time reclaim from their present worthless state millions of acres of rich productive soil. From Denver to Cheyenne is a ride of slightly over one hundred miles. On our return from Cheyenne—the latter, by the way, being the capital of the Territory of Wyoming—we were accompanied by Gov. Campbell, of Wyoming, who gave us many items regarding his little principality, the people of which have given the first test to female suffrage.[10]

At Denver we had the pleasure of renewing our acquaintance with Gov. Ed. McCook, of Colorado, lately our Minister at San Salvador. It was somewhat amusing to hear his story about the annexation of San Salvador to the United States. Gov. McCook began by sounding the present ruler of San Salvador, thinking it best to win him over to the project first. The Governor placed everything in its fairest light, and gave, as he supposed, his consent to spread eagleism, the clinching argument in favor of annexation by telling him that no doubt the United States Government would continue him as the Territorial Governor of San Salvador. The distinguished ruler of this desirable island then inquired "What is the salary of a Territorial Governor?" Upon being informed that it was $1,500 in greenbacks, he remarked that as his present position brought him in $40,000 in gold annually, he was unable to discover any particular advantage, so far as he was concerned, in becoming a citizen of the "best government the world ever saw."[11]

It had been decided that the day following our return from Cheyenne should be given up to the Denverites, who desired to celebrate the arrival of the first through train from the States, by dining and wining the entire party, and showing them all that was to be seen in their beautiful mountain city.

All this was very well and appropriate to the occasion, but there were four of us who determined to secede and get up an excursion of our own to the mountains. The regular programme for the party was to spend Monday in Denver and the next three days in the mountains, leaving Denver for the East on Thursday night. Stages had been procured to convey the entire party of one hundred and twenty-five on a three days' trip to the mining regions of Colorado. The four who determined on seceding were Hon. J. A. J. Creswell, Postmaster General; Hon. Giles A. Smith, Assistant Postmaster General; Col. Ely, the President's private secretary, and "yours truly." We took this step, if a trip through the mountains of a hundred and fifty miles can be called a step, not that we loved Denver less but that we loved the mountains more.

At 7 o'clock Monday morning our conveyance, called in Colorado a "jerkey," was in readiness. Stowing away our guns and what little baggage we required for the trip, we turned our backs on Denver and set out for the mountains, with visions of bear, trout and other enticements floating through our minds. Our chaperone was Hon. L. P. Bennett, formerly delegate from Colorado, now the postmaster of Denver. Our team was a splendid four-in-hand, the lines being held by Mr. Bogen, of Denver, who is largely engaged in the stage and mail routes centering in Denver. His knowledge of the country through which we passed and the people along our route was of great assistance to us, and placed us under many obligations to him. Our ride was frequently prevented from becoming monotonous by listening to Hon. L. P. Bennett relate episodes in his early

Colorado life, when the law of the land was then enforced by vigilance committees. As I stated at the commencement of this letter, there is material for half a dozen, but the great length to which this has grown warns us to be brief in referring to our mountain trip, which in many respects was the most interesting and by far the most novel portion of the entire journey. To sketch hurriedly, then, noon found us, after changing horses at "Trotter's," twenty miles from Denver, where we sat down to as inviting a dinner as an epicure could desire. Not only was every delicacy of the season spread before us, but the style of preparation was perfect. Soon are we rolling along in our "jerkey," with Idaho as our objective point.

We reached this little mining town about 4 P. M. Here is found the famous hot and cold springs of Colorado, and which at no distant day are destined to render this point the Saratoga of the mountains. Already two extensive bathing establishments have been fitted up and have been visited by thousands. Our little party, after brushing some of the dust of travel off, and partaking of a most refreshing supper, visited the springs, which are but a few minutes' walk from the principal hotel. The exact degree of temperature of the water we have forgotten; the heat, however, is so great that the hand can scarcely be held in it without pain. When conveyed to the bathing rooms the temperature becomes moderated. The medicinal qualities of the waters are acknowledged by all who have given them a test. We can well believe this reputation a deserved one, after having enjoyed a few invigorating baths and drank freely of the soda and sulphur springs. And we have no doubt but that Idaho will soon become a favorite resort for both pleasure and health seekers. [12]

From Idaho we went to Central City, the centre of another valuable mining region. After visiting some of the mines near by, we returned to Idaho for dinner, intending to drive to Georgetown in the afternoon. While at Idaho we were surprised to learn that Wigfall, the once belligerent Senator from Texas, was a sojourner of Idaho, having been there for several months engaged in mining. So far he has not realized anything, his time and money having been spent in the development of his mines, but there is now a fair prospect of his mines yielding him a rich return. [13]

From Idaho we drove to Georgetown, the most extensive and promising town we found in the mountains. Again we were fortunate in stopping at a hotel where the comforts of the inner man were most carefully looked after. Indeed, this was observable, much to our surprise, at every hotel we stopped. The rooms were neat, large and comfortable, while the table was bountifully supplied with the luxuries as well as the delicacies of life. At Georgetown we found raspberries in the greatest abundance and we were told that bushels could be plucked from the mountain sides. Of course we had mountain trout for breakfast—and such trout! [14]

The following morning, having been overtaken by the main portion of the excursionists, we rode to Bakersville, and from there to the base of Gray's Peak, the tallest of the entire range. The last three miles of the ascent could not be made on wheels. We transferred ourselves from the jerkey to the saddle, and in this manner, as one of the party remarked, in speaking of the great height "we approached nearer to heaven than we had ever been before." Gray's Peak has an altitude of 14,251 feet. A late writer, in referring to a visit to the summit of Gray's Peak, says: "From this sublime altitude the most wonderful panorama bursts upon your vision. These grand old mountains, in every conceivable form and on every side, confront you as you gaze on their snow-clad summits, on their bleak palisades, or lower down on their pine-bowered sides, at the beautiful peaks, or sources of mighty rivers flowing from the base, some to the Atlantic and some to the Pacific. Here in full view, are the sources of the Platte, Snake, the Blue, Arkansas, Colorado and other rivers. You can count also some seven or eight ranges of mountains. North, West and South, and away East, in full sight stretch the majestic Plains." While on the summit some of us arranged ourselves on the Pacific slope and began snowballing the others who were standing on the Atlantic slope, and yet but a few steps distant. As if Nature had made up her mind to entertain us with all her gifts and beauties, we witnessed a heavy snow storm before making the descent.[15]

From the summit of Gray's Peak we began our return to the States, spending that night at Georgetown, and reaching Denver the following afternoon at 4 o'clock. We found, although in the region of trout and bear, that our limited time would not permit us to attempt either fishing or hunting. But if all goes well, we organized a small party, whose intention is to go to the mountains next Summer, with our guns, dogs, and—God bless them— our wives, and we propose to devote a month to the mountains and peaks of Colorado. And as to the number of bear or pounds of trout we get, no estimate can now be made.

The Denverites gave the entire party a sumptuous banquet the evening we returned. After a number of happy speeches had been made by the speakers of the party, city and country, we bade adieu to Denver and its hospitable inhabitants, glad indeed that we had had the opportunity of renewing some old acquaintances and forming many new ones, well pleased with the evidences, which as a young and rapidly growing town Denver exhibited, and forming high estimates as to its future size and importance.

We left Denver for the East about midnight on Thursday, on the same train which had conveyed us to that place. Nothing occurred next day worthy of note, as we were passing over the ground for the second time. The active party was outspoken in commendation of the manner in which the Kansas Pacific Road has been built, far exceeding in its perfection of structure most new roads laid in the East. Every one realized for the first time the energy, perseverance and vast expense which had been called into requisition in building this second great route across the continent. The importance of this route will constantly increase with coming years, and there is no doubt but that it is to be the popular line of travel from the Eastern States to the Pacific. Particularly is this true of the travel which passes through Washington, Baltimore, Cincinnati and St. Louis. Another result of the completion of this road will be a more thorough development of our vast mining resources in Colorado, from which the nation is to receive untold wealth. And still another result equally beneficial to the nation is the opening up for settlement of millions of acres of rich valuable land, which hitherto have been neglected, because of their great distance from a market.[16]

Arriving at Hays City in the evening, fifteen of the excursionists accepted an invitation from "Nomad" to stop at his camp, and participate in a buffalo hunt on the following day. One of Pullman's palace cars was left at this point to bring the buffalo hunters back after the termination of their hunt. Among those who joined in the hunt were the three companions of yours truly, in the *Turf*, to the mountains. Gen. Creswell killed his buffalo, after considerable sport. Many of the representatives of the press entered heartily into the sport, and some of them proved themselves as skillful in the saddle as they are brilliant with the pen, and some of them—didn't.

We killed twenty buffalo, had plenty of sport, and reached the railroad in time for the departure, which had been fixed at ten o'clock that night. We accompanied the party as far as Topeka, where we reluctantly bade each and all of them adieu.

III

KENTUCKY, 1871-1873

". . . nothing but horse, horse, horse"

IN MARCH 1871, the bulk of the Seventh Cavalry left Kansas for Reconstruction duty in the Department of the South. There the regiment was scattered and over the next few years saw service principally in South Carolina and Kentucky, but also in Tennessee, Alabama, Mississippi, and Louisiana. Custer, with one company of the Seventh and a company of infantry, commanded the post at Elizabethtown, Kentucky, about forty miles south of regimental headquarters at Louisville.[1]

Judging from the frequency of their requests for leaves and leave extensions, most officers in the post–Civil War army found service in the West a hardship, and they sought any posting stateside that would release them from the monotony and isolation of frontier life. In some respects Custer was no different, but by 1871 he had come to relish service "on the plains" and did not welcome what he deemed "political" duty in the South. He was a Democrat, after all, and out of sympathy with many of the Republican policies he would be expected to enforce. Moreover, Reconstruction duty was unexciting, consisting mainly of furnishing details to assist state and federal officials in carrying out court orders and apprehending criminals. For the troops, this meant everything from breaking up illegal distilleries to suppressing the spread of the Ku Klux Klan. Custer's personal routine was even tamer. When he first arrived in September 1871, he had tried to put the best face on Elizabethtown in a letter to his wife, noting that its climate was "pure and healthful" and the citizens "cordial." "I enjoy this old-fashioned hotel, its quaint landlady who is everything in one," he wrote. "The meals are not so dreadful . . ." When she saw it for herself, Libbie was unimpressed, but, as always, she accepted her situation.

"This is a rest after our late excitement," she wrote. "But it is the stillest, dullest place."[2]

Elizabethtown's very quietness afforded Custer ample time to work on his memoirs of life on the plains, while the posting in Kentucky offered him another, enormous compensation. For part of his stay, Custer was detailed in Louisville on a board to purchase cavalry mounts, an assignment that took him to the Blue Grass country around Lexington where he could give free rein to his enduring passion for horses. It provided him an entrée onto some of the finest stock farms in the country and introduced him to many of the leading breeders in a horse-proud state. It gave him the chance to study up close and at leisure several fabled thoroughbreds and trotters. And it put him, an avid race fan, in the heartland of the reviving Southern turf.

Racing was experiencing a renaissance in the United States following its decline during the Civil War. By the early 1870's its popularity was marked both in the North, where the revival began, and in the South, where it had been delayed by the dislocations attendant upon war. Kentucky had been a fortunate exception. Throughout the fighting the Lexington Association managed to hold two or three meetings each year except 1862 when it was limited to a spring meeting. "Racing was kept up," a contemporary noted, "no matter what flag floated from the staff." During the period of Custer's residence in Kentucky, New Orleans, Memphis, Nashville, and Mobile were also hosting races, and there was every indication by 1872 that the Southern turf would rise again. Once more, rivalries between North and South would be decided on a bloodless field, as they had been in "the palmy days of the turf" before the Civil War when, to the cheers of their rabid partisans, great horses from each section fought mighty duels that instantly entered into folklore. Thoroughbred racing and trotting alike were on the threshold of a new golden age.[3]

Custer, long a fancier of fine horses, could hardly resist a personal involvement. Since the Civil War he had owned thoroughbreds and always cherished the dream of one day buying "a Blue-grass farm with blooded horses."[4] His two years in Kentucky were as close as he came to realizing it, and his first biographer claims that he followed temptation and "invested much of his private funds in race-horses" with "decidedly bad" results: "No sooner had he paid his money for a valuable mare, than the mare would be kicked by another, and get a leg broken, or fall sick and die; and in this way his horse ventures all came to grief and he lost some ten thousand dollars in a few years."[5] The evidence for such massive speculation in horses on Custer's part is slim, though there is no doubt that he bought some fine Kentucky thoroughbreds for his own use, notably Vic, the horse he would ride into his last battle. There is also firm evidence that he bought an expensive racing horse in 1872, Frogtown, the son of a distinguished sire, Bonnie Scotland, who, imported to New England in 1857, later proved his mettle at Nashville where he became champion sire in

1880. Frogtown had a great spring meeting at Lexington in 1872, winning the mile-and-a-quarter and mile–and–three-quarters dashes, both in record times. At Jerome Park that June he failed to meet expectations, finishing third in two races, but he regained his form in the September meeting at Lexington, winning both the mile-and-a-half and three-mile dashes. Custer acquired Frogtown shortly after and, since the horse was coming off a winning performance, must have paid handsomely for him. Apparently Custer hoped to race Frogtown at New Orleans in December, but his horse contracted an influenza that was then going the rounds and could not compete—a fact that might explain the sour tone of Custer's letter #13 on the Louisiana Jockey Club's abortive meeting.[6]

The five letters Nomad sent to *Turf, Field and Farm* between November 1871 and January 1873 are the most specialized and least generally interesting in the collection. But they do reveal the dimensions of a neglected facet of the General's character. Precious little has been written about Custer's stint in Kentucky—perhaps because precious little happened—and these five letters add to the record by indicating an obviously important outlet for his restless energies during not only the "stillest, dullest" but also the least-known years of his career.[7]

9. "Nomad in the Blue Grass Country— The Famous Breeding Studs"

NOVEMBER 26, 1871, Galt House, Louisville, Ky.

published December 1, 1871

Being desirous of taking a peep at the flyers of the Blue Grass region in their Winter quarters, I stepped aboard the early train from this city to Lexington, on Monday last, and after a charming ride of five hours found myself under the hospitable roof of the Phoenix Hotel, Lexington, where, according to previous agreement, I met Col. S. D. Bruce, of the *Turf, Field And Farm.*[1] After partaking of a good Kentucky dinner, such as the guests of the Phoenix are familiar with, our party, consisting of Col. Bruce, Col. Cook, U.S.A., Zeb Ward, and myself, started for Woodburn Farm[2] and its vicinity, fourteen miles west of Lexington—Mr. Ward and Col. Cook in one carriage, Col. Bruce and myself in another, for which we were indebted to the courtesy of Mr. Lowell, the gentleman who brought Blackwood to his greatest triumph as a three-year-old.[3]

A drive of two hours brought us to the residence of Mr. B. Gratz,[4] whose magnificent stock farm adjoins that of Mr. Alexander on the West. Here we not only found shelter, but luxurious comfort for man and beast. After supper the evening was spent in horse talk. The stranger is struck with the universal importance attached to horses and their history. Said a friend, "Did you ever hear anything like it? I have been here three days, and have heard nothing but horse, horse, horse." My only reply was that he might remain three months, or three years, and hear the same inexhaustible subject canvassed, past, present and prospective. And so it is; the youngest boy, white or black, can correctly trace the pedigree of every prominent horse, and give the time of each prominent race, with the place of each horse. He would not be a Kentuckian of the Blue Grass region if unable to do this. Desiring to make an early start in the morning, as we intended to devote the day to the distinguished stock of Mr. Alexander's immense farm, we retired comparatively early. Col. Cook and myself were assigned as room-mates.

In the morning the servant-girl, an overgrown fifteenth amendment, entered our room for the purpose of building a fire.[5] Col. Cook, arousing from a comfortable slumber, and anxious to learn the hour, inquired of the girl, "What time is it?" "Oh, de cows done gone long go." The Colonel, half awake, repeated his interrogatory, to which the ebony representative replied as before, "De cows done gone long go." Now as neither the Colonel or myself had ever informed ourselves at what hour Blue Grass etiquette required the cows to be "gone," we were left in ignorance of the hour of the morning. Our doubts on this point, however, were soon removed by Col. Bruce popping his head in at our door and inquiring if the "rattlesnake eater," (referring to one of our stories of the Plains of the night before) desired any breakfast. Breakfast served we were invited to witness the killing and preparation of meat according to the Jewish custom. Mr. Gratz, a most worthy descendent of this ancient people, although not a close or strict observer of their rights and customs, yet in some respects has not departed from the recognized faith. The process of killing simply requires that the animal shall not be bruised or shot. The throat must be cut in a transverse direction, and

then the animal is bled to death. If a fowl, the feathers around the neck are first plucked, the legs and wings securely tied to prevent bruising, then the throat is cut and the fowl bled to death.[6]

Inviting Mr. Gratz to join us, we seated ourselves in our carriages and drove to Mr. Alexander's, about one mile distant. Mr. Alexander, with his bride, is spending the winter in California, but his representative, Mr. Broadhead, who has supreme control of Woodburn Stock Farm and its valuable herds and stables, received us with that marked courtesy and cordial hospitality which has ever characterized the proprietors of this justly noted establishment.[7] Under his guidance we at once set about the object of our visit. As I propose to touch upon other subjects and places of interest the limits of this communication will not permit me to enter into a detailed description of the princely estate comprised in the Woodburn Stock Farm, embracing as it does four thousand acres of the richest and fairest soil in the world, with its trotting stables and exercising grounds at one point, its stables and walks for runners at another, while midway are to be found the immense stables and pastures of the fine herds of shorthorn cattle and Southdown sheep. Nor will I attempt a review of the stock itself—trotters or runners— further than a brief reference to a few of each. If I fail, however, to impart desired information as to the coming ones, I can refer all anxious inquirers to Col. Bruce, of our party, whom I saw carefully and critically studying and examining, with pencil and notebook in hand, the points of the thoroughbred weanlings preparatory to selecting at the annual sale in June next the winning colts for his Eastern friends, in the same manner as two years ago he selected the yearling, Harry Bassett, for that successful turfman Col. McDaniel, paying for the colt $315. Harry Bassett is but one of the many successful selections made by Col. Bruce.[8] In this connection I recall the greeting of the sable old functionary who has been born and bred among the thoroughbreds of Woodburn:

"Ah, Colonel, you're cum to look at de colts agin, has ye. You beats dem all a namin' de fastest ones."

What is the precise meaning of the mysterious phrases which the Colonel jotted down in his note-book after the pedigree of each colt I know not. It looked very much like the process of arranging the slate for a political election. This much I do know: the Colonel has promised to name to us the colts which will prove winners, and with this much we are for the present content.

The first stable we visited was that of the trotters. We were just in time to see the two great trotting sires and sires of trotters—Woodford Mambrino and Belmont—taking their morning walk. Woodford Mambrino is a wonderful horse, he was foaled in 1863 by Mambrino Chief, dam by Woodford; he is fifteen hands three inches in height, dark brown in color, with no white marks; he is a horse of great power and muscular development, close-ribbed, strong shoulders with good slope, broad loins, short back and immense breadth of haunches, good arm and leg, fine neck, with a head denoting great intelligence and mildness of disposition. He has never been handled sufficient to test his great speed, but after serving forty-five mares the past season he was han-

dled for a short time, and trotted one mile in 2:23. Mr. Alexander has refused $30,000 for him. Belmont, to the casual observer might be considered the better horse of the two; he certainly is a first-class horse in every respect, and in style greatly surpasses Woodford Mambrino. The latter looks and acts the trotter. Belmont, while being a trotter, looks the thoroughbred. He is a bright bay, 15.3 in height; he was foaled in 1864, and is by Abdallah, dam by Mambrino Chief, 2d dam by Bellfounder. Belmont has shown great speed as well as endurance. He served, during the past season, forty-five mares, and afterward trotted a third heat in 2:28⅓. The colts of both these noted stallions show great promise as trotters. We saw some weanlings and yearlings which are certainly destined to become fast ones.[9]

From the trotting stables we drove to the thoroughbreds. First we looked at a herd of brood mares. Among them were many who, having first achieved honor and reputation as runners on the turf, are now wearing new chaplets of fame by becoming the dams of successful racers. Among them Idlewild, whose four-mile record of 7:26¼ is excelled by but that of Lexington, Canary Bird, dam of Harry Bassett, Eagless, dam of Grey Planet, Novice, dam of Norfolk and Newry, Dolly Carter, and others of equal fame. Then we passed to the weanlings. Among them I saw a full brother to Grey Planet, Mr. Belmont's recent $10,000 purchase.[10] The weanling is said to be a perfect likeness of his two-year-old brother at same age. In the next lot was a full brother to Kingfisher, resembling the latter not a little. These two colts will undoubtedly cause lively bidding at the coming June sale. Then we saw some good ones by Planet; indeed, we are not certain that we saw better ones than some of those included in the get of Planet. Some young Asteroids also looked well; but as yet, if we except Stockwood, who ran a good second to Harry Bassett, the get of Asteroid has not been entitled to much favorable consideration. However, Asteroid is yet young in the stud, and should, and undoubtedly will, get winners.

After thoroughly reviewing the weanlings, we repaired to the stallion stables. First we saw Asteroid in his pasture, little looking as we saw him in his four-year-old form, when he ran his great race against Loadstone over the Woodlawn Course in 1865. His owner confidently expects him to become noted as the sire of race-horses. And why should he not? sired by Lexington, dam Nebula by Glencoe.[11]

From the son we repaired to the stable of the sire, the greatest horse, whether on the turf or in the stud, which this country has yet produced; and whose brilliant four-mile record of 7:19¾, has stood for more than three racing generations uneclipsed and untouched, notwithstanding the necessarily great improvement of the running horse in America since Lexington's racing career, and we safely venture the prediction that when four miles are run in less time than Lexington required, 7:19¾, it will be by a descendant of this gallant old king of the turf; and Lexington, instead of losing his long worn and well-earned laurels, will only add another by proving his reputation as a sire, like that as a racer, to be unparalleled. As his groom drew back the bolt and opened the door which admitted us into the distinguished presence of this famous horse, we involuntarily felt like lifting our cap, and with uncovered head and respectful mien approach this great steed as if we were in the sacred presence of royalty. Age has dealt lightly with him, his form is still youthful, his limbs clean and sinewy as those of a three-year-old, his sightless eyes alone seem to appeal for sympathy and pity. As he stood in his comfortably bedded stall our entrance seemed to attract his attention, but unlike other horses, who would turn their heads to see who it was who thus disturbed them, Lexington assumed an attitude of intent listening, pricking his ears as if to determine by the sounds of the voice who we were and the occasion of our visit. Thus proving, as in the human species, that when one sense is lost the other becomes more acute. Lexington was led from his stall and his blanket removed; his appearance was but little different from what would be imagined judging from the pictures taken of him years ago.[12]

Bidding him adieu we then visited Planet, who was browsing in his pasture near by. He was foaled in 1855, sired by Revenue, dam half sister to Lexington; he is a bright sorrel, and although he left the turf with a racing record considered as a whole, second to that of no other horse in this country, yet he has the points which go to make up the trotter, and under proper trotting management should get trotting colts. Imported Australian came next for inspection, and we found him with his Winter coat and looking well. He is undoubtedly a good horse, and to use a Kentucky expression, he should get colts "that would run as fast as anybody's horse," yet we would greatly prefer to breed to either Lexington or Planet.[13] We were then shown the two-year-old colt purchased at Mr. Cameron's recent sale of imported stock for

Mr. Alexander's stud. His name was The Reaper before being imported, but Mr. Alexander has given him the name of Glen Athol, as a sort of indication, I presume, of the name of his sire, Blair Athol. He is a large, powerfully made colt, his greatest fault, to my eyes, being in his fore legs. He is what might be termed cut away below the knees. I was not favorably impressed with this colt, yet, from his pedigree I would judge that Mr. Alexander, in selecting a strain of blood to cross with his present stock could not have done better. This colt's ancestry extends through a long and almost continuous line of winners.

Concluding our inspection of the thoroughbreds, by glancing at the weanling fillies, we next proceeded to the Alexander mansion, where we sat down to a most refreshing dinner. Two items—important ones, too—I must mention. A piece of Southdown mutton, served in the perfectness of Southern style, and Alderney milk of such rare and exceeding richness as to cause one only accustomed to city living to wonder whether he had ever really tasted pure milk before.[14]

After dinner our entire party, including Messrs. Gratz and Broadhead drove to the stock farm of Mr. Swigert, stopping by the way to take a glimpse of some thirty or forty weanling trotters, all, or nearly all, by Woodford Mambrino or Belmont out of thoroughbred mares. I think this lot of colts, without exception, is the finest I ever saw. They were in finer condition than the thoroughbreds as a lot, although the latter were treated individually with more consideration, having each a pasture lot to itself. We were well repaid by our visit to the stables of

Mr. Swigert, and if space would allow us we would gladly enter into a description of his stock. Among the many fine ones we saw there was one two-year-old colt by Lexington Dam, the dam of Stonewall Jackson, which, from his remarkable likeness to his grand old sire was particularly noticeable. He has the exact color and white marks of Lexington, and even now resembles him in form. Mr. Swigert justly holds him in high esteem; and I understand that, barring accidents, Grey Planet will have to look to his laurels in the coming three-years-old stakes, as this son of Lexington will certainly be there to see.[15]

Spending a most enjoyable evening and night under Mr. Alexander's roof, thanks to the courtesy and genial hospitality of Mr. Broadhead, as well as to Messrs. Gratz and Evans, we bade adieu to Woodburn next morning, promising to avail ourselves of an invitation to return at some future time, when we will take a peep at the shorthorns and Southdowns. We saw one two-year-old heifer for which Mr. Alexander refused $8,000 in gold. From Woodburn we drove to the stock farm and residence of "Old Uncle John Harper," the owner of Longfellow. Of course we were eager to see both stable and owner.

First among the horses to be interviewed was Longfellow, favorite son of a favorite sire. I had seen him at the Spring meeting at Lexington, when he had a walk over. Again I saw him in his wonderful contest with Kingfisher at Saratoga, when in the dash of two and a quarter miles he easily vanquished the favorite of Mr. Belmont's extensive stable, and ran one of the best races ever run in this country, making the first mile in the unprecedented time of 1:40. He had laid aside his running trim and donned his Winter condition. As it may be of interest to the lovers of the turf, I take pleasure in stating that Longfellow appeared in splendid condition, and exhibited every evidence of good health. From a close examination, and also by inquiry, I am satisfied that Longfellow's condition, in every respect, is all that his many friends can desire.[16]

Next to be looked at was Lyttleton, whose two-mile record of 3:34½ is within one quarter of a second of the best ever made. Although not in as fine condition as Longfellow, there could be no fault found. In writing of Longfellow, I omitted to state that Mr. Troye is now engaged in painting a likeness of that celebrated horse.[17]

Glancing at Express, Exchange and others we must devote a little space to Uncle John Harper. The horrible murder of his aged brother and sister is of too recent occurrence and of such horrible details to cause it to have been forgotten by the public; but a few facts have come to light recently, which, so far, seem to have failed to reach the knowledge of any but the immediate neighbors of Mr. Harper. We found Uncle John at home. His wealth, though estimated at nearly a million dollars, has not induced him to exchange the simple hut or cottage in which he, with his murdered brother and sister so long resided, for a more comfortable and modern dwelling. The stock farms of Messrs. Alexander and Harper lie side by side; one observes a vast difference in the possession and accompaniments of the patrician Alexander and those of the plebeian Harper. We found Uncle John occupy-

ing the room in which but a few weeks ago his brother, aged about seventy, had been so heartlessly murdered, while to reach this room we had to pass through another with low, dark ceiling, in which the sister, Miss Betsy was murdered. The owner of Longfellow, a feeble old man of near the allotted term of life, has been an invalid for several weeks, having been confined to his room from the effects of a fall. He is recovering, however, and will soon, I hope, be able to give his personal attention to his stock.

The subject of his horses, particularly Longfellow, seems the only one to interest him. After some preliminary conversation I asked Uncle John to give what he considered an explanation of Longfellow's defeat by Hembold. His explanation seemed perfectly satisfactory; too long for repetition, it amounts to this: He, no longer fearing that Kingfisher could contend in the four-mile race, imagined that there would be no opposing horse, and that Longfellow would simply have a walk over; he was allowed to get out of condition and to take on too much fat, increasing his weight from the time he ran with Kingfisher more than two hundred pounds. He came to the starting post wholly unfit to run any race, let alone a four-mile one, and as a consequence was beaten in very slow time. Uncle John said that Longfellow was not even in fair running condition when he met Kingfisher at Saratoga, and but for the fact that Kingfisher, as he says, was also out of condition, Longfellow would have been beaten.

"But," continued the old veteran, warming to his subject, "If I get out of this all right (referring to his temporary confinement to his room) I'm agoin to have Longfellow in fix to run next year, and when I get him ready I'm agoin to fetch him East; then you'll see what he kin do. I tell ye ye've never seen that horse run yit, gentlemen."

I asked Uncle John if he intended to match Longfellow against Harry Bassett? His reply was: "I don't say I am agoin to run agin any particular horse, but I do say that I am goin to git my horse ready, and when the time comes I am agoin to the races at Long Branch and will run Longfellow agin any horse what wants to run agin him, and, gentlemen, thar's no livin horse can run with my horse if he is in fix to run."

I was greatly struck by the confidence felt in Longfellow, as expressed by his owner. I have since learned from good authority that Mr. Harper has pledged the owners of the course at Long Branch that Longfellow will be there next year to run against Harry Bassett. If such an event comes to pass, there will be the greatest gathering of turfmen that has been witnessed for many years. I doubt even if a race between Harry Bassett and the English horse Sterling would attract so many people. Harry Bassett would have the odds as matters now stand, but if the race is made a dash of two miles and a quarter or less, the backers of Harry Bassett can get their bets taken freely. It will be a betting race, and if Longfellow is in condition my impression is that the son of Leamington will vanquish the favorite son of Lexington. In a four-mile race, however, Harry Bassett against the field. Longfellow is surely going East the coming season, if he and his owner escape accidents.[18]

The theory of the neighbors regarding the murder of the brother and sister of Uncle John Harper is, that instead of being committed by negroes, as was

at first suspected, the real perpetrator of the horrible deed is a relative. The two brothers, John and Jacob, and the sister, had made wills leaving their share of the vast estate to that one of the three who should survive the other two. It is supposed that in John's absence at the races in Lexington, his brother and sister were murdered and an attempt made by the murderer to find and destroy the wills of each, in which event the estate would then be divided by law between Uncle John and the heirs of a third brother, deceased some years ago. The wills were not found, having been carefully concealed. Uncle John discovered them on his return, so that he became the sole possessor of the entire estate. By the advice of friends, and to guard against his own assassination, he has employed some young men to remain in his house.

From Harper's we drove to Lexington. That evening and night I spent at McGrathiana, where I sat down to a champagne supper, which Delmonico could not have excelled. There were some choice spirits there besides those which were bottled. There was Charlie Woolley, of Cincinnati, whom Bottle Butler tried to unbottle; there was a Joe Elliott, of the New York *Herald*, *en route* to New Orleans to write of the races; there was Gen. Robinson, the jovial proprietor of the Phoenix Hotel; there was Col. Morgan, brother of Gen. Morgan, of Confederate fame; and last but not least there was the Prince of McGrathiana, and a "jolly old soul was he."[19]

The following day Col. Bruce and I drove out to see Dr. Price's famous yearling colt, by Ericsson, dam a Pilot mare. This colt is a marvel. He trotted in the presence of numerous witnesses, and timed by several experienced timers, one mile, in harness, 3:12. A yearling trotting in three minutes and twelve seconds! Dr. Talbot's yearling, by Herr's horse, trotted a mile, in harness, some weeks ago, in 3:28, and this was justly esteemed a wonderful performance; but here is a record sixteen seconds faster than has ever been trotted by the same age before. What may we not expect?[20]

From Dr. Price's we went to the stock farm of Mr. Enoch Lewis, near Lexington, where Ericsson, the sire of this wonderful colt, is kept. While here we saw this noted horse whose record as a four-year-old still stands unequalled. He is the property of Hon. K. C. Barker, Detroit, Mich. His colts are attracting great attention. Unfortunately he was kept for several seasons in Michigan where but few good mares were served by him, but since coming to Kentucky he is every day growing in the esteem of the lovers of the trotting horse. He is a large powerful horse plainly showing the Mambrino traits, and in the opinion of horsemen is one of the surest getters of trotters now in the stud. On Mr. Lewis' farm are several promising young Ericssons, one a yearling, half brother to Price's colt, trotted a quarter, in July, in :50. The death of several Mambrino stallions the present year, will be another inducement for breeders to look after Ericsson. Ericsson is half brother to Lady Thorne, who, but for her accident on the cars a year ago, would undoubtedly have eclipsed Dexter's time.[21]

10. " 'Nomad' with the Blue Grassonians"

[AUGUST 1872] *published August 30, 1872*

The time for the Fall meeting of the Kentucky Association is rapidly drawing near, and the prospect is that first-class sport may be anticipated. Nearly all the races promise to fill well, and among the entries thus far are some known good ones, while among the unknown a racing wonder may be found. The first race of the opening day has nine entries for the Phoenix Hotel Stakes for three-year-olds, and will bring together several already well-known to fame. Among others, there are two which will puzzle the betting fraternity not a little, provided both come to the stake in fine fettle. I refer to Zeb Ward's Planetarium, and Robinson & Morgan's Bazaine. Both proved themselves racers and winners at the Spring meeting, although Bazaine did not do so well at the East as was expected of him. There will be two races each day of the race week, commencing Monday, the 16th of September, and continuing through the week. Planetarium and Bazaine are also among the

entries in the Produce Stakes for three-year-olds, which will be run as the first race on Friday. In the second race for Friday, a sweepstakes for two-year olds, single dash of one mile, there are seventeen entries. There will be three interesting races the last day—the first a selling race, the second a consolation purse for beaten horses, the third a dash of three miles, to name and close the first day of the meeting.[1] With the greatly improved arrangements in stands and grounds, and under the liberal and strictly honorable management of the high-toned gentlemen who control the Lexington course, the lovers of real sport can assemble at the coming meeting, fully assured that everything will be conducted in the most correct manner and *pro bono publico*, and that in every race the best horse will win, which is saying a good deal more than can be justly said of many of the meetings which are held throughout the country.[2]

And while on this subject, I desire

[84]

to call the attention of the readers of the *Turf, Field And Farm* to the recent trotting races at Eminence, in this State. Such conduct as was permitted there is just what brings discredit and disgrace upon the trotting world, and should receive an unqualified rebuke from all honest lovers of sport. From the *Farmer's Home Journal*, of Lexington, Ky., a paper earnestly devoted to the interests of the stock breeders, and conducted with marked ability and candor, I clip the following comments on the race of the 13th inst., between Sentinel, Morrissey, Burger and Lottie:

"The horses in the first heat did a good deal more running than should have been allowed; but, as all did about the same amount, it was overlooked. Lottie came in first, Burger second, Morrissey third, and Sentinel fourth. *The time was 2:33⅗, and was so announced from the judges' stand.*

The horses got off well together in the second heat. Sentinel took the lead and kept it throughout, coming home first, Morrissey second, Lottie third and Burger distanced. Burger was lame, and it was owing to this, doubtless, that he was distanced. It was now apparent to all that Sentinel could win the race; but the drivers of Morrissey and Lottie decided to do all they could to prevent it, as proved by their subsequent acts.

Of all the jockeying we ever saw in scoring and in the heats throughout, this took the lead. Each made an effort to crowd Sentinel off the track, and would dash up beside him, it mattered not whether he was reached in a run or a trot. They tried to work him down in scoring, by making false starts. As an evidence of the collusion of the drivers of these two horses and the desperate game they were playing to defeat Sentinel, one cried out to the other, 'Don't let him pass,' as he was about to pass them on the backstretch. Sentinel managed, however, to win the third heat, notwithstanding the means resorted to to defeat him.

After several false starts the word 'go' was given for the fourth heat, and Sentinel got the lead and kept it to the end of the mile, amid the applause of the whole crowd. *Sentinel had many friends from the fact it was observed by all that a high-handed game was taken to defeat him. While*

we do not censure the association for the way this race was conducted, we are frank to say they were entirely too lenient with drivers who were not disposed to trot the race upon fair and honorable principles.

In the beginning of the race it was announced that it would be according to rule. The distance was marked off, and a distanced judge with his flag, to shut the distanced horse out, was placed there. Regular timers and judges of the race were selected. The first heat was trotted and won in 2:33⅗ by Bob Johnson's bay mare Lottie; the time was announced from the judges' stand, and Mr. Johnson came up and asked that the time be recalled, as he did not wish to have his mare to have the record against her. The time was recalled, and the association made a great mistake by it. If the association wishes to prosper, it must not suppress time simply to please an individual. Suppressing time is a direct violation of well-established trotting rules. The gentlemen of the trotting turf will not patronize grounds where the whims of every jockey are carried out as he suggests.

This was a public race for the consideration of $500, and we believe the time made by Lottie must hold good against her, and we believe it will be so decided by the Board of Appeals, or any set of intelligent gentlemen.

It has been stated (but we hope it is not so) that one of the judges had $100 bet on Lottie. This does not sound well, and it would be exceedingly mortifying to us to know that a Kentuckian would consent to act as a judge when he had money staked on the results."

Could anything in the conduct or management of a race be much more disgraceful? I cannot agree with the *Home Journal*, when it says "while we do not censure the Association for the way the race was conducted," etc., etc. The Association is chiefly deserving of the censure which such dishonorable management calls forth. I blame the Association rather than the drivers, dishonorable and unprincipled as the drivers of Lottie and Morrissey proved themselves to be, because it is to the judges of a race, not to the drivers, that the public, particularly that portion of it which has great interests at stake, looks to see that everything which smacks of knavery or unfairness shall be at once put down, and the guilty parties summarily punished. I do not, I am happy to say, know who the judges on this occasion were, but taking the comments of the *Home Journal* as my guide, I would not hesitate to pronounce the judges as utterly unfit to discharge the responsible duties of judges of a race, particularly when money was at stake, and their conduct, as above related, shows they ought never to be admitted to a judges' stand, or recognized on any respectable trotting course. They have clearly violated, not only the rules of honor, independent of the turf, but the rules intended to secure fair and honorable conduct in the management of races. As to the mare Lottie owned by a man named Bob Johnson, let the facts be known, and let it be published to the trotting fraternity, so that it will be known on every trotting course in the United States, that this bay mare Lottie trotted in a race "according to rule," and so announced from the stand before the race, and that she won the first heat in 2:33⅗, which record was publicly announced by the judges from their stand at the termination of the heat. Afterwards the owner of the mare asked the judges to recall this announcement, giving as a reason for this request that *"he did not wish to have the record against her,"* which request the judges either through ignorance or something worse, pretended to grant. I say pretended because it is well known that it is not in the power, happily, of the judges of a race to recall or alter a record once regularly made and announced, as it was in this instance.

So long as transactions like the above are permitted to occur, and not only permitted, but participated in by those whose duty it is to frown them down by punishing the guilty parties, just so long will the trotting turf be a reproach and a byword in the mouths of those who are ever seeking to destroy it. And it is the duty of all who take delight in the contests of the turf, as well as those interested in the breeding and training of superior horses, to allow no opportunity to pass unimproved of administering unqualified rebuke to those who would prostitute either themselves or their official position, or both, as was done in the above instance, to change or influence unfairly the results of a race. I am happy to say that, so far as my experience proves, such examples of high-handed unfairness as that just referred to are of rare occurence in this part of the country.[3]

The week preceding the races at Lexington beginning with Tuesday, the 10th, will be full of interest, as the Kentucky Agricultural and Mechanical Association of Lexington holds its annual fair. The trials of speed made under its auspices will be over the course of Mr. Richard Lowell, the proprietor of Mentella Stock Farm. Any person desiring to see fine stock of all kinds, embracing horses, thoroughbreds and trotters, Alderney and all the varieties of short-horn cows, mutton and wool-producing sheep of the finest grades, hogs which weigh a good deal more than they ought—to all such people I say attend the Lexington Fair.

I omitted to mention the greatest attractions offered by the Blue Grass region, and even now I hesitate to refer to them; but you know, dear *Turf*, that "from the abundance of the heart the mouth speaketh," or, as they say in military parlance, "words to that effect." Admitting, however, the great superiority justly claimed by the Blue Grass people for their Lexingtons, Longfellows, Blackwoods, Patchens, and Ericssons; acknowledging that they can, on their beautiful green sward, produce the finest mutton, the richest milk, the choicest vegetables and the purest *Bourbon*, yet the greatest pride of the Blue Grassonians is to be found, and justly so, in the unparalleled loveliness of their women. The beauty of the women of the Blue Grass region seems to have been developed like the speed of its thoroughbreds, so as to eclipse that of all other lands. The women are as charmingly beautiful as the men are proverbially chivalrous, which is saying not a little, while both are as truly hospitable as warm hearts and welcome hands can be.

Take it the world over, there is no hospitality which surpasses that of the true Kentuckian, and he is not a true Kentuckian who is not hospitable. The Kentucky style of beauty is found wherever beauty is a thing to be prized or admired, but Louisville, the great metropolis of Kentucky, generally aims to furnish the real type by which the fair sex of the State shall be judged. I will admit that there is a great deal of true womanly beauty in Louisville, if one could only get at it. That is, if one could get through the disguises and be allowed to form an unbiased opinion. How beautiful the Louisville girls really are is one of those puzzling questions which, as Dundreary says, "No fellah can find out."[4] For if ever a human contrivance was gotten up with malice aforethought and intended to deceive, it is the Louisville girl of the period.

Nature is but little occupied so far as controlling the outward appearance of the Louisville belles is concerned. Pencil, paint and hair-dye are the three predominant qualities of her mind. I say her mind, for she occupies it with but little else. It is something of a curiosity to see one of them promenading on some of the fashionable streets ornamented in their peculiar style. As for taste, they exhibit but little, so far as dress goes. They appear in street costumes which combine every color of the rainbow, the material and styles of making being far better adapted to a drawing-room reception than a shopping excursion. Blonde is the predominent style of beauty *adopted*, and, as a consequence, a stranger strolling through any of the popular promenades of Louisville is very apt to imagine that Lydia Thompson, with an increased troupe of English blondes, has just arrived. It is thought to be quite the thing with some of the dark-haired belles to wear a very light-colored wig in front and a chignon of dark hair. Contrasts are striking, you know. Society is not led or controlled by married ladies, but by young girls. Mothers are not recognized as a necessary element in the social circle, and if the Louisville girls are regarded by strangers as inclined to be a little the opposite of slow, it is not surprising Louisville does not lie within the circle of the Blue Grass region. In the latter the girls display more beauty because of less paint, Lydia Thompsonisms, etc., etc., and furnish the true type of Kentucky beauty. And while their feet may not have received the thorough training given to those of their blonde rivals of the Falls City, the education of their heads and hearts makes them superior women to the others.[5]

I have written only of the Girl of the Period as she is to be seen in Louisville, with her bad grammar, cheap diamonds, and horribly flashy dresses; but do not understand me as representing that no other style is to be met with in this beautiful city. I would be doing a gross injustice to many a charming and accomplished fair one of my acquaintances, whose simple but elegant tastes and manners eminently fit them to adorn and brighten the highest walks of educated and refined society. Louisville has representatives among her young ladies of the fairest types of womanhood, and can proudly hold them up as such, but she ought, from the vast numbers of young ladies, to have a greater number answering to this description.

11. "The Kentucky Association"

[OCTOBER 1872] *published October 11, 1872*

The Kentucky Association, after maturely deliberating upon the subject, have concluded to take a step which ought to have been taken long since. They have determined to open their course to the trotting fraternity, and with this view they will have their first meeting, commencing October 16, and continuing four days. There will be from two to three trotting races each day, mile heats, three in five; entrance money ten per cent of the purse offered.

This is a step in the right direction, and will be found to be a benefit not only to the Association financially, but of incalculable benefit and importance to the breeders and owners of trotting stock in Kentucky, particularly in the Blue Grass region. The vast amount of capital invested in the producing and training of stock in Kentucky demands that annual meetings at least be held upon first-class grounds, but, more important than all, under a management that will rebuke fraud and rowdyism such as too frequently prevail on the

trotting courses. From a personal acquaintance with the officers of the Association, and after conversations with them regarding the proposed experiment—for it is to be an experiment—I am satisfied that the meeting in October will be a new era in trotting affairs as usually witnessed in this section of the country, and as exhibited at the recent trot given on the old track near Lexington, when several of the drivers, and some of the judges, should have been ruled off of all trotting courses on account of their behavior. Nothing bordering on improper conduct, whether on the part of drivers, owners, stable-boys or spectators, will be permitted on the grounds of the Kentucky Association. The control of the trotting meeting is to be under the present officers of the Association, with Gen. Breckenridge to preside. The first attempt at fraud, or even the ordinary annoyances to which the public are subjected to at trotting races, in the way of starting horses, bickerings between drivers, or not allowing horses that are able to do so to win, will result then and there in the summary expulsion of the guilty parties from the grounds of the Association. In this connection, I would suggest to the officers of the Kentucky Association that they join the National Association before the October meeting comes off, so that parties ruled off the Lexington course will thereby, as they deserve, be ruled off every respectable track in the United States.

Too much must not be expected from this first meeting in the way of success. In the first place, the limited time between the announcement of the meeting and the day it commences will prevent many owners of horses from having their stock in readiness to compete for purses; second, the size of the purses offered will not attract so many horses as large amounts properly divided would. It will be enough if the meeting is held even with slim attendance of men and horses, to show, that in the proper hands, a trotting meeting can be held, and the same fairness, propriety and good order enforced that characterizes the running meetings held under the same management. Of one thing the drivers and owners of horses that are to contend for the purses offered by the Kentucky Association may rest assured. Either they will conduct themselves with the utmost propriety and honesty, or they will be subjected to such summary treatment as they have not seen practiced on most of the trotting courses.

It is a great triumph for the trotting turf to have the Kentucky Association open its gates to trotting contests. Let those most interested in the breeding and training of trotting stock leave nothing undone to make this first step

a success, and incalculable benefit will result to both the Association and to those whose wealth and pleasure are largely connected with trotting horses.

While on the subject of trotters, I recall the subject of the pedigree of the famous horse Jim Irving, whose owner has recently offered to match him against any horse in the world, mile heats, best three in five, or two-mile heats. In my notes on the Buffalo meeting, written after witnessing his wonderful race there in August, I stated that it was reported at Buffalo at the time that Jim Irving was a thoroughbred, but believed him to be by Melbourne, and out of a common mare. I took pains to learn all that is known as to the breeding of this horse. I cannot furnish this information to the readers of the *Turf, Field and Farm* in a better manner than by giving the letter of A. Keene Richards, a gentleman who has devoted a fortune to the importation and production of fine stock of all kinds, and whose word and character are ample guarantee of the authenticity of the pedigree as given:

"Georgetown, Ky., Sept. 21, 1872 GEN. CUSTER—*Dear Sir*:—The facts in connection with the pedigree of the trotting gelding Jim Irving will soon be put in proper form and furnished you. The mare that produced Jim Irving was bred to Melbourne while Mr. Lewis kept him. She was a common wagon mare, used for farm purposes, and was by a well bred stallion known as Leah's Sir William; he was out of a mare by imported Contract, son of Catton, the sire of Trustee, &c., &c. The dam of Irving was out of an Ohio mare, pedigree not ascertained, but of cold blood without doubt. Jim Irving probably has no trotting cross or cold cross except this Ohio mare; the other crosses are probably of the best racing blood. Judging from the form, color, temper and action of Irving, we may safely say that he has bred back to the thoroughbred crosses in his pedigree, and is owing to what Darwin would call "atavism," or reversion. The disposition of Jim Irving to run instead of trot, he does not get, I'm sure, from his dam, and if he had a Canadian cross on his sire's side the tendency would be to mix his gait, and to pace or rack. The proof that the mare was bred to Melbourne, and that the time of foaling came to the time of service, will soon be furnished you, and some facts in reference to the dam of Jim Irving, which will astonish those who believe in the theory about the Earl of Morton's mare that produced the striped foals, and the well bred pointers that produced brindle pups.

I am yours truly,
A. KEENE RICHARDS.[1]

This will settle the question conclusively as to how Jim Irving is bred.

Would it not be a good idea for the owners of trotting mares to patronize Melbourne? I saw Melbourne last spring, before Jim Irving had been heard of in public, and remarking upon his formation, I said he ought to trot well, but did not imagine he was already the sire of one of our most remarkable trotters—one that would challenge the world. Melbourne and Jim Irving are not unlike in form or color. To-night I start for Nashville, to attend the meeting which opens there to-morrow.

12. " 'Nomad' Makes Some Good Suggestions"

[**NOVEMBER 1872**] *published November 8, 1872*

In my haste to catch the mail with my last letter, containing notes on the inaugural trotting meeting given by the Kentucky Association over their course at Lexington, I necessarily was forced to omit many suggestions which might well be considered.

Regarding it as a fixed fact that trotting meetings will hereafter be events of at least annual occurrence upon the Lexington course, it may not be amiss to throw out a few hints looking to the success of the proposed meetings. I mean not only the success of the Kentucky Association, under whose auspices and able management the meetings should be held, but to that of the breeders and producers of trotting stock in Kentucky, at the same time keeping in view the interests of that large class of purchasers to whom the breeder must look for success. That programme should be adopted by the Kentucky Association which will pro-duce the greatest amount of generous, but earnest, competition between the breeders of trotters. It is in the power of the association to establish such a system of tests as will cause success upon their grounds to be the almost certain and unquestioned stepping-stone to public favor, so that purchasers from other States will regard the annual meetings of the Kentucky Association as the most fitting time to make their selections, and those families or strains of trotting blood which appear to greatest advantage during the meeting will be most likely to receive greatest consideration and encouragement from the public.

The Kentucky Association is in the midst of influences differing materially from those bearing upon any other prominent course in the United States. It is located in the centre of a section of country already famous, and each year becoming more so, as the source from which the great majority of our distinguished horses come. So true is this that in other states a peculiar and enhanced valuation is placed upon the horse if it can be claimed for him that he is of Kentucky birth. No other association could so truthfully claim as one of its objects "The Improvement of Horses," this being the set phrase which usually precedes or heads the programmes of other associations. At any of our prominent trotting meetings, such as at Buffalo, Mystic Park, Prospect Park, or elsewhere, except in Kentucky, it would be a difficult, if not impracticable matter to place upon their regular programme a moderate proportion of colt stakes and have them well filled, while at Lexington the reverse of this would be true. Contests between colts of two, three and four years of age might, and probably would, be made the distinctive feature of the annual meetings. I purposely omit yearlings, as I cordially agree with the *Turf, Field And Farm* when, referring to the "wonderful performance" of the yearling which trotted, as is alleged, the first mile in 3:05, the second in 3:02, making the *two miles* in 6:07, it does not fail to utter its condemnation of "the cruelty involved in speeding a tender yearling such a distance in so short a time." Elsewhere than Kentucky, speeding a two-year old for even a mile would be condemned, but when we consider that the two-year old of Kentucky is as fully developed as the average three or four-year old of other States, it does not seem so open to criticism. Other associations do well to offer such purses and conditions as will call together the greatest number of celebrated aged horses, while the Kentucky Association should aim to bring together in

competition the largest number of two, three, four and five-year-olds, the get of stallions which have made seasons in the Blue Grass country. This would encourage, almost compel, the owners of every stallion claimed as the sire of trotters to handle, or have handled, at least one of each year of his horses' get, and in this manner a true and impartial development of the various trotting families would be brought about, while the public would be enabled to judge knowingly of their respective merits, and both breeder and buyer be benefited thereby.[1]

How can this programme be made to operate effectually, and to the success, financially, of the association and all interested? If the gratifying results of the first and recent meeting were obtained upon such limited notice, and such moderate-sized purses as were given, it is but fair to assume that by deciding upon the holding of the meeting at as early a period as practicable, and offering liberal purses, the success would be correspondingly increased. The members of the Kentucky Association, whose experience in turf matters has generally been confined to the thoroughbred running horse, should bear in mind that it is but just that a larger purse should be offered to trotters than to runners, if for no other reason than this: A running colt may compete for any prize, no matter how limited in value, and in doing so may make a record which eclipses all former time, and yet he not only increases his value, but is still as eligible for a race of the same kind or of any other as he was before, whereas a trotting colt, in making a record, is debarred from entering again in any race except for horses which, like himself, have not beaten in public his best time; hence the owner of a promising trotter is naturally unwilling to enter his horse in a race in which the purse offered is so small that by winning it his horse makes a record which is more damaging to him than would be the loss of the race. This is not altogether applicable to the owners of stallions, who in many cases (and financially are justified in so doing) are willing to trot their colts, not for the possession of the purse offered, but for the reputation it will give to the sire.

This fact alone will enable the Association to offer two purses for the same ages. I believe that results will justify them in offering what might well be termed handsome amounts, to be trotted for by the youngsters. Assuming that the trotting meeting would immediately follow the running meeting in September, let them offer a sweepstakes for two-year olds, of $50 entrance, play or pay, to close the 1st of June, the Association to add $——, best two in three, second horse to save his entrance. I venture to say this stake, independent of the amount added by the Association, would be worth to the winner at least $1,000 in money, as it is but a moderate estimate to say twenty would be the number of hopeful owners of green two-year olds who would be confident that their particular colt could trot faster than "any man's" colt. Then I would suggest a Breeders' Stake for two-year olds, $100 entrance, play or pay, to close the 1st of June, open to any two-year old owned and to be entered by the owner of the sire, second horse to save his entrance. The winner of this stake would not only be compensated by gaining a handsome amount of money, for the subscribers would undoubtedly be numerous, but what would be more gratifying, and in the end remunerative, he

would be winning reputation and increased patronage for his stallion.

Races of almost the same condition could be made for the three, four and five-year olds. Then, upon the closing day, and as the end of the programme, let there be offered a handsome piece of plate for the stallion whose get received during the meeting the greatest number of purses, value considered. An equally valuable piece of plate to the best trotting stallion, as a stallion, pedigree, style, action and speed the test. When purses are offered, and a fair percentage required as entrance money, the amount obtained from the latter will go far towards reimbursing the Association for the expenses of the meeting. The entries, nominations or subscriptions to all races should close in advance of the opening day. The experience of the last meeting, no doubt, proves this.

To insure success, nothing is more necessary than that the Association should, as soon as is practicable, fully consider the questions connected with their next meeting, and publish their programme extensively. This is due to those who will have, or desire to have, colts to compete for the various purses or stakes offered. Breeders and owners of colts, unlike the owners of aged or trained racers, will desire time first to look over their stock from time to time, and choose those that they consider most promising for early training; second, after having made their selections, to be able to gradually develop the speed of their youngsters without resorting to that forcing process which would be necessary if allowed but a few weeks of preparation, and which would almost certainly result in the permanent injury of their colts. Three races could easily be given each day, two of them being contests between the youngsters, the third being a race open to all horses that had not beaten—minutes, or a free-for-all race. To have three races in one day, it would be necessary, and the Association would find it most satisfactory and interesting, as the experience of other associations proves, to have the heats of two of the races trotted alternately. In this way the public are kept comparatively free from the tiresome delays between heats which are otherwise unavoidable.

If, as was suggested in my last letter, the prominent stock sales of the breeders of trotters in the Blue Grass region were united with and made part of the trotting meeting, the number of people and purchasers from other States would probably exceed the entire number which visit Kentucky in a whole year, owing to the increased facilities, not to mention the pleasure, of visiting and inspecting the prominent breeding stables. As in most branches of business one sure aid to success is ample advertising, so in this case let the Kentucky Association promptly decide upon its programme, and then announce it to the public.

To change the subject, I wish to refer to your editorial in last week's number, headed "High Prices For Trotters." In conversation with one of our most prominent breeders, I find an unfavorable impression produced by it. He regarded it as prejudicial to the interests of the breeders of trotters, and as one result predicted that his annual sale, which had not then taken place, would be injured by it. His view, which I hope is an exceptional one, I take as unfounded. I mean as to the effect. On the contrary, I think your editorial remarks ought to stimulate and increase the number of buyers. While all that

you stated is true, you undoubtedly did not state all that is true, or which you might have stated and have left the mind of the breeder of trotters at rest—not only at rest, but delighted at the prospect. Your editorial says, speaking of former years, that "the trotter was bred in a hap-hazard sort of way, and the flyer was the result of chance." "An offer of $30,000 for a 2:20 horse was not out of the way, since a horse of the kind was so exceptional as to be worth the money." "But the 2:20 flyers came at such rare intervals that the supply was never equal to the demand, and consequently the price remained unchanged. In the last two years, however, the change has been marked. Where one trotting stud existed fifteen years ago one hundred can be counted now, and a horse that can go low down in the twenties is no longer exceptional." "Clearly the horse that sold for $30,000 five years ago is not worth $30,000 now." "We cannot go on paying the high price for a 2:20 horse when horses that are two and three seconds faster are more numerous than the former class were when the prize was first offered."[2]

Admitting all this to be true, as it is, there is nothing in it to alarm the breeder as to his present and future prospects. Considered in the aggregate there is scarcely any branch of business in which the annual increase of money invested has been so great as that invested in trotters during the past few years, and while it may be true that the purchase of a trotter to-day at the high price of $30,000 is exceptionable, yet the great number of purchases at from $1,000 to $20,000 more than compensates the breeder by their frequency for what might be considered the rarity of a $30,000 sale. And if we could be furnished with the statistics during the years in which the trotting interests have grown from their infancy to their present huge proportions, I think it would appear evident that the per cent profit derived now, as compared with that derived a few years ago, is largely in excess of the latter. Years ago it was the "exceptional" breeder who was fortunate enough to dispose of an "exceptional" horse at a strikingly large figure. To-day there are few breeders of prominence but can exhibit a string of young trotters, ranging in price from $500 to $15,000, some even going beyond these figures, and there are still people who demand such prices and people willing to pay even higher ones. Look at the sale of the three-year-old *gelding*, Prospero, a few days ago, for *twenty thousand dollars*.[3] And where the sale of a trotter for $30,000 took place, proba-

bly, once or twice in a period of five years but a decade past, at least half a hundred, on an average, are now sold, within the same period, at figures ranging from $10,000 to $20,000.

Surely the signs of the times contain nothing portentious of evil to the breeder of trotters. Two prominent sales of the present year suggest themselves to me. I will not at this date attempt to be accurate as to figures, but having attended both sales, my recollection is that at each sale there were from fifteen to twenty yearling and two-year-old head of trotting stock sold, mostly yearlings, and that the average price brought at auction was between $500 and $1,000. So long as breeders can sell at anything like these prices, the margin of their profits must surely satisfy them.[4]

13. " 'Nomad' on the Louisiana Jockey Club —Anecdote of Lexington"

[JANUARY 1873] *published January 10, 1873*

With the tame events of the Fall meeting of the Louisiana Jockey Club your readers are already familiar. Notwithstanding the possession of one of the best and handsomest courses in the entire country, and the offer of most liberal purses and stakes, with the population of one of our largest and greatest pleasure-loving cities in convenient proximity, the late meeting was a decided failure.

The combination of circumstances which operated against a successful meeting was formidable and difficult to overcome. When the time advertised for the races to take place arrived, the horses of the various racing stables represented on the ground were well and in good condition to make splendid running, but the epizootic had reached New Orleans and the public and private stables in the city, including those of the streetcar lines, were paralyzed, thus preventing the citizens from reaching the racecourse, had any been so disposed. The races were postponed from time to time, until the recovery of the livery and car animals restored the usual means of conveyance to the course. But by this time the thoroughbreds in nearly all the running stables were in condition to run well—only at the nose. Of those allowed to start in the few races ran, it is safe to say that on the last day not one was free from the epizootic, and four out of five of those led to the cooling ground between heats were coughing badly.[1]

The attendance at no time exceeded three hundred persons, although on the last day of the meeting the facilities for reaching the grounds were ample, and the running, considering condition of track and other unfavorable circumstances, was good and the races well contested.[2] The intense interest and excitement resulting from the great political movements then taking place daily, or, more properly speaking, nightly—as every prominent step in the movement was taken near the hour of midnight, as if shunning the light of open day—no doubt exercised an unfavorable influence upon the success of the meeting.[3]

Yet, admitting the many obstacles which stood in their way, it seemed to an outsider that the club itself was lacking in that enterprise and judgment necessary to command success. Any association, independently of its ability or merits, succeeds, provided fortune throws every element of success in its way. Success achieved under these circumstances, when failure is almost impossible, reflects no particular credit upon the managers; it is only when obstacles are encountered and surmounted or swept aside that success becomes the criterion of merit. The hesitation and lack of energy, almost of interest, displayed by the Louisiana Jockey Club in their late meeting were deserving of and calculated to bring about just such a complete failure as was witnessed. There was but one person connected with the club who seemed at all interested as to whether the races came off or not, or whether the club carried out its published programme or not, and that person was Captain W. M. Connor, clerk of the course, who devoted his entire time to the matter, and but for whose indefatigable exertions no meeting would have been held.

The club had ample excuse for finally abandoning the attempt to have a race meeting, because the racehorses themselves were not present in sufficient numbers and fully recovered from the epizootic to justify the continuance of the races. This excuse did not exist, however, when the races began, as advertised, on the first day. The racers were in fine trim, and owners eager to run their horses and get them safely located for the Winter. The postponement was first made in reality because the public stands were not filled with spectators, or, in other words, to adopt the language of a prominent turfman present, the stewards had counted over the gate-money and found that the club was not making money, and, like a country cross-road association, they proposed to wait a few days, and try and drum up enough gate-money to pay expenses, at least. It was then predicted that the club would abandon its published programme, if any excuse for so doing could be discovered by delays. The excuse came in the shape of the epizootic throughout the racing stables. The club was thus justified, although they had not been at first, in giving up their feeble attempt to hold a Fall meeting.

From the concurrent opinion of nearly all the owners of horses there I was led to the conviction that December is too late in the season to run horses even at New Orleans. First, the weather is nearly always too cold and unpleasant to encourage a large attendance, besides being unfavorable and dangerous to horses. Second, it leaves too brief a period to devote to the rest and recuperation of the horses, preparatory to engaging in their Spring work.

The *Turf, Field And Farm* for Dec. 27 has this moment been placed upon my table, from which it will be read that the Louisiana Jockey Club has relinquished its grand idea of offering $20,000 in the great four-mile race, so long advertised as to come off in the Spring. This announcement will take none of the horse owners by surprise who attended the last meeting, any one of whom felt confident that the purse would never be hung up. Recalling the dispatch of Capt. Billy Connor published some months ago, to the effect that the $20,000 race had become a fixed event, and the Louisiana Jockey Club assumed the responsibility for it, some inquiring mind may hereafter, in view of the past vacillation of the Louisiana Jockey Club, when told that the aforesaid Louisiana Jockey Club assumes the responsibility, inquire "Who assumes the responsibility for the Louisiana Jockey Club?" and I have no doubt some such responsible person will be necessary. "Oh, for the restoration of the grand old Metairie!" will be the exclamation of more than one. There are many experienced turfmen in the South who believe that two racing associations would succeed better (worse it could not be) than one at New Orleans. Rivalry and competition would produce a little of that plucky determination and enterprise now so lacking. Imagine the officers of the grand old Kentucky Association, or of any of our first-class racing clubs, postponing advertised races, with good day, good track and plenty of entries, simply because people could not be induced to attend the races in as great numbers as had been expected.

I know that the *Turf, Field And Farm* is the determined and outspoken enemy of everything which tends to debase the sports of the turf, and it never misses any fair opportunity to administer rebuke to any unusual practices or customs which, in themselves or by their influences, act so as to prevent the best and most refined classes of society from lending the sanction of their presence to the excitement and pleasure of the turf contests. There is one practice of the Louisiana Jockey Club

which, in any city North of the Gulf States, would prove fatal, as it deservedly should to the success of any racing club, no matter what might be the respectability and high character of the officers and members of the club. I refer to the official and public sanction given by the club to gambling in its worst forms. This is done by the club selling to the highest bidder the privilege of that portion of the grand stand allotted to gambling. This privilege is bought generally by one or more wealthy gamblers, the price realized by the club amounting to thousands of dollars. The gambler who leases this privilege sub-leases it to dozens of other gamblers of lesser pretensions. These, after being allotted the space set apart for them, are privileged to carry on their nefarious practices in such manner and according to such schemes as they see fit. I saw no less than half a dozen roulette tables, with numerous other fleecing game tables, all in full blast in the grand stand of the Louisiana Jockey Club during the last meeting. These were in full view of every spectator of the races who chose to cast his eyes toward that part of the grand stand, and were kept running during and between the heats. I was not surprised that there were not more than a dozen ladies present either day of the races. Anywhere but in New Orleans this licensed gambling by the club, and the little regard paid to public sentiment would be sufficient excuse for deterring any lady and most gentlemen from countenancing the meetings by their attendance.[4]

I trust the Louisiana Jockey Club will not issue their programme for a Spring meeting until they have positively decided that such a meeting will be held. Should they announce a few more important events such as their last meeting and the "grand $20,000 race, four-mile heats," with like results, their name, without altering their initials, should be the Louisiana Joking Club. I hope they will decide upon a spring meeting and that all the circumstances, including themselves, may work to insure the success of the meeting. There is no reason why New Orleans in the future, as in the historic past, should not be one of our greatest racing centres. And with all my criticism I wish the Louisiana Jockey Club the greatest success, but hope it will deserve it more in the future than it has in the past. I have referred to the members of the club collectively. Individually, I found all with whom I was brought in contact, from the courteous President, Col. Breaux, down to the subordinates, gentlemen whom it is a delight and an honor to know. Success attend them heartily, say I.

While in New Orleans, and taking a peep almost daily at the various stables collected there, many were the legends of the turf related to me by the various habitues of the course always found about the stables during a race meeting. Among others, I recall a story relating to that matchless racer and sire of racers, Lexington, which you may have heard, but was new to me. I repeat it for your readers, to show what an irremediable loss the racing world barely escaped. When on the track one morning, watching the galloping of the thoroughbreds, the early exploits of Lexington became the subject of conversation, and very naturally, too, as New Orleans was the scene of his great triumph over time, and, so far, of posterity.

Henry Brown, the well-known trainer of Mr. Geo. Cadwallader, and who, at the time referred to, lived with Dr. Warfield, the owner of Lexington, near Lexington, Ky., relates how, as was almost his daily custom, the Doctor one day mounted his saddle mare (then in season) and started on a ride through the pastures to take a look at his stock.[5] Finally he came to the field containing five two-year-old thoroughbred colts, one of which was Lexington, then unnamed. No sooner did the young stallions discover the tempting presence of the mare than the entire lot of five charged towards her. The Doctor, divining their purpose, headed the old mare towards the bars and gave her her head, at the same time brandishing his cane towards the colts to frighten them back. Their blood was up, however, and they were not to be turned aside from their purpose so readily.

By this time the Doctor had got the old mare down to nearly a two-minute gait, closely followed by the colts. Seeing some of the servants near the bars, he shouted, "Throw down the bars! throw down the bars!" but before any but the uppermost bar could be removed the Doctor, riding at a John Gilpin rate,[6] had reached them. There was no time to pull rein; so, giving the old mare a free hand and a persuader with his cane, over he went as if riding a hurdle-race, and landed safely on the other side the bars. The servants checked the colts, but it was not to end here. The Doctor's blood was up, and he declared that every one of those colts should be castrated then and there. The order was put in train of execution at once, and four of the five colts were castrated. The ropes were placed on the fifth, and he was thrown to the ground. The operator (Henry Brown, my informant) took his position, knife in hand, and had already taken the testicle in his left hand; but just when preparing to cut a slit in the scrotum the colt struggled, and the point of the knife entered the hand of the operator, cutting a vein. The bleeding from the latter was so profuse that the castration of the colt was deferred, the ropes were removed, and the colt was returned to his pasture. The colt was Lexington, afterwards to astonish the sporting world by his remarkable performances, both on the turf and in the stud.

I read with great interest the communication of "Warwick" in the *Turf, Field And Farm* of the 27th, upon the subject of vaccination of dogs to prevent distemper. I have probably the finest pack of Scotch staghounds in this country, and each year had lost many valuable dogs from distemper, until I concluded to try vaccination. My young dogs were vaccinated; it took well, and I have not had a case of distemper since. I am a strong believer in the saving merits of vaccination. The best place to perform the operation is inside the fore leg, close to the body, as this point is beyond the reach of the mouth, and prevents disturbance after the vaccine has produced a painful sore. Before adopting this method of prevention, I each year lost the greater portion of each litter of puppies from distemper alone. One of my bitches dropped a litter of eleven. These I caused to be vaccinated as soon as old enough, and every one grew finely and are still alive and well.

IV

DAKOTA TERRITORY, 1873-1875

"... into the field again"

IN FEBRUARY 1873, an exuberant Nomad received the orders that would start him on his life's last journey: the Seventh Cavalry was to be transferred to the Department of Dakota for service against the Sioux on behalf of another railroad building across Indian country, the Northern Pacific. Elizabeth Custer recalled the joyous response the news elicited:

> When orders came for the 7th Cavalry to go into the field again, General Custer was delighted. . . . [Duty in the South] seemed an unsoldierly life, and it was certainly uncongenial; for a true cavalryman feels that a life in the saddle on the free open plain is his legitimate existence.
>
> Not an hour elapsed after the official document announcing our change of station had arrived before our house was torn up. In the confusion I managed to retire to a corner with an atlas and surreptitiously look up the territory to which we were going. I hardly liked to own that I had forgotten its location. When my finger traced our route from Kentucky almost up to the border of the British Possessions, it seemed as if we were going to Lapland.[1]

But the General was ecstatic about the new posting, and as he swung his wife about the room knocking over furniture in his excitement, his enthusiasm, as always, proved contagious. Steamboats carried the various components of the Seventh Cavalry up to Cairo, Illinois, where they were assembled for a train ride to the end of track, at Yankton, D.T. The last 350 miles to Fort Rice were covered on horseback, proof positive that the regiment had finally left civilization and its amenities behind.

The troops arrived at Fort Rice on June 10; ten days later they were off with eleven companies of infantry, artillery, and a wagon train on the Yellowstone Expedition under the command of General David S. Stanley. Its task was to protect the survey crews of the Northern Pacific and, by its size and strength, give the Indians warning that the white man's road would be built despite their opposition. If it was action Custer wanted, he found it on this expedition in two dangerous brushes with the Sioux, one of which he alludes to in letter #14. The Yellowstone Expedition ended for Custer and his direct command when they arrived at winter quarters, the newly constructed Fort Abraham Lincoln, across the river from Bismarck, on September 21.

Thereafter, while companies of the Seventh would be stationed at Fort Rice and Fort Totten, and regimental headquarters would remain at Fort Snelling in Minnesota, Fort Lincoln would be the Custers' home. From it a major expedition into Sioux country departed on July 2, 1874, and though the Black Hills Expedition proved uneventful from the standpoint of Indian fighting, it was of primary importance as an exploratory probe into a gold-rich area and in future Sioux-white relations. It was while on this expedition that Custer "reached the hunter's highest round of fame. . . . I have killed my Grizzly." He proudly posed behind the fallen bear for a photographer but chose not to regale the readers of *Turf, Field and Farm* with an account of his feat, perhaps because there was some dispute as to who actually fired the fatal shot and all the members of the hunting party were included in the picture.[2]

Though 1875 shaped up as another busy year for the cavalry, events worked out so that the Seventh got a respite from extended field service. Consequently, Custer spent part of the spring and most of the fall visiting in the East. During the summer, with not much to do, he dashed off his shortest and, as it proved, final letter to *Turf, Field and Farm*. The next year he led his regiment as one of the cavalry components of the massive Sioux Expedition designed to thrash hostile bands of Sioux and Cheyennes into submission. Along with the five companies of the Seventh that constituted his direct command, on June 25, 1876, he was killed near the Little Big Horn River. Nomad would wander no more.[3]

14. "Letter from 'Nomad'"

[OCTOBER 1873] *published October 17, 1873*

Have you forgotten that once upon a time you numbered among your correspondents a certain "Nomad," whose roving, restless habits at least, well corresponded with his name? Having reason to believe that you have erased that name from the tablets of your memory, and more important still, from your subscription list, this epistle is penned and forwarded to your address in order that you may no longer rest under the impression that your quondam friend and scribe has departed from the scenes of this earth, and been wafted, or dragged, to that region where all entries depend upon previous records, and where neither time, distance, nor second money are taken into consideration. I will admit that I have been in that locality since we last exchanged friendly greetings in the Blue Grass regions, but a miss is as good as a mile, and thanks to the speed and bottom of a high-mettled steed, bred and brought up on blue grass pasture, and for being the proud possessor

of which I owe my thanks to my friend Swigert, I saved my distance and shut out all my opponents.[1] As the race did not come off over the course of any regularly organized association, unless Uncle Sam, in his present disengaged and demoralized condition may be considered regularly organized, I presume you do not care for an account of the affair, particularly as there was no money up and no time taken—at least I took no time in getting away. Everything, however, but the money, was up; I was up, the Indians were up, and for a little while, I thought it was "all up" with me. It was a dash race. I'm glad it wasn't heats. I won the dash, but might have lost the second heat. I am in favor of dashes. But I did not set out in the commencement of this letter to refer in vague terms to an Indian fight in which I barely did what you enjoined me to, and hoped I might do, in the last note I received from you just previous to my departure for the "Far West," viz.: saved my "hair." That story is a long one, and will keep until the Winter evenings set in.[2]

But I must give you my score in hunting, premising it with the explanation that in making up the score of game animals killed I only aimed at and brought down single animals, and did not fire into herds. I left the Missouri River, June 20, at Fort Rice, Dakota, rode Westward through Dakota and parts of Montana, crossing and ascending the Yellowstone River; then continuing Westward to the Muscle Shell River, down which beautiful stream I proceeded about one hundred miles; then struck East for the Yellowstone and Missouri Rivers, arriving at Fort Lincoln, Dakota, on the Missouri River, Sept. 21, having been on the wing three months and one day. I seldom went far out of the regular line of march to hunt, for two reasons: first, the hostility of Indians rendered such a course imprudent;[3] second, one route was as good as another, so far as game was concerned. The following is my score during the time referred to:

Antelope 41
Elk 4
Buffalo 3
Black-tail deer 4
White wolf. 2
Red fox 1
Porcupine 1
Wild cat 3
Geese, ducks, prairie chickens and sage hens without number.

The antelopes, buffaloes, black-tail deer and white wolves were brought down by my rifle, and without the assistance of other hunters. The fox I caught with Scotch stag-hounds. The porcupine I caught alive by hand, or, rather, by throwing a blanket over it. Two of the wild cats were killed outright; the third was taken alive, and

with the porcupine now constitutes a portion of the animal kingdom with which I have surrounded myself.

As I write these lines, in the wee sma' hours of the night, I can hear the porcupine gnawing vigorously in the endeavor to make his way through the large box in which I keep him confined in rear of my tent, while, as an occasional passer by in front of my tent stumbles, in the darkness, near a box of smaller dimensions than that containing his porcupine majesty, I can hear the low, determined growl of his or her feline highness, the wild cat. Fortunately I am no somnambulist, or I might, in my midnight wanderings, furnish a supper for this domestic menagerie. I suppose you, or the reader, wonder what on earth any sane man wants with a wild cat on one side of him and a porcupine on the other. Well, what I particularly want with reference to these two amiable specimens of the animal kingdom is to be let alone until the first favorable opportunity to reach the station of the Northern Pacific Railroad, just across the river, when I propose to label them properly, and send them, per Adams' Express, to Central Park, there to join company with the cinnamon bear I forwarded some time ago, and to gratify the curiosity of the youthful metropolitans.[4]

The porcupine and cat story has proved a digression. The largest of the four elk included in my score measured over fifteen hands in height, eleven feet and a half from point of the nose to hind heels, as he lay naturally on the ground after being killed, and when dressed his estimated weight was eight hundred pounds. I preserved his skin entire, from his antlers to and including his hoofs. His antlers are the handsomest I ever saw. I propose shipping him, in a few days, to our mutual friend, Hon. K. C. Barker, President of the Audubon Club, Detroit, to be mounted and set up in the rooms of the latter, where I hope you may some day drop in and review the exceedingly fine collection of game animals and birds, considering the short time since the first organization of the club. Should I be there, I will take delight in pointing out to you the King of the Forest, for such was the appellation bestowed upon the magnificent elk of which I write.[5] And with a hunter's pride I will ask you to glance at the long, deep scars on the ears and sides while I recount to you how, after being wounded by my rifle and pursued by my noble stag-hounds, the elk was forced to leap into the river, followed by the dogs—the same dogs who, as I write, are gathered near my camp-stool, some hugging the fire, others at my feet, while Maida, my favorite, has exercised her prerogative and stretched herself at full length on the buffalo covering of my camp-bed.[6]

The combat in the water was one of the finest and most exciting hunting scenes I ever witnessed. As I stood on the bank, rifle in hand, and within twenty paces of the quarry, I trembled for the lives of my brave dogs. The water was of such depth as enabled the elk to stand on *terra firma* while the dogs were compelled to swim in order to reach him. Nothing daunted, however, on they plunged; and like a charge of well-drilled cavalrymen, they dashed at the huge buck as if their battle-cry had been, "Up, dogs, and at him!" In vain did the elk make his way, always fighting, to where the water was deeper, almost covering his back. It only enabled his shaggy but silent foes to attack him at greater advantage, for see!

First Blucher, then Cardigan, leap from the water and clamber upon his back. What can be their object, as they endeavor to balance themselves upon the back of the now thoroughly infuriated animal—infuriated because the comrades of Blucher and Cardigan are pressing their attacks front and rear, so that no time can be spared from them to devote elsewhere? Look at Blucher as, like an expert and daring rope-walker, he eagerly but steadily makes his way towards the head. He has gone as far as he can, but still his aim is unaccomplished. I have it! Faithful and determined to the last, his favorite, in fact, his only hold when contending with smaller game is the ear, and it is to secure this hold now that he is struggling. Watching his opportunity, when the elk has thrown his head back to avoid the teeth of those dogs swimming in his front, Blucher makes a half plunge or spring, and his large, powerful jaws close like a huge vise upon the ear of the elk, thus to remain until either one or the other is vanquished. The struggle now became desperate in the extreme. The elk devoted his entire efforts to freeing himself from the fangs of the dog. At last, becoming maddened with pain, he, as a last resort, would plunge his entire head and neck deep down into the water, in his fruitless efforts to force the dog to release his hold. One moment I would see the head and neck of the buck thrown erect, high in the air, Blucher clinging grimly to the ear; the next, antlers, head, neck and dog would descend into the water, and disappear until I thought both animals must surely drown. Cardigan all this time was far from idle. Watching this conflict, and each moment becoming more anxious and excited for the safety of my dogs, I scarcely knew what I was doing or where I was. I called wildly to the dogs to come away—almost beseeched them as if they were human, and understood my every word. "You'll all be killed! you'll all be killed!" was my oft-repeated exclamation as I saw dogs and elk all floundering and fighting in the deep water. I kept my rifle in my hand all the time and would have terminated the combat long before, but that the rapid movements of the dogs prevented me from firing at the elk without endangering their lives. Finally, I was forced to choose between the risk of firing and that of having one or more of the dogs killed, or drowned by the buck. The latter seemed the most to be dreaded, so bringing my rifle to my shoulder and running my eye along the barrel, I waited a time when I could send a shot through a vital part. Presently it came; the loin was uncovered for an instant. Quick and sharp rang the report of my rifle, and at the same instant the immense body of the elk sank slowly down in the water, and the battle was over.[7]

Oh! for a Landseer to have grasped and preserved the exciting features of that combat![8] It was some two miles from camp. I sent for a wagon and men to transport the elk to camp. Without mutilating him in the least, he was carried and deposited on the green grass in front of my tent. Fortunately, among the other representatives of science who accompanied the party, under the auspices of the Government, was an experienced photographer, with com-

plete apparatus, &c., for taking hunting pictures. In a few moments everything was ready. The elk looked as natural as if enjoying a gentle slumber. Seated on the ground by his side, with a rifle thrown carelessly across the knee, while one hand rested on the antlers of the elk, was "Nomad." A splendid negative was obtained from which prints will be made after the arrival of the plate in Washington, D. C., when I hope to enclose a proof to the *Turf, Field and Farm* as confirmatory evidence of the truth of this story.[9]

My score was made with a Remington hunting rifle, calibre, 50; cartridges containing 70 grains of powder, I seldom killed at a less distance than 150 yards, running up from that distance to 630 yards, at which range I shot a fine buck antelope just nine days ago. The average distance at which I killed the 41 antelopes exceeded 250 yards. I usually measured the range after each successful shot. I retain momentoes of my antelope hunting in the shape of the preserved heads, necks and horns of about half a dozen of the finest bucks, one of which I intend to forward to the *Turf, Field and Farm*, provided some of its sporting friends have not anticipated me in this matter.

I have given you my score. I might have greatly increased it by including game which I only assisted in killing. Now, then, I want to hear from the "next." Can it be beaten by the correspondent of any other paper of by "any other man?" If so, hold up your right hand.[10]

15. *"Letter from 'Nomad'"*

AUGUST 23, 1875, Fort Lincoln, D.T. *published September 3, 1875*

In your issue of the 13th "W. H. S." puts forth some ideas in regard to "deer driving, with cross-bred dogs, pointer or setter, and hound," which I do not believe will find many supporters among the real lovers of sport. I have ridden in Texas after a pack of good hounds which had as an accompaniment one of "W. H. S.'s" cross-bred dogs, pointer and hound, and the combination was anything but desirable. It was true, however, as "W. H. S." states, the cross-bred dog, at the start, would lead the pack, but a stiff run of a couple of hours would leave him behind out of sight and hearing fortunately; and as for the "shrill squeal" by which "W. H. S." correctly designates the tongue of the half-bred, surely no one with half an ear for music will claim that the high and discordant yelping of the pointer adds to the inspiriting notes of a well-mated pack, for, after all, I believe the greatest pleasure of the chase, so far as dogs are concerned, is to be derived from the music which fills the air, as, like a well-trained orchestra, the deep-toned bass, harmonizing with the clear bugle tones of the higher-keyed voices, literally enables the hunter to realize that "there's music in the air," and who that has ridden after a well-matched pack, bestriding a steed,

"Upon a well-grown hoof, and strong,
Proud of the sport, with too much fire to yield,"

but could enthusiastically respond to the lines:

—"Now, my brave youths,
Flourish the whip, nor spare the galling spur,
But in the madness of delight forget
Your fears. For o'er the rocky hills we range,
And dangerous our course, but in the brave
True courage never fails."

In such a moment of sportsman's bliss surely one would not want to hear the "shrill squeal" of any mongrel disturbing the harmony of sound or sight.[1]

Nor will I admit that even if our only object is, as expressed by W. H. S., to make the deer "git up and git," that a cross-bred dog is the better able to do it. On the contrary, I have in my pack two fox-hounds, a gift from my friend Price McGrath, that can take a pace in running a deer which would kill any half-bred dog inside of an hour. Hanging against the wall, and spreading over my head as I write, are the beautifully branched antlers (twenty-three prongs) of a lordly buck driven to a standstill in less than an hour by the two dogs I have mentioned, Driver and Ferguson.[2]

As well attempt to harmonize the discordant notes of a fishmonger's horn with the silvery tones of Levy's cornet[3] and call it music, as to combine the yelping of a cur or cross-bred dog with the full cry of a well-mated pack. I am one of those persons who believe in preserving the points of each breed of animals, and, with the exception of the mule, am loth to admit that any animal, the result of a cross between two defined and distinct breeds is an improvement on the original stock. But if "W. H. S." insists on cross-bred dogs for driving deer, and desires speed in the produce, let him cross a fox-hound bitch with a Scotch deer-hound dog, and the result will be a large, powerful dog, fleeter than the pointer hound and nose enough to run any trail. I have in my kennel Scotch deer-hounds, fox-hounds and pointers; but I prefer to keep them pure.[4]

So much for dogs. Now an item on horses. You have been publishing from time to time the past season the results of the racing at Jerome Park, Long Branch and Saratoga, and have told the world that time has been cut down in this and that race, until there seems to be no limit to the capabilities of our thoroughbreds; but I desire to place on record the performance of a thorough-

bred saddle-horse that I brought from Kentucky, mention of which I made in your columns some months ago. He is a son of Uncle Vic, a grandson of old Lexington. I was absent from home for a few weeks, during which time some repairs were made in the stable occupied by horses. In the stable is a well thirty-two feet deep, the water usually being about four feet deep. It became necessary in making the repairs referred to to temporarily remove the well curb, and owing to some neglect or forgetfulness on the part of those whose duty it was to attend to it, the curb was not replaced at night. It so happened that on that night—of course—my horse Vic got loose in the stable, and in roaming about in the darkness fell down the well, tail first. He was missed at daylight the following morning, and as the door was open it was supposed he was running at large. Search was made for him, but it was several hours before it was discovered that he was at the bottom of the well. A large force of men was at once assembled, ropes and pulleys prepared, and a man was lowered into the well for the purpose of attaching the ropes to what was supposed was the worthless or broken remains of a once-valuable horse. Ropes were placed under his body in rear of his fore legs, while another was attached to the head to keep the latter in proper place. After considerable time and labor the horse was drawn to the surface and placed on *terra firma* once more. He evinced his joy and gratitude by a distinct whinney. Upon examining him, to discover his broken bones or other injuries, he was found to be in comparatively as sound condition as before his visit to the bottom of the well, the hair being rubbed away in but two places on a strip as large as a little finger on the eye, and a slightly larger place on one of his hips. Considering the distance and direction of the course, and the conditions of his performance, I believe Vic's exploit is unequalled.

NOTES

INTRODUCTION

1. Robert M. Utley, "The Frontier Army: John Ford or Arthur Penn?" in *Indian-White Relations: A Persistent Paradox*, ed. Jane F. Smith and Robert M. Kvasnicka (Washington, D.C.: Howard University Press, 1976), pp. 133–145. The essay has been reprinted as a separate pamphlet, *Good Guys and Bad: Changing Images of Soldier and Indian* (Crow Agency, Mont.: Custer Battlefield Historical & Museum Assoc., 1978).

2. For the social life and diversions of the rank and file in the West, see Oliver Knight, *Life and Manners in the Frontier Army* (Norman: University of Oklahoma Press, 1978), esp. chap. 4; and Don Rickey, Jr., *Forty Miles a Day on Beans and Hay: The Enlisted Soldier Fighting the Indian Wars* (Norman: University of Oklahoma Press, 1963), esp. chaps. 6, 10. On the matter of inviting guests out West, it is worth noting that officers tended to be very accommodating hosts generally, often entertaining distinguished and influential visitors at the behest of the top brass. The army after the Civil War was hard-pressed financially and under almost continuous assault by Democratic members of Congress eager to reduce its size as an economy measure; consequently, every opportunity to cultivate good will was to be grasped, even when it meant requesting officers to extend the hospitality of the post to total strangers—a point made in Nomad's letter #6.

3. See Rollin G. Osterweis, *Romanticism and Nationalism in the Old South* (New Haven: Yale University Press, 1949), pp. 96–98; and Knight, *Life and Manners in the Frontier Army*, pp. 71–76, 142–143. If army officers, unlike the prewar planters, were not modern lords presiding over a feudal domain tenanted by slaves instead of serfs, they were masters of their own domain, the army post, with enlisted personnel to do their bidding. In their everyday social intercourse they fancied themselves knights of the Round Table and vied with one another in playing the gallant where women were concerned; in the field, of course, they aspired to be *chevaliers sans peur et sans reproche*; in practice, they frequently fell far short of both ideals. Nevertheless, the chivalric code was part of their way of life.

4. Elizabeth B. Custer, *Following the Guidon* (New York: Harper & Brothers, 1890), p. 245.

5. See F. W. Benteen, "Trouting on Clark's Fork," *Recreation* 3 (November 1895): 234–235. Benteen contributed several other sporting reminiscences to *Recreation* that did not find acceptance but that have recently been published: John M. Carroll, ed., *Cavalry Scraps: The Writings of Frederick W. Benteen* (Bryan, Tex.: Guidon Press, 1979).

6. Beginning on August 3, 1876, with an article headlined "Crook's Command: Inactivity of the Troops in the Presence of the Hostile Sioux," the *New York Herald* launched a two-month campaign of vituperation against Crook for his alleged failure to take action. While he had his defenders—for example, "General Crook and the Newspapers," *Morning Oregonian* (Portland), August 14, 1876, p. 2—even a loyal officer thought he wasted time "hunting & picnicing" instead of pressing on after the Indians (Harry H. Anderson, "Charles King's *Campaigning with Crook*," *Westerners Brand Book* [Chicago] 32 [January 1976]: 66, letter of October 6, 1876. Also see Lewis F. Crawford, *Rekindling Camp Fires: The Exploits of Ben Arnold (Connor)* (Bismarck, N.D.: Capitol Book Co., 1926), chap. 28; John Gregory Bourke, *On the Border with Crook* (Chicago: Rio Grande Press, 1962 [1891]), pp. 321–329; and Oliver Knight, *Following the Indian Wars: The Story of the Newspaper Correspondents among the Indian Campaigners* (Norman: University of Oklahoma Press, 1960), chaps. 8–9.

7. Elizabeth B. Custer, *"Boots and Saddles"; or, Life in Dakota with General Custer* (New York: Harper & Brothers, 1885); *Tenting on the Plains; or, General Custer in Kansas and Texas* (New York: Charles L. Webster & Company, 1887); and *Following the Guidon.*

8. For the creation of the heroic image of Custer emphasizing Whittaker's role, see Robert M. Utley, *Custer and the Great Controversy: The Origin and Development of*

a Legend (Los Angeles: Westernlore Press, 1962), pp. 51–56, 121–123, 155–158; and Bruce A. Rosenberg, *Custer and the Epic of Defeat* (University Park: Pennsylvania State University Press, 1974), passim. In the year Custer died, Whittaker published a poem, an article, and a biography, *The Complete Life of Gen. George A. Custer* (New York: Sheldon & Company), paying tribute to the fallen hero; he also became embroiled in a lengthy newspaper controversy on Custer's behalf and in 1882 added a dime novel biography of the General to his list of publications.

9. On the transformation of Custer's image from hero to villain or fool, see Paul A. Hutton, "From Little Bighorn to *Little Big Man*: The Changing Image of a Western Hero in Popular Culture," *Western Historical Quarterly* 7 (January 1976): 19–45; and Brian W. Dippie, *Custer's Last Stand: The Anatomy of an American Myth* (Missoula: University of Montana Publications in History, 1976), pp. 65–69. Van de Water's biography was *Glory-hunter: A Life of General Custer* (Indianapolis: Bobbs-Merrill, 1934).

10. William E. Curtis, *Chicago Inter-Ocean*, July 9, 1874, in *Prelude to Glory: A Newspaper Accounting of Custer's 1874 Expedition to the Black Hills*, comp. Herbert Krause and Gary D. Olson (Sioux Falls, S.D.: Brevet Press, 1974), pp. 101–102.

11. Donald F. Danker, ed. *Man of the Plains: Recollections of Luther North, 1856–1882* (Lincoln: University of Nebraska Press, 1961), p. 185 and, for additional observations on Custer's boasts, pp. 105–106, 187. Also see George Bird Grinnell, *Two Great Scouts and Their Pawnee Battalion: The Experiences of Frank J. North and Luther H. North . . .* (Cleveland: Arthur H. Clark, 1928), pp. 241–242.

12. G. A. Custer, *My Life on the Plains; or, Personal Experiences with Indians* (New York: Sheldon & Company, 1874). I have seen no explanation why "My Life on the Plains" was not published in book form

until two years after its original appearance. But a note at the end of the book suggests that it was released in 1874 to coincide with popular interest in the expedition under Custer to the Black Hills.

13. *Turf, Field and Farm* began publication in 1865 and was soon one of the leading turf weeklies and sportsman's papers in the United States. In 1903 it was absorbed by a new journal, *Sports of the Times.* See Frank Luther Mott, *A History of American Magazines,* 5 vols. (New York: Appleton, 1930; Cambridge: Harvard University Press, 1938–1968), III, 215, IV, 373; also letter #9, n. 1, for additional information.

14. Jay Monaghan, *Custer: The Life of General George Armstrong Custer* (Boston: Little, Brown, 1959), p. 332.

15. Custer, *My Life on the Plains,* p. 256.

16. Custer, *"Boots and Saddles,"* pp. 44–45.

17. Lawrence Barrett, "Personal Recollections of General Custer," in Whittaker, *Complete Life of Gen. George A. Custer,* p. 636.

18. Custer, *"Boots and Saddles,"* p. 152.

19. See Paul L. Hedren, "The Custer Library," *Little Big Horn Associates Research Review* 8 (Winter 1974): 5–11.

20. Frederick W. Benteen, ca. 1895, annotations in his copy of *Wild Life on the Plains and Horrors of Indian Warfare* (1891), in a private collection.

21. G. Custer to E. Custer, September 28, 1873, in Custer, *"Boots and Saddles,"* p. 298; ibid., pp. 151–153.

22. On this, see Custer's bantering letter to his wife, June 26, 1873, in ibid., p. 276, and her own comments, p. 149; also Barrett, "Personal Recollections," p. 635. For *The Galaxy* and its rates to contributors, see Mott, *History of American Magazines,* III, 13–15, esp. n. 24, and pp. 361–381.

23. G. Custer to E. Custer, June 9, June 17, 1876, in Custer, *"Boots and Saddles,"* pp. 308, 311; and W. S. Edgerly to E. Custer, October 10, 1877, in Marguerite Merington, ed., *The Custer Story: The*

Life and Intimate Letters of General George A. Custer and His Wife Elizabeth (New York: Devin-Adair, 1950), p. 302. Seven installments of Custer's "War Memoirs" appeared in *The Galaxy* in 1876, three posthumously. They were first reprinted, with notes by E. Elden Davis, in Paul A. Hutton, ed., *Garry Owen 1976: Annual of the Little Big Horn Associates* (Seattle: Little Big Horn Associates, 1977), pp. 14–96, but can be found most conveniently in John M. Carroll, comp., *Custer in the Civil War: His Unfinished Memoirs* (San Rafael, Calif.: Presidio Press, 1977), pp. 70–158.

24. Silas Farmer, *History of Detroit and Wayne County and Early Michigan: A Chronological Cyclopedia of the Past and Present* (Detroit: Gale Research Co., 1969 [1890]), p. 708.

I. KANSAS, 1867

1. G. Custer to E. Custer, April 4, 1867, in Custer, *Tenting on the Plains,* p. 525.

2. For secondary accounts of the Hancock Expedition and Custer's role in it, see William H. Leckie, *The Military Conquest of the Southern Plains* (Norman: University of Oklahoma Press, 1963), pp. 30–56 (highly critical of Hancock's conduct); Lonnie J. White, "Warpaths on the Southern Plains, No. 3: The Hancock and Custer Expeditions of 1867," *Journal of the West* 5 (July 1966): 355–378 (Hancock and Custer both failed to meet the goals they had set); Lawrence A. Frost, *The Court-martial of General George Armstrong Custer* (Norman: University of Oklahoma Press, 1968), pp. 3–89 (Custer was made the scapegoat for Hancock's costly blundering); Minnie Dubbs Millbrook, "The West Breaks in General Custer," *Kansas Historical Quarterly* 36 (Summer 1970): 113–148, and "Custer's First Scout in the West," ibid., 39 (Spring 1973): 75–95 (Custer was new to Indian campaigning in 1867 and made many beginner's mistakes); and Robert M. Utley, *Frontier Regulars: The United States Army*

and the Indian, 1866–1891 (New York: Macmillan, 1973), chap. 8 (sympathetic to the dilemma of an undermanned army on a vast frontier). For the Indian perspective on the events of 1867, see George Bird Grinnell, *The Fighting Cheyennes* (Norman: University of Oklahoma Press, 1956 [1915]), chap. 19; and George E. Hyde, *Life of George Bent, Written from His Letters*, ed. Savoie Lottinville (Norman: University of Oklahoma Press, 1968), chap. 9. All of Custer's biographers have had their say on the Hancock Expedition and his service in Kansas, 1866–1871, but the most useful works on the subject are the most recent, especially for 1867: the two articles by Minnie Millbrook cited above; Blaine Burkey, *Custer, Come at Once! The Fort Hays Years of George and Elizabeth Custer, 1867–1870* (Hays, Ka.: Thomas More Prep, 1976), pp. 1–33; and Robert M. Utley's splendidly edited *Life in Custer's Cavalry: Diaries and Letters of Albert and Jennie Barnitz, 1867–1868* (New Haven: Yale University Press, 1977).

3. [George E. Pond], "The New Indian Hostilities," *Nation*, January 17, 1867, p. 51. Robert G. Athearn has written extensively on the Indian scares of 1867–68: "The Montana Volunteers of 1867," *Pacific Historical Review* 19 (May 1950): 127–137; "Early Territorial Montana: A Problem in Colonial Administration," *Montana Magazine of History* 1 (July 1951): 15–21; "The Fort Buford 'Massacre,'" *Mississippi Valley Historical Review* 41 (March 1955): 675–684; "Colorado and the Indian War of 1868," *Colorado Magazine* 33 (January 1956): 42–51; and *William Tecumseh Sherman and the Settlement of the West* (Norman: University of Oklahoma Press, 1956), chap. 7. Also see James L. Thane, Jr., "The Montana 'Indian War' of 1867," *Arizona and the West* 10 (Summer 1968): 153–170.

4. Sherman to Hancock, March 14, 1867, cited in Athearn, *William Tecumseh Sherman and the Settlement of the West*, p. 131.

5. A. Barnitz to his sister-in-law, March 29, 1867, in Utley, ed., *Life in Custer's Cavalry*, pp. 21–22.

6. Hancock to Davis, March 10, 1867, in Robert Taft, *Artists and Illustrators of the Old West, 1850–1900* (New York: Charles Scribner's Sons, 1953), p. 300, n. 48.

7. G. Custer to E. Custer, May 6, 1867, in Merington, ed., *The Custer Story*, p. 202.

8. On Custer's court-martial, see Robert A. Murray's concise account, "The Custer Court Martial," *Annals of Wyoming* 36 (October 1964): 175–184. The complete transcript of the proceedings can be found in Frost, *Court-martial of General George Armstrong Custer*, pp. 96–246, though there are some significant printing errors —pointed out in Don Russell's review in the *Westerners Brand Book* (Chicago) 25 (August 1968): 45—that scramble the court's findings. Though the court modified certain of the specifications and thereby cleared Custer of the charge that his actions were solely motivated by a desire to get to Fort Riley—that is, to his wife—I find the evidence suggesting as much convincing. See A. Barnitz to J. Barnitz, July 28, 1867, in Utley, ed., *Life in Custer's Cavalry*, p. 86; Millbrook, "The West Breaks in General Custer," pp. 136–147; and Burkey, *Custer, Come at Once!* pp 31–32. Indeed, the judge advocate general, in his review of the court's findings, remarked: "The conclusion unavoidably reached under this branch of the inquiry, is that Gen. Custer's anxiety to see his family at Fort Riley overcame his appreciation of the paramount necessity to obey orders which is incumbent on every military officer; and thus the excuses he offers for his acts of insubordination are afterthoughts" (quoted in Murray, "Custer Court Martial," p. 184).

9. "Statement of General Hancock before the Indian Peace Commission, Fort Leavenworth, Kansas, August 12, 1867," in *Proceedings of the Great Peace Commission of 1867–1868* (Washington, D.C.: The Institute for the Development of Indian Law, 1975), p. 27.

1. September 9, 1867

1. It is worth remembering that Custer was writing in 1867, two years before the Union Pacific and Central Pacific Railroads were joined and a host of travelers began making the pilgrimage across the continent and filling the nation's journals and bookstores with their observations. Custer's mention of *The Black Crook* launches an extended conceit in which he likens the plains Indians to the cast of a musical comedy (actually, burlesque) that was then all the sensation in New York City. *The Black Crook* opened at Niblo's Garden on September 12, 1866, and became an immediate *cause célèbre*, attracting nationwide attention and so thoroughly outraging morals that it remained in continuous production for almost thirty years. Its great attraction, and the source of its notoriety: a corps de ballet of one hundred girls wearing, the *New York Times* observed, "no clothes to speak of." Thus Custer, an avid theater-goer and a fancier of the well-turned female form, was quick to compare *The Black Crook*'s performers, clad in revealing, flesh-colored silk tights "and as little else as the law will permit," to the troupes of bare-skinned Indians he had encountered in the West. *The Black Crook: An Original Magical and Spectacular Drama in Four Acts*, by Charles M. Barras, is reprinted, with a useful introduction, in *The Black Crook and Other Nineteenth-Century American Plays*, ed. Myron Matlaw (New York: E. P. Dutton, 1967). Also see William C. Young, *Famous Actors and Actresses on the American Stage: Documents of American Theater History*, 2 vols. (New York: R. R. Bowker Co., 1975), I, 1075–1076.

2. This phrase was borrowed from Alexander Pope's *Essay on Man* (1734): "Lo, the poor Indian! whose untutor'd mind / Sees God in clouds, or hears him in the wind!" "Lo, the poor Indian" became the standard derogatory term for the native out West and was meant to mock Eastern sentimentality about the "noble savage."

The phrase was so familiar that it was commonly shortened to "Lo" or "Mr. Lo." The only discussion of the origin and spread of this usage that I have encountered is a fascinating note in Taft, *Artists and Illustrators of the Old West*, pp. 300–301, n. 49. He concludes that Horace Greeley was wont to echo Pope as early as 1843 but is less certain about the date when "Lo" came into general use as a proper noun.

3. By act of Congress, July 20, 1867, an Indian Peace Commission was appointed to negotiate treaties with the hostile Western tribes, keeping in mind three objectives: to remove the causes of warfare, where possible; to secure the safety of the frontier settlements and the transcontinental railroads then building; and to "suggest or inaugurate some plan for the civilization of the Indians." Assigned these ambitious tasks were, as Custer notes, Lieutenant General Sherman; General William S. Harney, an old Indian-fighter who was brought out of retirement; and Senator John B. Henderson of Missouri, chairman of the Senate Committee on Indian Affairs. In addition, there was another army officer, General Alfred H. Terry, commander of the Military Department of Dakota under Sherman, and three more civilians: Nathaniel G. Taylor, Commissioner of Indian Affairs; Samuel F. Tappan, like Taylor a prominent advocate of a policy of peace with the Indians; and John B. Sanborn, a Minnesota lawyer. On the premise that, humanitarian considerations aside, "it costs less to civilize than to kill" Indians, the commission proposed to test the wisdom of "conquest by kindness." Accordingly, Sherman ordered his department commanders to adopt a purely defensive posture. "I want the deliberation of the Commissioners to be as little disturbed by acts of our troops as possible, so that the effort to settle the Indian question peaceably may have a fair chance of success," he wrote, though he did not disguise his own opinion that the commis-

sion was a waste of time. Most of his officers, including Custer, agreed. See "Report of Indian Peace Commissioners" (January 14, 1868), *House Exec. Doc. No. 97*, 40 Cong., 2 sess., pp. 1, 15; Athearn, *William Tecumseh Sherman and the Settlement of the West*, pp. 171–184; Utley, *Frontier Regulars*, chap. 9; and Leckie, *Military Conquest of the Southern Plains*, pp. 58–62. For the actual councils, see Douglas C. Jones, *The Treaty of Medicine Lodge: The Story of the Great Treaty Council as Told by Eyewitnesses* (Norman: University of Oklahoma Press, 1966); and *Proceedings of the Great Peace Commission of 1867–1868*.

4. The commission originally intended to meet with the Sioux near Fort Laramie, on the North Platte River, about mid-September and with the southern tribes near Fort Larned, Kansas, a month later. This schedule had to be altered when attempts in August and September to lure the hostile Sioux in for negotiations proved futile, and the commissioners were left talking with "friendlies" along the Missouri and North Platte Rivers. Despite Custer's prediction that it would "end with a farce," the council held in October south of Fort Larned on Medicine Lodge Creek was considerably more successful. Some five thousand Indians participated, and while the Cheyennes at first held back, understandably suspicious given the events of the spring and summer, they too came in to negotiate (and get their share of "Uncle Sam's *presents*") after the Kiowas, Comanches, and Kiowa-Apaches signed a treaty on October 21. Seven days later the Cheyennes and Arapahos concluded a treaty of their own. Attempts to lure the warring Sioux into Fort Laramie proved no more fruitful in November than two months earlier, and another year would elapse before the last—and most important—of the hostile Sioux leaders deigned to "touch the pen" at Fort Laramie.

5. In letters #3–#5 Nomad would provide the readers of *Turf, Field and Farm* with an account of his activities during the first stage of the Hancock Expedition, but he saved the sequel for his later series in *The Galaxy* magazine. The "swing around the circle" is a casual but apt reference to an episode that, like the summer's Indian campaign, cost Custer in popular prestige and opened him to criticism in the press. Reduced to his regular army rank of captain, though he was a brevet major general, Custer found himself in Washington in the spring and summer of 1866 at a critical juncture in his career and with time heavy on his hands. While he was casting about for a suitable career opportunity, he became actively involved with the National Union Party, which was supporting the Reconstruction policies of Abraham Lincoln's successor Andrew Johnson against a concerted onslaught by the "Radicals" in the Republican Party. It was a calculated risk for Custer but one congruent with his own beliefs as a postwar Democrat and one that he hoped would yield prompt returns. Though he was commissioned lieutenant colonel of the Seventh Cavalry on July 28, he had wanted more and in mid-August wrote directly to President Johnson seeking a colonelcy—even in the infantry if need be, though he drew the line at service with a black regiment. Nothing came of this initiative, but Custer's fame and his willingness to support Johnson brought him into the presidential orbit, and when Johnson, seeking to drum up popular support for his policies, left Washington in late August on a speaking tour that would take him to Chicago and St. Louis before returning to the capital in mid-September, the Custers were among the dignitaries invited on the "swing around the circle." At first it was a heady experience for the impressionable young couple to be traveling with the chief executive's party, but soon its charm began to pall. Launched in the name of sectional reconciliation, the "swing" was strictly partisan in nature since Johnson hoped to persuade the electorate along the way to de-

feat the radical candidates in that fall's congressional races, thereby reducing the opposition to his policies. In effect, he was running against a powerful element in his own party, and as the tour progressed he was met by increasingly unfriendly crowds. His speeches degenerated into exchanges of insults as words like *traitor* and *treason* flew back and forth. It was a sobering experience for Custer, and he and his wife were doubtless happy enough to leave the presidential party before it completed its return journey. A year later, as his wry reference points out, he had completed another "swing around the circle," with results that were even more personally devastating. See Kenneth M. Stampp, *The Era of Reconstruction, 1865–1877* (New York: Alfred A. Knopf, 1965), pp. 114–117; Eric L. McKitrick, *Andrew Johnson and Reconstruction* (Chicago: University of Chicago Press, 1960), pp. 428–438; Monaghan, *Custer*, chap. 20; and Merington, ed., *The Custer Story*, pp. 185–190.

6. Of the several colloquialisms that Custer employs in his letters, this is one of the few still commonly used today. In the seventeenth century Hobson operated a livery stable in Cambridge, England, and was noted for his inflexible insistence that his hacks be let out in a set rotation. Thus, his customers had the option of taking what they were offered or nothing —Hobson's choice.

7. A reference to Alaska, purchased from Russia in June 1867 for $7.2 million. Custer's tone suggests that he agreed with those who thought Secretary of State William H. Seward had made a preposterously bad deal and called Alaska "Seward's Folly" and "Seward's Icebox." Seward was along on the "swing around the circle" the year before, and Elizabeth Custer, thrilled by the chance to chat and dine with a man so venerated in her father's house that she was "almost surprised to see him eat and drink like other mortals," could not ignore the "ineffaceable marks" of his common humanity—

visible scars on his face and throat left by an assassination attempt the night Abraham Lincoln was murdered (Merington, ed., *The Custer Story*, p. 189).

8. Andrew J. Smith (1815–1897), commander of the Military District of the Arkansas and colonel of the Seventh Cavalry, was, until his retirement in 1869, Custer's immediate superior. A genial and kind-hearted man, Smith allowed his more vigorous subordinate effective field command of the Seventh, thereby establishing the relationship that Custer would enjoy with both of the regiment's colonels until his death in 1876. Custer's reference to Smith as "my friend" is especially revealing when it is remembered that it was Smith who ordered him arrested on July 21 and preferred the original charges against him. However, Custer chose to see these as Hancock's doing, arguing that "although signed by other officers" they were brought "at the instance of General Hancock. He being considered the prosecutor, the law prevented him from issuing the order for my trial, consequently it was issued from the War Department." In his own submission to the court Custer was critical of Smith's role in bringing the charges against him, but he did not make his grievances public; against Hancock, whom he saw as possessing an ulterior motive, he was willing to wage war in print. See G. A. Custer, letter of December 21, 1867, to the Sandusky, Ohio, *Register*, reprinted in the *Westerners Brand Book* (Chicago) 25 (August 1968), p. 47; Millbrook, "The West Breaks in General Custer," pp. 142–143; and Frost, *Court-martial of General George Armstrong Custer*, pp. 226–228.

9. Custer's rattlesnake repast makes for a good story from the wild-and-woolly West, though he was not the only officer with the expedition to sample such reptilian fare—nor the only correspondent to dish it up for a presumably squeamish audience of Easterners. Theodore Davis, who covered the entire campaign for

Harper's and was with Custer's column in June wrote:

During the march from the Saline River to Fort McPherson the command was camped for one night on ground that was subsequently discovered to be perforated with the holes of rattlesnakes. The shelter tents were just pitched when the snakes made their appearance. The soldiers were quickly at work with sabres and sticks. . . . My tent companion, Major Elliot [Joel H. Elliott], murdered five good-sized rattlesnakes in the vicinity of our tent; but inasmuch as the Major was caterer of our mess, it was in a measure his duty to secure all the prairie-eels that might come within reach. The cook for our mess . . . was averse to snakes of all kinds, and particularly so to rattlers. On this occasion he was rushing wildly from one point to another to escape the neighborhood of snakes, and finally returned to the mess-tent, to discover five or six large snakes lying at length on the mess-chest. His horror knew no bounds. He was absolutely frightened out of his wits.

But when a rattler that invaded the cook's tent late that night was dispatched and "broiled for breakfast," the cook "took revenge on the bones . . . From that time there was not a more energetic snake-hunter in camp . . ." Rattlesnake feasts no doubt provided a welcome change of diet for readers who had about had their fill of Indian kettles brimming with stewed puppy dogs, the other Western delicacy commonly served up in traveler's tales. Custer, as the reader will discover, got around to his version ere long. See Theodore R. Davis, "A Summer on the Plains," *Harper's New Monthly Magazine* 36 (February 1868): 299–300; and, for Elizabeth Custer's version of the General's tale, *Following the Guidon*, pp. 305–306.

10. This comment serves as a remarkably disingenuous lead-in to the story Custer was about to unfold. At the time, on April 16, he was supposedly leading the Seventh Cavalry in hot pursuit of several hundred Sioux and Cheyennes. He was not on a pleasure trip, in short, as his letters #4–#5 make abundantly clear.

11. Kirkland C. Barker (1819–1875), the affluent owner of a tobacco factory and mayor of Detroit from 1864 to 1865, was an ardent sportsman and president of the city's Audubon Club. "He is so fond of dogs and horses and hunting," Elizabeth Custer wrote after a visit at the Barkers' Grosse Ile home. "Autie [General Custer] and he are great friends . . ." Custer's letters to Barker do bespeak a close relationship based on shared interests, and it seems likely that Barker was in some way connected with Custer's original decision to contribute to *Turf, Field and Farm.* Certainly his name is prominent in the Nomad letters. See Farmer, *History of Detroit and Wayne County and Early Michigan,* pp. 140, 826; and E. Custer to Rebecca Richmond, December 6, 1866, in Minnie Dubbs Millbrook, ed., "Mrs. General Custer at Fort Riley, 1866," *Kansas Historical Quarterly* 40 (Spring 1974): 64. Excerpts from Custer's letters to Barker appear in Custer, *Following the Guidon,* pp. 9–10, 216–217, 219–220, and a complete letter, January 6, 1870, in Joseph G. Masters, *Shadows Fall across the Little Horn: "Custer's Last Stand"* (Laramie: University of Wyoming Library, 1951), pp. 61–62. All reflect the mutual concerns of the two men.

12. Custer's choice of words here is interesting given the ill-advised adventure he was recounting. In relating the same tale in his memoirs five years later, he frankly conceded that he had been "rashly imprudent" in chasing after the antelope and had compounded the error by then engaging in a one-man buffalo hunt (*My Life on the Plains,* p. 37).

13. "Man proposes, God disposes": one of those comforting nineteenth-century homilies which, like its twin, "Man appoints, God disappoints," was often uttered to console the bereaved. Custer goes on to provide a model definition when he notes of his near-fatal mishap that it gave him pause to consider "the uncertainty of all human calculations."

14. The horse that he killed had been his

wife's favorite, "a fast pacer named Custis Lee, the delight of my eyes and the envy of the General's staff while we were in Virginia and Texas . . ." (*Tenting on the Plains*, p. 334 and, for her keen sense of loss, pp. 542–543).

15. Custer had ample cause for sober reflection, not only because of his predicament—unhorsed, alone, and potentially lost in hostile Indian country—but also because of the whole course of action that had landed him there. He had killed his wife's beloved mount, though she would forgive him anything and years later chose to make his misadventure a prominent episode, illustrated with a pen drawing by Frederic Remington, in her reminiscences of their life together in Texas and Kansas, *Tenting on the Plains*. But his superiors might not be so understanding, especially if they knew the full particulars. At the outset of the expedition, General Hancock had issued a strict injunction against "straggling" and the discharging of firearms "without authority. For hunting, details may be made, but permission for such purposes will be requested, from these headquarters, which will be granted, as a rule, only to procure meat when necessary." Of course, Custer had an independent command on April 16, and the officers with him were apparently happy to get in some hunting of their own. But he was supposed to be pursuing Indians, and, while he had all but abandoned the chase the previous evening, his reports to superiors concealed that fact and instead gave the distinct impression that his command had pressed on after the foe and put in an arduous day marching and countermarching. While Nomad related the story of his first buffalo hunt as a good joke on himself, he was discreet about the date and circumstances for reasons that may have had something to do with the court-martial looming before him less than a week away. He reported the same incident to his wife, less humorously but at considerable length, in the letter she later pub-

lished in *Tenting on the Plains*, and he included it as an "entirely personal" aside in *My Life on the Plains*, which was otherwise almost devoid of hunting stories. Two noteworthy variations appear in these other versions. His letter indicates that he had a prior experience with buffalo when his hounds ran down a calf which he shot and butchered for his evening's meal; such a feat would hardly merit mention in a sportsman's journal, however, and anyway, as he wrote his wife, the buffalo that starred in his story was the "first large one" he ever saw—or hunted. In *My Life on the Plains* Custer greatly dramatized the tale by stressing the peril in which he had placed himself. With Indians lurking everywhere he hid in a ravine, trusty dogs at his side, and anxiously studied an approaching dust cloud to determine whether it heralded friend or foe. At last, relief! Through his field glasses he could make out a stars-and-stripes guidon floating above the distant riders. A hundred Western movies never did the scene better. In his letter to his wife it was a much more mundane sight—the "tops of the wagons as they were making their way up a small ravine"—that first told him rescue was at hand. See Millbrook, "Custer's First Scout in the West," pp. 77, 85–89; Burkey, *Custer, Come at Once!* p. 4; G. Custer to E. Custer, April 20, 1867, in *Tenting on the Plains*, pp. 564–570; and *My Life on the Plains*, pp. 37–39.

2. September 29, 1867

1. Custer's comment establishes the important link between the sportsman's skills and the martial virtues: the "successful buffalo-hunter" would be, by definition, the ideal cavalry officer. In his memoirs Custer elaborated on this theme: "I know of no better drill for perfecting men in the use of firearms on horseback, and thoroughly accustoming them to the saddle, than buffalo-hunting over a moderately rough country. No amount of riding under the best of drill-masters will give that

confidence and security in the saddle, which will result from a few spirited charges into a buffalo herd" (*My Life on the Plains*, p. 47). Theodore R. Davis, who was with him through much of the campaigning in 1867, made a similar point in "The Buffalo Range," *Harper's New Monthly Magazine* 38 (January 1869): 154.

2. Here again Custer makes the case for buffalo-hunting, that most American of sports, as a natural means of military training on the plains. Conducted at a break-neck speed and spiced with more than a little danger, it reminded him of nothing so much as a full-tilt cavalry charge. It would even allow a noncombatant a chance to taste the thrill of battle, and he wrote his wife: "I wish you were here to go buffalo-hunting. I know you will enjoy it. You will be carried away with excitement. Nothing so nearly approaches a cavalry charge and pursuit as a buffalo-chase." Upon calm reflection Custer decided that the risk was too great to permit women along on the hunt, but he did make one exception that he recounts in letter #6. See G. Custer to E. Custer, May 2, 1867, in *Tenting on the Plains*, p. 579.

3. After his unsuccessful pursuit of fleeing Sioux and Cheyennes, fully described in letters #4–#5, Custer put in at Fort Hays on April 19 expecting to find a twenty-day supply of forage for his horses exhausted from 154 miles of marching in less than five days. He intended to leave again at dark and press on in search of the Indians but learned to his intense irritation that the fort could provide forage for only one day. So the Seventh was forced to go into camp nearby awaiting supplies. It would be April 27 before adequate forage arrived, and, except for a single futile foray in mid-May, June 1 before Custer again took the field. Among the many causes for this long period of inactivity one stands out: Custer seems to have suffered an extended bout of depression. Plains service had so far proven monoto-nous and unrewarding, and the separation from his wife unendurable. Casting about for alternatives, Custer clutched onto one straw that floated by—the possibility that the Seventh would be reassigned to Fort Garland in the mountainous country of Colorado where, in Custer's imagination, the streams were full of fish, game was bountiful, the scenery was superb, the climate was bracing—and the duty soft enough that families could be stationed together. All this, in contrast to the dreary sameness, the furnace heat, the unhealthiness of Kansas where warlike Indians prevented family life at the remote Western posts; all this, if only General Hancock could be made to see the light and the current misunderstanding with the Indians be speedily resolved. As Custer watched his hopes dashed against the reality of a spreading Indian war, he nurtured the animosity toward Hancock that would become evident later and he sank deeper into despondency. "You cannot imagine or realize the state I have been in for the last ten days," he confided to his absent wife on May 2. It was to lift the General's spirits, as well as to alleviate the boredom, that the buffalo hunt described in this letter was planned for May 7 and 8. See G. A. Custer, report of April 19, 1867, in "Difficulties with Indian Tribes" (April 6, 1870), *House Exec. Doc. No. 240*, 41 Cong., 2 sess., pp. 73–74; A. Barnitz, journal entry for April 19, 1867, letter to his wife, April 20, 1867, in Utley, ed., *Life in Custer's Cavalry*, p. 37; G. Custer to E. Custer, May 2, 1867, in *Tenting on the Plains*, p. 577; Millbrook, "The West Breaks in General Custer," pp. 117–122; and Burkey, *Custer, Come at Once!* pp. 6–17. The rise and fall in Custer's Fort Garland dream can be traced in *Tenting on the Plains*, pp. 326–327; in his letters to his wife, April 8, 12, 22, 1867, and her letter to him, May 7, 1867, in ibid., pp. 527–528, 555, 571, 546–547; A. Barnitz echoed Custer's hopes in letters to his wife, April 9 and 30, 1867, and gave vent

to his growing disenchantment after Custer plunged into his black mood and became, in Barnitz's judgment, "billious," "obstreperous," capricious, "unpleasant," "very injudicious," "generally obnoxious," a "petty tyrant," cruel, discourteous, "arbitrary," an "incarnate fiend" who abused his authority, "unfeeling," "unworthy of the respect of all right-minded men," and "a martinet" (Utley, ed., *Life in Custer's Cavalry*, pp. 28, 30, 44–46, 50–53). Fort Garland, it might be added, while pleasantly located, may not have proven as much to Custer's liking as he believed. See Duane Vandenbusche, "Life at a Frontier Post: Fort Garland," *Colorado Magazine* 42 (Spring 1966): esp. 143–144.

4. The match hunt, as it was termed, pitted officers of the Seventh Cavalry against others from the postmaster's division. The majors who headed the teams selected seven officers each. The rules stipulated that the parties would go out on successive days, leaving camp at sunrise and returning by sunset. All shooting had to be done from horseback and the tally was to be verified by bringing back the buffalo tongues. Custer, as he notes, was with the party that went out on the first day, May 7. See Theodore R. Davis in *Harper's Weekly*, July 6, 1867, quoted in Burkey, *Custer, Come at Once!* p. 12; and Custer, *Tenting on the Plains*, p. 610.

5. Custer's reasoning here goes against one traditional explanation for the behavior he noted which assumes that it was precisely because the buffalo relied more on his nose than his eyes that he ran against the wind when alarmed: what he could not see he could scent, and thus running into the wind warned him of any new danger ahead. In addition, since hunters almost invariably approached a herd from downwind, when the buffalo took fright they naturally ran into the wind, which is to say away from the hunters. Another explanation is that buffalo habitually sought relief from the insects infesting their range by facing into the breeze.

Startled, they would run in the direction they were already pointing. See Frank Gilbert Roe, *The North American Buffalo: A Critical Study of the Species in Its Wild State* (Toronto: University of Toronto Press, 1951), pp. 140–141.

6. Custer fails to mention the embarrassing fact that this horse, lent to him by one of his officers, suffered a fate similar to Custis Lee's. "He could not run as fast as the buffalo," Custer wrote his wife when he returned to camp, "and after about five miles developed blind staggers, and was about to fall with me when I dismounted. In doing so my pistol accidentally discharged into his free shoulder, entirely disabling him." Such a mishap was acceptable the first time out, but it was not supposed to become a habit; thus, it was not admissible in a letter designed to show that, since "that most unsuccessful" initial chase, Nomad had become an old hand at buffalo hunting and now "generally came off the winner." See G. Custer to E. Custer, May 7, 1867, in Merington, ed., *The Custer Story*, p. 203. The same letter also appears in *Tenting on the Plains*, p. 581, with this passage deleted. Indeed, the two versions are so different that it is difficult to recognize them as the same letter, which introduces a general problem in Custer historiography. His correspondence with his wife reproduced in her three volumes of reminiscences and in the collection by Merington has been heavily edited and there is no one entirely reliable version. Mrs. Custer, for example, routinely omitted much personal matter, especially the baby talk and romantic endearments in which her husband indulged, thereby shaping an image of a mature and responsible military officer; Merington, in contrast, tended to preserve the element of breathless romanticism and bring out the boy in the Boy General but often condensed or eliminated interesting matter not related to Custer directly. Neither left the student with an authoritative text.

7. Nomad omits another detail which sug-

gests that despite his reputation as something of a martinet he was sensitive about the impression that would be created if he were to reveal the treatment commonly accorded enlisted men, who were described by one officer's wife as "perfect slaves." In his letter home, Custer described what happened after he disabled his horse: "Soon Sergeant King who always accompanies me came, looking for me. Together we took off my saddle and fastened it atop his, and so footed our way toward the column. On our way we came upon a small herd. The Sergeant then carried my saddle while I rode his mount, bringing down a fine one. My horse—or rather, his—was too fatigued for a second run." See J. Barnitz to her mother, February 26, 1867, in Utley, ed., *Life in Custer's Cavalry*, p. 15; G. Custer to E. Custer, May 7, 1867, in Merington, ed., *The Custer Story*, p. 203.

8. Probably Dr. I. T. Coates, acting assistant surgeon, who figures prominently in an anecdote in letter #3.

9. All the contemporary accounts indicate that Custer's party brought back twelve tongues, with Captain Louis M. Hamilton the individual champion, having procured four of them himself. See Theodore Davis, in Burkey, *Custer, Come at Once!* p. 12; G. Custer to E. Custer, May 7, 1867, in Merington, ed., *The Custer Story*, p. 203 (and, in *Tenting on the Plains*, p. 581, the same letter but with the usual discrepancies).

10. At the time, Custer told his wife that his party had devised an even craftier strategy. Asked by a member of the rival team what their tally was, they "kept it a secret," and when the inquisitor approached an orderly who was with them, he was told, "Four." "He smiled his peculiar smile and said he expected his party to bring in six, on the morrow, adding 'won't you all feel badly if we should bring in ten!' Well, we had twelve to our credit" (G. Custer to E. Custer, May 7, 1867, in Merington, ed., *The Custer Story*, p. 203).

11. It is quite possible that the second team outnumbered the first, though it seems more likely that the two sides started out evenly matched, at eight apiece. Custer's party was reduced to seven hunters soon after their departure because one of their number proceeded to get "so beastly drunk he could scarcely sit on his horse" and had to be sent back to camp. See Theodore Davis, in Burkey, *Custer, Come at Once!* p. 12; and G. Custer to E. Custer, May 7, 1867, in Merington, ed., *The Custer Story*, pp. 202–203.

12. Theodore Davis, who was along on the hunt and reported it in words and pictures for *Harper's Weekly*, concurred: "The buffalo are thin now, and capable of running faster at this season of the year than during the fall or summer" (quoted in Burkey, *Custer, Come at Once!* p. 12).

13. Though she was not present, it being a stag affair, Elizabeth Custer provided a vivid description of the banquet that was held on the evening of May 21: "Two wall-tents were put together so that the table, made of rough boards, stretching through both, was large enough for all. Victors and vanquished toasted each other in champagne, and though the scene was the plainest order of banquet, lighted by tallow candles set in rude brackets sawed out of cracker-box boards and fastened to the tent-poles, and the only draping a few cavalry guidons, the evening brightened up many a dreary day that followed." She did not report an incident that interrupted the festivities and reminded the revelers of the hard realities of service on the plains—"a shower of balls through camp" as four deserters returned the fire of the guards before riding off into the night. See Custer, *Tenting on the Plains*, p. 612; A. Barnitz, journal entry, May 23, 1867, in Utley, ed., *Life in Custer's Cavalry*, p. 53.

3. October 26, 1867

1. Winfield Scott Hancock (1824–1886), a graduate of West Point in 1844, a Mexican War veteran, and a brigadier general

in the Civil War, was commander of the Military Department of the Missouri (embracing the area of Kansas, Colorado, New Mexico, and Indian Territory) from August 1866 to September 1867. Custer's attitude toward Hancock seems to have vacillated over the years. Before the 1867 expedition he evidently entertained a high opinion of him, and for all the difficulties the expedition encountered in April, the two men were still on friendly terms in early May. Perhaps preparing her for a prolonged separation, Hancock told Mrs. Custer that her husband was indispensable to the Indian campaign: "I do not know what we would do without Custer; he is our reliance." But as the summer wore on, with the expedition generally acknowledged a failure and Custer in arrest awaiting trial, relations between Hancock and Custer soured. Nomad's letters to *Turf, Field and Farm* became sarcastic and biting as the two officers engaged in mutual recriminations. Five years later, in "My Life on the Plains," Custer quieted his criticisms and even argued the case that Hancock merely did what soldierly duty dictated in 1867. There the matter might rest were it not for the posthumous publication of Custer's account of the battle of Williamsburg, fought in May 1862. In it, he depicted Hancock as a hot-tempered, impatient, superbly brave officer who was, moreover, guilty of a gross insubordination that would undoubtedly have ended his career had he not managed to carry the day and erase all memory of his defiance of "positive orders." Custer's Civil War memoirs had been appearing in *The Galaxy* throughout the spring of 1876 in regular installments. After his death the magazine noted that it had received and would be publishing two additional chapters "written on the march." In fact, it carried three more chapters, the last with another explanatory note: "This article, a continuation of the series of 'War Memoirs,' is a portion of a manuscript found among General Custer's papers since his death." It in-

cluded the discussion of Williamsburg, and its rather querulous portrayal of Hancock might be accounted for by the fact that it was possibly written much earlier than the rest of the series, perhaps during the winter of 1869–70 before Custer softened his attitude in "My Life on the Plains" and while the sting of reprimand from his court-martial was still relatively fresh in mind. See E. Custer to James W. Forsyth, January 25, 1867, in Lawrence A. Frost, *General Custer's Libbie* (Seattle: Superior Publishing, 1976), p. 160; E. Custer to G. Custer, May 7, 1867, in *Tenting on the Plains*, p. 546; G. A. Custer, "War Memoirs: Yorktown and Williamsburg," *The Galaxy* 22 (November 1876): 684–694; and Whittaker, *Complete Life of Gen. George A. Custer*, p. 473.

2. On November 29, 1864, Colonel John M. Chivington, commander of the Military District of Colorado, led a force of 700 to 800 regular and volunteer cavalrymen against a Cheyenne village of perhaps 600 inhabitants camped thirty-five miles from Fort Lyon under what they assumed were assurances of peace. However, feeling had been running high in Colorado that the Indians must be severely punished for past transgressions, and the Cheyenne village provided a convenient target. The battle was a blood bath in which the village was utterly destroyed and 150 to 200 Indian men, women, and children were killed. Westerners welcomed the news of what they considered just punishment meted out to the Cheyennes, while Easterners generally expressed shocked outrage at a slaughter that was conducted with undeniable ferocity. For their part, the plains Indians formed an abiding distrust of white men and their professed desire for peace. Thus Custer was aligned with opinion in the East, and especially in the Indian Bureau, when he attributed Cheyenne and Sioux skittishness about allowing Hancock to approach their camp to their memories of Sand Creek. The Indians in their parleys

with Hancock said as much. "They feared us; feared another massacre like Chivington's," Custer noted at the time. See G. Custer to E. Custer, April 15, 1867, in *Tenting on the Plains*, p. 560. The substantial literature on Sand Creek is surveyed in Michael A. Sievers, "Sands of Sand Creek Historiography," *Colorado Magazine* 49 (Spring 1972): 116–142. The standard account is Stan Hoig, *The Sand Creek Massacre* (Norman: University of Oklahoma Press, 1961).

3. Actually the fourteenth of April. The date is important in determining whether Hancock acted precipitately in holding Indians from this village responsible for depredations committed on the fifteenth fifty miles away. To set the chronology straight, Hancock's expedition left Fort Riley on March 26, arriving at Fort Larned on April 7. Major E. W. Wyncoop, agent for the Cheyennes, notified Hancock that the Sioux and Cheyennes camped on Pawnee Fork had agreed to meet with him at Fort Larned on the tenth. A snow storm and the evident reluctance of the Indians to move their village closer to the fort resulted in a delay, and by the time a small party of warriors and two chiefs showed up to parley with Hancock on the evening of the twelfth he had already decided to march on the village the next day. He covered twenty-one of the approximately thirty-two (not twenty, as Custer estimates) miles to the Indian camp before another parley was arranged. This time Hancock extracted a promise that all the leading men would be on hand for a council the following morning. When they failed to turn up, Hancock resumed his march on the fourteenth, and it is at this point that Custer picks up the story. By compressing this record of events, it should be noted, Custer fosters the impression that Hancock was unreasonably impatient in his dealings with the Indians.

4. In a letter written on April 14, Custer set the number of Indians at three hundred, while Captain Barnitz estimated three to four hundred, and the correspondent Theodore Davis guessed "about three hundred." One other eyewitness, James W. Dixon, who was with the Fourth Artillery, later came up with the improbable figure of "about fourteen hundred" warriors. Dixon was writing almost twenty years after the event, and while his article is occasionally cited by historians, much of it was simply borrowed without acknowledgment from Custer's *My Life on the Plains*. The Indian numbers are of interest because the spectacle of the battle line impressed all who saw it and was one rarely repeated in the experience of army officers in the West despite the fact it became a staple in Hollywood westerns. See G. Custer to E. Custer, April 14, 1867, in *Tenting on the Plains*, p. 559; A. Barnitz to J. Barnitz, April 14, 1867, in Utley, ed., *Life in Custer's Cavalry*, p. 32; Davis, "A Summer on the Plains," p. 295; and James W. Dixon, "Across the Plains with General Hancock," *Journal of the Military Service Institution of the United States* 7 (June 1886): 197.

5. *My Life on the Plains*, pp. 26–27, offered a radically different version: "After a few moments of painful suspense, General Hancock, accompanied by General A. J. Smith and other officers, rode forward, and through an interpreter invited the chiefs to meet us midway, for the purpose of an interview. In response to this invitation Roman Nose, bearing a white flag, accompanied by Bull Bear, White Horse, Gray Beard, and Medicine Wolf on the part of the Cheyennes, and Pawnee Killer, Bad Wound, Tall Bear that Walks under the Ground, Left Hand, Little Bear, and Little Bull on the part of the Sioux, rode forward to the middle of the open space between the two lines." Here, Hancock *initiates* the parley—a version in accordance with what Captain Barnitz wrote the same day. In Indian accounts, it was Agent Wyncoop who played the role of peacemaker, calmed down the situation, and arranged for the parley. See A. Barnitz to J. Barnitz, April 14, 1867,

in Utley, ed., *Life in Custer's Cavalry*, p. 32; and Grinnell, *Fighting Cheyennes*, p. 250.

6. Edmond Guerrier, a mixed-blood Cheyenne, who appears as Gayere and Gayen (an obvious error in transcription) in Custer's reports and as Gurrier in *My Life on the Plains*.

7. *My Life on the Plains*, p. 27, downplays any bellicosity on Hancock's part: ". . . we shook hands with all of the chiefs, most of them exhibiting unmistakable signs of gratification at this apparently peaceful termination of our rencounter. General Hancock very naturally inquired the object of the hostile attitude displayed before us, saying to the chiefs that if war was their object we were ready then and there to participate."

8. *My Life on the Plains*, p. 27, notes: "The interview then terminated, and the Indians moved off in the direction of their village, we following leisurely in rear." This gives the impression that, since the troops did not mean to threaten the Indians, they did not hurry after them to make certain that they honored their promise. Only a few months after the Nomad letter appeared, Theodore Davis also contradicted it, writing that Hancock "did not move forward for some time, as he expressed himself anxious that the Indians should reach the village and inform the inhabitants of his peaceful intentions before the command came in sight of it" (Davis, "A Summer on the Plains," p. 295).

9. In *My Life on the Plains*, p. 27, Custer wrote that "our tents were pitched within half a mile of the village. Guards were placed between to prevent intrusion upon our part. A few of the Indian ponies found grazing near our camp were caught and returned to them, to show that our intentions were at least neighborly." Nevertheless, the village panicked and four Cheyenne leaders rode in to inform Hancock that their women and children had fled. "General Hancock insisted that they should all return, promising protection and good treatment to all; that if the camp was abandoned he would hold it responsible. The chiefs then stated their belief in their ability to recall the fugitives . . ." By actual count the village consisted of 111 Cheyenne and 140 Sioux lodges, with an estimated 25 more removed before the count was made ("Difficulties with Indian Tribes," p. 71).

10. *My Life on the Plains*, pp. 27–28: "I had retired to my tent . . . when a messenger . . . awakened me with the information that General Hancock desired my presence at his tent. . . . General Hancock briefly stated the situation of affairs, and directed me to mount my command as quickly and as silently as possible, surround the Indian village, and prevent the departure of its inhabitants." Here, instead of an emotionally immature and indecisive commander, we have Hancock as the model of swift action. No mention is made of a two-hour delay between his receiving the intelligence that the Indians were pulling out and his summoning Custer. While the story Custer was about to recount at some length became an even more dramatic adventure in *My Life on the Plains*, it did not strike anyone at the time as extraordinary. See G. Custer to E. Custer, April 15, 1867, in *Tenting on the Plains*, p. 560; A. Barnitz to J. Barnitz, April 17, 1867, in Utley, ed., *Life in Custer's Cavalry*, p. 34; and Davis, "A Summer on the Plains," pp. 295–296.

11. Oddly, in *My Life on the Plains*, pp. 28–29, Custer changed this bright moonlit night: "The moon, although nearly full, kept almost constantly behind the clouds, as if to screen us in our hazardous undertaking. . . . Taking a campfire which we could see in the village as our guiding point, we made a detour so as to place the village between ourselves and the infantry. Occasionally the moon would peep out from behind the clouds and enable us to catch a hasty glance at the village. . . . The same flashes of moonlight which gave us hurried glimpses of the village enabled us to see our own column of horse-

men stretching its silent length far into the dim darkness. . . . No sooner was our line [around the village] completely formed than the moon, as if deeming darkness no longer essential to our success, appeared from behind her screen and lighted up the entire scene." One reason for changing the status of the light was obviously dramatic, to add suspense; another, to answer the question why, if the cavalry was able to surround the camp under full moonlight without being detected, it did not immediately assume that the Indians had fled.

12. This little story is eerily reminiscent of one of the most popular jokes about Custer's Last Stand: As he was falling fatally wounded, the General uttered his immortal last words, "Take no prisoners, men!" Contemporary Indians particularly like to tell it. See Vine Deloria, Jr., *Custer Died for Your Sins* (New York: Macmillan, 1969), p. 149.

13. These events are considerably embellished in *My Life on the Plains*, pp. 29–31, with Custer assuming a more prominent role therein. "Directing the entire line of troopers to remain mounted with carbines held at the 'advance,'" Custer *dismounted* and, with *three* others, crawled on hands and knees toward the village. "It became a question of prudence with us, . . . how far from our horses and how near to the village we dared to go. . . . When we had passed over two-thirds of the distance between our horses and the village, it was deemed best to make our presence known. . . . Gurrier [Guerrier] called out at the top of his voice in the Cheyenne tongue. . . . We had approached near enough to see that some of the lodges were detached some distance from the main encampment. Selecting the nearest of these, we directed our advance on it. . . . there was scarcely one of us who would not have felt more comfortable if we could have got back to our horses without loss of pride. . . . Cautiously approaching, on all fours, to within a few yards of the nearest lodge, occasionally halting and listening to discover evidence

as to whether the village was deserted or not, we finally decided that the Indians had fled before the arrival of the cavalry, and that none but empty lodges were before us. . . . Arriving at the first lodge, one of our party raised the curtain or mat which served as a door, and the doctor and myself entered." So—here we have a nerve-jangling hands-and-knees crawl through the darkness toward the village, and a tense initial entry into a lodge by Custer and one other. Instead of high drama, however, the whole episode, to borrow Custer's earlier imagery, may have more closely approximated farce, since there is evidence that the scout who hallooed the camp, Guerrier, was perfectly aware it was empty, having concealed the information from Hancock until his Cheyenne relatives got a good headstart on the troops. See Hyde, *Life of George Bent*, pp. 260–261; Guerrier's own account, given to George Bird Grinnell in 1908, mentions no such deceit on his part: *Fighting Cheyennes*, pp. 252–253.

14. With a few changes in emphasis this anecdote survived relatively intact in *My Life on the Plains*, p. 31, where the doctor (I. T. Coates) and Custer are still in the first tipi entered, and Guerrier walks in just as the doctor asks, "What can this be?" In a letter to his wife written a few weeks after the incident, Custer reported the story as one he had heard, with the doctor *thinking* the thoughts Custer later had him verbalize. Also, the doctor is credited with an almost professional sangfroid, "coolly" responding when he is told he is eating dog, "I don't care; it's good, any how" (G. Custer to E. Custer, May 2, 1867, in *Tenting on the Plains*, pp. 577–578). "Esculapius," usually rendered Aesculapius or Asclepius, was the Greek god of healing.

15. This passage entails a gross misrepresentation, since the deserted Indian village was not actually destroyed until April 19—as Custer tacitly admits in letter #5. Here Custer stresses Hancock's baffled fury and his intemperate decision to

burn the village as immediate revenge; in *My Life on the Plains*, p. 33, we have: "General Hancock, on learning the situation of affairs, despatched some companies of infantry to the deserted village, with orders to replace the cavalry and protect the village and its contents from disturbance until its final disposition could be determined upon." When Hancock *did* destroy the village, a few days later, Custer quotes his reasons for doing so and defends his action as justifiable "retribution" (pp. 42–43). Because Custer was making a case against Hancock at the time, he omitted a detail from his Nomad letter that he had mentioned to his wife and would elaborate upon in *My Life on the Plains* and that was also prominent in other contemporary accounts: the discovery in the deserted village of a young mixed-blood girl who had been repeatedly raped before she was abandoned by the departing warriors. In his letter to his wife, Custer was wrought up enough by the discovery to write, "Wo be unto these Indians, if ever I overtake them!" But in the letter to *Turf, Field and Farm* written half a year later he avoided even mentioning the subject, presumably because, in the mental climate of the age, such brutal treatment of a young girl would have seemed ample justification for Hancock's destruction of the village and the ensuing Indian war. See G. Custer to E. Custer, May 2, 1867, in *Tenting on the Plains*, p. 578; *My Life on the Plains*, p. 32; A. Barnitz to J. Barnitz, April 17, 1867, in Utley, ed., *Life in Custer's Cavalry*, p. 35; and Davis, "A Summer on the Plains," p. 296.

4. November 11, 1867

1. The implication here, that Hancock should have known better than to burden the cavalry with wagons, was not repeated in the parallel discussion in *My Life on the Plains*, p. 33.

2. At twenty minutes to three on the morning of April 15, moments after receiving orders from Hancock to pursue the absent Indians, Custer dashed off a letter to his wife brimming with confidence: "I do not anticipate war, or even difficulty, as the Indians are frightened to death, and only ran away from fear. If I can overtake them, which I believe I can, their horses being in very poor condition, I can at least try to disabuse their minds of an idea of harm . . ." Chastened by the hard summer of futile pursuit that followed, Custer in his *Turf, Field and Farm* letter was openly pessimistic that the army could ever run down the Indians and bring them to bay. But by the time he wrote up his memoirs in 1872, with the successful winter campaign of 1868–69 behind him and his reputation as an Indian-fighter firmly established, Custer spoke from a broader base of experience: ". . . in making a rapid pursuit after Indians, much of the success depends upon the lightness of the order of march. . . . Never was the old saying that in Rome one must do as Romans do more aptly illustrated than on an Indian campaign. . . . [The Indian] divests himself of all superfluous dress and ornament when preparing for rapid movements. The white man, if he hopes for success, must adopt the same rule of action, and encumber his horse as little as possible" (G. Custer to E. Custer, April 15, 1867, in *Tenting on the Plains*, pp. 560–561; *My Life on the Plains*, p. 33).

3. The long description of tracking that follows was tailor-made for *Turf, Field and Farm*'s readership. As Custer observed on the same topic in *My Life on the Plains*, p. 35, when the Indian scouts set out to discover a trail, their method "resembled not a little the course of a thorough sportsman, who, with a well-trained pointer or setter, thoroughly 'ranges' and 'beats' the ground in search of his coveted game." The powers that Custer attributes to the Indian trackers seem almost out of the novels of James Fenimore Cooper and are amusing in light of his opinion that to Cooper's writings "more than to those of any other author are the people speaking

the English language indebted for a false and ill-judged estimate of the Indian character" (p. 11).

4. Frontier types like James Butler "Wild Bill" Hickok (1837–1876) delighted Custer. They smacked of the Wild West and made excellent copy for Eastern readers, as Custer's reference to the recent article on Hickok suggests (George Ward Nichols, "Wild Bill," *Harper's New Monthly Magazine* 34 [February 1867]: 273–285). In *My Life on the Plains*, pp. 33–34, Custer expanded his treatment of Wild Bill, touting him as "the most prominent man" among the army's scouts in 1867. For Hickok and his career during the period Custer knew him, see Blaine Burkey, *Wild Bill Hickok, the Law in Hays City*, rev. ed. (Hays, Kans.: Thomas More Prep, 1975). The standard biography is Joseph G. Rosa, *They Called Him Wild Bill: The Life and Adventures of James Butler Hickok*, rev. ed. (Norman: University of Oklahoma Press, 1974).

5. December 15, 1867

1. Custer here refers to his court-martial sentence, issued on November 20, that he "be suspended from rank and command for one year, and . . . forfeit his pay proper for the same time." In public, Custer accepted the judgment jauntily. A sympathetic correspondent for the *New York Times* remarked that the sentence gave Custer "a respite that he has desired for a long time, not perhaps in this precise way, but he seems to be satisfied to take his blessings as they come. He proposes to remain in Leavenworth during the Winter and visit Europe in the Spring. It may be, too, that some of this wished-for leisure time will be devoted to the preparation of a work that will be decidedly interesting to those who have followed the fortunes of the General through his many campaigns." Mrs. Custer wrote that she and her husband were "the wonder of the garrison" at Fort Leavenworth, "we are in such high spirits,"

and he made his literary intentions clearer in a letter to a friend: ". . . I am preparing to execute a long-projected plan— to write a memoir of my experience from West Point to Appomattox. Arrangements for this are concluded with Messrs Harper & Brothers. I have fifty pages of the script completed." Though Custer kept a smiling face to the world during the period of his court-martial and sentence, his bitter denunciation of Hancock in the Nomad letters indicates that he was deeply wounded by the end result of his first Indian campaign, and he said so quite openly in *My Life on the Plains*, p. 23:

General Hancock, with the artillery and six companies of infantry, reached Fort Riley, Kansas, from Fort Leavenworth by rail the last week in March; here he was joined by four companies of the Seventh Cavalry and an additional company of the Thirty-seventh Infantry. It was at this point that I joined the expedition. And as a fair sample of the laurels which military men may win in an Indian campaign by a zealous discharge of what they deem their duty, I will here state . . . that after engaging in the expedition . . . and undergoing fatigue, privations, and dangers equal to those of a campaign during the Rebellion, I found myself at the termination of the campaign again at Fort Riley *in arrest*. This is not mentioned in a fault-finding spirit. I have no fault to find. It is said that blessings sometimes come in disguise. Such proved to be true in this instance, although I must say the disguise for some little time was most perfect.

See also Russell, "From the Plains," *New York Times*, December 7, 1867, p. 2; E. Custer to Rebecca Richmond, November 20, 1867, and G. Custer to Mr. Walker, [1867], in Merington, ed., *The Custer Story*, pp. 214–215; and, for a graphic description of the promulgation of the court-martial sentence, see Stan Hoig, *The Battle of the Washita: The Sheridan-Custer Indian Campaign of 1867–69* (Garden City, N.Y.: Doubleday, 1976), pp. 19–20.

2. Such a person was John Burkman, Custer's striker, or orderly, from 1870 until the General's death. Elizabeth Custer described Burkman, an illiterate, dull-witted but intensely loyal fellow, as "slow of speech, thought, and movement . . . The man lived in a world by himself, with little in common with his comrades, going along a dull, beaten path at snail's pace . . . I have a photograph of him standing between and holding . . . [Custer's two favorite mounts]. The dogs stand or lie about the group . . ." Burkman "may have had a past," she noted, but "his horizon encompassed two horses, some dogs, and one yellow-haired officer." His own story, told when he was a truculent old man still living in the past and devoted to the memory of the General and "Miss Libbie," was published nine years after his suicide in 1925. See Custer, *Following the Guidon*, p. 331; Glendolin Damon Wagner, *Old Neutriment* (Boston: Ruth Hill, 1934).

3. The "Editor's Drawer," featuring contributions or "deposits" of light verse and amusing or instructive anecdotes, was a regular feature at the back of each issue of *Harper's New Monthly Magazine* beginning with the fourteenth number, July 1851.

4. In *My Life on the Plains*, p. 36, with its fairly pronounced anti-Indian tone, Custer replaces "natural sagacity" with the more connotative phrase "proverbial cunning."

5. The story recounted here with such relish was fundamentally transformed in *My Life on the Plains*, pp. 39–41. The "young officer" who here is the butt of the joke becomes an experienced old hand, and the whole point of the story is consequently altered. In the Nomad version, which was in accordance with what Custer told his wife a few days after the fact, a brash young officer receives his comeuppance for his know-it-all attitude. In contrast, in his memoirs Custer wrote: "Had the officer in command been young and inexperienced, his mishap might have been credited to these causes; but here was an officer who had grown gray in the service, familiar with the Plains and with Indians, yet so completely misled by appearances as to mistake his camp, which he had left but an hour before, for an Indian village." Now it was "the deceptive effects produced by the atmosphere on the Plains" and the propensity of those who are lost to wander in circles that set up the moral of the story: "This little incident will show how necessary experienced professional guides are in connection with all military movements on the Plains." Why the changes? Perhaps propriety dictated them, since the officer involved in the incident was apparently Captain Louis M. Hamilton. He was indeed young at the time—not quite twenty-three—and he would fall a year later at the battle of the Washita. Custer may well have wanted to eliminate any clue that would link his story to the dead officer. While the matter is trivial in itself, it serves as a salutary warning that other incidents in *My Life on the Plains* were also shaped to ends other than strict historical accuracy. Custer's conversations with scout "California Joe" Milner —rendered in the richest border dialect—were doubtless partially invented for their humorous effect, while his description of a meeting with the father of Lieutenant Lyman S. Kidder, in which they together find the evidence that will allow the lieutenant's remains to be identified, rearranges the actual record of events for dramatic purposes. These factual alterations made for the sake of more-vivid storytelling are quite distinct from the self-justifying distortions noted by Minnie Millbrook, among others, but they do need to be kept in mind by the reader who might otherwise accept Custer's words uncritically. See G. Custer to E. Custer, April 20, 1867, in *Tenting on the Plains*, pp. 563–564; Millbrook, "Custer's First Scout in the West," p. 90;

Barton R. Voigt, "The Death of Lyman S. Kidder," *South Dakota History* 6 (Winter 1975): 18, n. 14; Custer, *My Life on the Plains*, pp. 100–101; and Millbrook, "The West Breaks in General Custer," pp. 137, 140.

6. Actually the Union Pacific Railway Company, Eastern Division, later (March 1869) the Kansas Pacific Railway. Its on-again off-again progress through Kansas on the way, as events worked out, to Denver was a background to the Indian fighting in the area from 1867 to 1870, when the line was completed. In recognition of his services on the railroad's behalf, Custer would be one of the dignitaries invited aboard for an inaugural excursion to Denver in September 1870. See letter #8.

7. In *My Life on the Plains*, p. 42, this picture of men nervously huddling at each station in response to a "big Indian scare" that had yet to materialize is very much changed: "The stage stations were erected at points along the route distant from each other from ten to fifteen miles, and were used solely for the shelter and accommodation of the relays of drivers and horses employed on the stage route. We found, in passing over the route on our eastward march, that only about every fourth station was occupied, the occupants of the other three having congregated there for mutual defence against the Indians, the latter having burned the deserted stations." The impression Custer conveys here is of an Indian war already well underway—an impression confirmed shortly after when the ruins and remains of the stationkeepers at Lookout Station are discovered.

8. The subject touched on here was at the crux of the whole controversy over the Hancock Expedition's responsibility for inciting an Indian war. In his letter #3 Nomad had left the distinct impression, contradicted here, that General Hancock, furious over what he considered the Indians' treachery in deserting their village the evening of April 14, had caused it to be burned the next morning. In fact, Hancock had been prepared to take just that step but, dissuaded by cooler heads, had agreed to wait until he had positive evidence that the village's late inhabitants were engaged in raiding and were not simply fleeing in fright. It was up to Custer to provide this evidence one way or the other, and it came in his report, dated April 17, 9:30 P.M., at Downer's Station: "There is no doubt but that the depredations at Lookout were by some of the same Indians who deserted their lodges on Pawnee Fork, and whose trail I followed until they broke up into small bands." Upon receiving this intelligence from Custer late the next day, Hancock ordered the destruction of the abandoned village, which was carried out on the morning of the nineteenth. That same day, Custer added an unsettling postscript to his follow-up report. He had decided after personal investigation that "Lookout Station was burned and the men massacred on Monday the 15th, which clears those Indians who were at Pawnee Fork the day of our arrival from the charge of being present at the murder. I am confident, however, that the act was committed with their knowledge and approval, which accounts for their hasty flight." This left Hancock in an embarrassing position, and in his report to General Sherman he put the best face he could on the matter, arguing that the warriors who committed the depredation *could* have been from the village he destroyed, likely were, and anyway it was not "of much importance" for he was "satisfied that the Indian village was a nest of conspirators." Indian testimony indicates that Hancock was right—a band of Sioux from the village did burn Lookout Station—but Custer was also right in maintaining that only *some* of the Indians could be blamed, not *all*, and certainly not the Cheyennes whose 111 tipis were put to the torch along with those of the Sioux. Hancock

knew that burning the Indian village would be "a cheap victory" with costly consequences: "It is war against the Cheyennes and Sioux, between the Arkansas and Platte," he advised his immediate subordinate, Andrew Smith. But Custer, in his desire to get at Hancock, was less than candid in saying that it was "known at the time" Hancock ordered the Indian village destroyed "that the burning of the station occurred before the Indians had deserted their village," and he was actively deceitful in saying that, "as the two were hundreds of miles apart, it was not possible that the occupants of the village could have been the perpetrators of the outrages at the station," when the actual distance between the two points (in contradistinction to the distance Custer marched his men in pursuit of their will-o'-the-wisp quarry) was nearer fifty miles. Nothing is more striking than Custer's about-face in *My Life on the Plains*, pp. 22, 42–43, where he chose to let Hancock speak for himself on the objectives of the expedition and, more critically, on the much mooted question "as to which party committed the first overt act of war": "When I learned from General Custer, who investigated these matters on the spot, that directly after they had abandoned the villages they attacked and burned a mail station on the Smoky Hill, killed the white men at it, disembowelled and burned them, fired into another station, endeavored to gain admittance to a third, fired on my expressmen both on the Smoky Hill and on their way to Larned, I concluded that this must be war, and therefore deemed it my duty to take the first opportunity which presented to resent these hostilities and outrages, and did so by destroying their villages." "This act of retribution on the part of General Hancock was the signal for an extensive pen and ink war, directed against him and his forces," Custer added, unmindful of his own role in that paper war back in 1867. See "Difficulties

with Indian Tribes," pp. 66–77; also Burkey, *Custer, Come at Once!* pp. 4–6; and Millbrook, "Custer's First Scout," pp. 90–95.

II. KANSAS, 1869–1870

1. See Carl Coke Rister, *Border Command: General Phil Sheridan in the West* (Norman: University of Oklahoma Press, 1944), chaps. 3–9.
2. Custer, *My Life on the Plains*, pp. 124–125.
3. The battle of the Washita bulks large in all the histories of the plains Indian wars and Custer's Seventh since it was the regiment's first major offensive success against the natives and the basis of Custer's reputation as a skilled Indian-fighter. Washita was controversial in its time because it raised the specter of total war against a mixed Indian population and, some argued, involved a fairly peaceable village of Cheyennes. It was controversial in another sense as well because, of the twenty soldiers killed in the battle, all but three died with Major Joel H. Elliott on an incautious pursuit of fleeing Indians. Custer, pressed by Indian reinforcements, made no effort to locate Elliott's detachment or determine its fate, and this episode effectively divided the regiment along lines that had already been laid down during the hapless campaign of 1867. For a recent study, see Hoig, *The Battle of the Washita*.
4. Whittaker, *Complete Life of Gen. George A. Custer*, p. 472.
5. P. H. Sheridan to G. Custer, April 7, 1869, in Merington, ed., *The Custer Story*, p. 228.
6. E. Custer to Rebecca Richmond, October 16, 1869, in Frost, *General Custer's Libbie*, p. 184.
7. Whittaker, *Complete Life of Gen. George A. Custer*, p. 474.
8. Ibid.
9. Custer, *Following the Guidon*, p. 308.

6. September 12, 1869

1. Two days before the battle of the Washita, K. C. Barker wrote Custer lamenting his long absence from the columns of *Turf, Field and Farm* and urging him to resume his contributions since "they would add greatly to the interest of the paper." But the events of the winter and spring of 1869 gave Custer little time for literary pursuits, while the summer was spent relaxing with a succession of visitors and hunting buffalo. By now the General was perhaps a little jaded, though he still thought buffalo hunting "the most exciting of all American sports," understood its appeal to the novice, and hosted any number of guests eager to add a buffalo tail to their trophies. Two hunts in 1869 stuck out in Custer's mind, and because the individuals involved would be of interest to *Turf*'s readers, Nomad sent along the particulars. Custer would hunt in distinguished company again—notably in January 1872, when he was invited to join the party accompanying Grand Duke Alexis of Russia—but he did not choose to describe another buffalo hunt. The "succession of incidents" that he mentions as having befallen him since his last appearance in *Turf* were left to be recorded in *My Life on the Plains*, about half of which is given over to his Indian experiences subsequent to 1867. See K. C. Barker to G. Custer, November 27, 1868, in Frost, *General Custer's Libbie*, p. 179.

2. John M. Schofield (1831–1906) was confirmed as secretary of war in 1868, replacing the controversial Edwin M. Stanton for the balance of Andrew Johnson's presidency. Subsequently, Schofield commanded the Military Department of the Missouri from 1869 to 1870, then the Division of the Pacific, headquartered in San Francisco, from 1870 to 1876 and, following a stint as superintendent of West Point, again from 1882 to 1883. With Sheridan's death in 1888, Schofield became commanding general of the army and in February 1895, seven months before he retired, lieutenant general. His was, in short, a spectacular career.

3. September 7, 1869.

4. William Thomas Gentry, a graduate of West Point in 1852, served with the Seventeenth Infantry throughout the Civil War. He was unassigned to a regiment from May 27, 1869, to February 15, 1870, on duty with General Sheridan's staff. Brevetted a lieutenant colonel in 1865, he achieved it as his regular rank with the Twenty-fifth Infantry a year before his death in 1885.

5. The identity of these two young lords has remained elusive. There is consensus that Lord Paget was Lord Berkeley Paget, while Blaine Burkey has ventured the guess that Lord Waterpark was Henry A. Cavendish, Baron Waterpark. Custer's mention of Paget's martial forebears is irresistible, so often was his own Last Stand compared to Waterloo and Balaclava. Scores of American poets, in paying tribute to the dead hero, found their inspiration in Tennyson's "The Charge of the Light Brigade" and echoed the immortal lines that Custer himself was wont to quote:

Theirs not to make reply;
Theirs not to reason why;
Theirs but to do and die.

In death, Custer was frequently likened to Lord Cardigan, who lived on, a hero in some minds, a fool in others. Lord George Paget, the uncle to whom Custer refers, held Cardigan responsible for the decimation of his command in "the valley of death" because of his failure to leave "no stone unturned" in trying to find Paget to let him know that the first line was retreating. Nevertheless, Paget considered Cardigan a man of "courage and daring" whose subsequent fall from popular favor resulted not from his actions at Balaclava but from an ambitiousness and vanity that "led him astray"—opinions that Custer likely heard secondhand from his young guest. See Burkey, *Custer,*

Come at Once! p. 83, n. 30; G. A. Custer, "War Memoirs," *The Galaxy* 21 (March 1876): 321; and Gen. Lord George Paget, *The Light Cavalry Brigade in the Crimea* (London: John Murray, 1881), chap. 7.

6. The Marquis of Hastings (1842–1868) has gone down in the annals of horse racing as a rather pathetic n'er-do-well, more to be pitied than censured. By the time he was twenty he was involved in racing and in 1864 enjoyed an especially good season which he capped by eloping with Lady Florence Paget just before she was to marry another. At his height, the Marquis owned fifty race horses and was well regarded as a gentleman of the turf. But he made several errors of judgment, notably a heavy bet against the horse owned by his wife's former fiancé in the 1867 Derby. The horse won, the Marquis lost a fortune, and his path to ruin was completed the next year when he scratched a horse he had entered in the Derby on the eve of the race to the outrage of its backers and the consternation of the racing establishment. Later that year, at the age of twenty-six, the Marquis died—an apparent casebook study in the fate that moralists loved to warn awaited all who frequented the track. See Roger Longrigg, *The History of Horse Racing* (London: Macmillan, 1972), pp. 130, 126.

7. Lexington (1850–1875) was, hands down, the most celebrated American thoroughbred in the second half of the nineteenth century. On April 2, 1855, at the Metairie course near New Orleans, a crowd of racing enthusiasts from across the Union gathered to watch Lexington race against the clock. On a fast track, with a running start, pacemakers, and a slightly overweight jockey aboard, Lexington made the four-mile run in 7:19.75, a time so astounding that it held up for two decades. Consequently, Custer, like every other devotee of the turf, could still quote it from memory fourteen years after the fact. Custer subsequently had the opportunity to see the famous old horse in retirement, and he provided *Turf, Field and Farm* with his impressions in letter #9. See Longrigg, *History of Horse Racing*, pp. 214–216.

8. It is uncertain just when the Seventh Cavalry formally adopted "GarryOwen" —an Irish quickstep and a boisterous drinking song with a martial tradition dating back to about 1800—as its regimental air. Tradition has it that Custer personally chose "GarryOwen" for the Seventh at the suggestion of one of his Irish officers, but since the regimental band was the brainchild of Major Alfred Gibbs, it seems just as likely that he was responsible for adopting the tune. Whatever the case, "GarryOwen" has been closely identified with *Custer's* Seventh ever since he ordered the band to strike it up when he gave the signal to charge at the Washita. "At once the rollicking notes of that familiar marching and fighting air sounded forth through the valley, and in a moment were reechoed back from the opposite sides by the loud and continued cheers of the men of the other detachments, who, true to their orders, were there and in readiness to pounce upon the Indians the moment the attack began," Custer recalled. "In this manner the battle of the Washita commenced" (*My Life on the Plains*, p. 163). For "GarryOwen," see Edward S. Luce in Melbourne C. Chandler, *Of GarryOwen in Glory: The History of the Seventh United States Cavalry Regiment* (Annandale, Va.: Turnpike Press, 1960), pp. 412–415.

9. "Another Richard appeared upon the field": while the phrase was used to suggest that a rival claimant for place of honor had made an appearance, it originally had a quite different connotation. In Colley Cibber's 1700 version of *The Tragical History of King Richard III*, one of the king's retainers, worried by Richard's broodiness on the eve of battle ("Methinks the King has not that pleas'd Alacrity / Nor cheer of Mind that he was wont

to have"), is reassured: "The meer effect of business— / You'll find him, Sir, another Man i'th' Field . . ." The other Richard, in short, was Richard's other side. Custer followed this usage elsewhere when he said of himself after recovering his composure following the near-fatal mishap on his first buffalo hunt, "Another horse, and Richard was himself again . . ."—a specific allusion to a later line in Cibber's play when king Richard declares:

Conscience avant: Richard's himself again.
    Hark! the shrill Trumpet sounds, to Horse: Away!
    My Soul's in Arms, and eager for the Fray.

See *My Life on the Plains*, p. 39; C. Cibber, *The Tragical History of King Richard III* (1770), Act, v, Sc. 3.

10. This reference eludes me. It might be to Mr. Toodle, the classically poor-but-proud family man who pops in and out of Charles Dickens' *Dombey and Son* (1848), but I cannot locate the line quoted by Custer in that mammoth novel. Custer did not enjoy most fiction but was partial to Dickens. A copy of *A Tale of Two Cities* was in his library, and he quoted Mr. Micawber, from *David Copperfield*, in a letter to a friend. See Hedren, "The Custer Library," p. 7; and G. Custer to Mr. Walker, 1867, in Merington, ed., *The Custer Story*, p. 215.

11. The exceptional courtesy shown such a large party of excursionists no doubt had something to do with the fact they were from Ohio, Custer's native state. Too, some of the officers and excursionists enjoyed a previous acquaintance dating back to Civil War days. See Frank Talmadge, "Buffalo Hunting with Custer," *Cavalry Journal*, January 1929, quoted in Minnie Dubbs Millbrook, "Big Game Hunting with the Custers," *Kansas Historical Quarterly* 41 (Winter 1975): 436.

12. Charles Lever (1806–1872), a Dublin-born author, published a string of novels between 1839 and 1872, many of them depicting life in the Irish regiments during the Napoleonic wars. Tradition has it

that Custer read them furtively behind his geography book while a student in Monroe. Commenting on Lever's popularity, Don Russell has noted that one of his early novels, *Jack Hinton, the Guardsman* (1843), has reference to the band of a British dragoon regiment's striking up "the well-remembered air" of "Garry-Owen" as they rode through the streets of a French village. Custer, familiar with Lever's work, may also have become acquainted with "GarryOwen's" tradition in his pages. See Lionel Stevenson, *Dr. Quicksilver: The Life of Charles Lever* (New York: Russell & Russell, 1969 [1939]); Whittaker, *Complete Life of Gen. George A. Custer*, p. 8; and Don Russell, "Garry-Owen," *Westerners Brand Book* (Chicago) 34 (October 1977): 43.

13. The officer involved in this incident, Lieutenant Myles W. Moylan (1838–1909), had to endure his share of slights in a status-conscious officers corps because, with an excellent Civil War record in the volunteers behind him and with Custer's backing, he was commissioned from the ranks on July 28, 1866. When he was ostracized because of his service as an enlisted man, Custer literally took him into his home and, through example, made him one of the Seventh Cavalry "family." For a man who often experienced animosity from older officers without a West Point training, Custer throughout the Moylan episode acquitted himself admirably, demonstrating that he was more interested in good officer material than in paper credentials. Moylan served as regimental adjutant from February 21, 1867, to December 31, 1870. See Custer, *Tenting on the Plains*, pp. 415–419; and Robert Utley's informative biographical note on Moylan in *Life in Custer's Cavalry*, pp. 268–270.

14. Miss Talmadge, the seventeen-year-old daughter of one of the Ohio excursionists, was permitted to accompany the buffalo hunters. This was in violation of Custer's usual rule against allowing women to participate in the sport on the

grounds that the risk of a serious fall was too great. But when Miss Talmadge was told that she would have to ride in the ambulance with the other women, she remonstrated so vigorously that Custer, impressed by her demonstrated skills as a rider and pistol shot, and ever the gallant, relented. See Talmadge, "Buffalo Hunting with Custer," quoted in Millbrook, "Big Game Hunting with the Custers," pp. 436–437; and E. Custer to Laura Noble, September 19, 1869, in Frost, *General Custer's Libbie*, pp. 184–185.

15. This is probably the same scene described by Mrs. Custer in *Following the Guidon*, pp. 203–204. In her version, the General swept up the young lady of the party and placed her on top of the buffalo's carcass, where she received help in cutting off a tuft of hair from the animal's head as a trophy. This may have been Miss Talmadge, whose later feats Custer goes on to record.

16. The horse Custer was riding at the time, Dandy, had become his favorite in the year since he selected him for the Washita campaign. Mrs. Custer remembered that Dandy was "so quick, strong, and intelligent that he was accounted as good a buffalo-horse as there was in the regiment." But he, too, had his close calls, and on this particular hunt Dandy "pursued a buffalo down the side of a ravine, where the footing was insecure and narrow. The furious beast . . . suddenly wheeled, and before horse or rider could escape or even turn General Custer felt himself poised in air. The huge animal had actually lifted both man and beast on his strong vicious horns. It was only by Dandy's sudden leap to one side, and the coolness of both, that General Custer and his favorite gained a place of safety . . . on their return that day, Dandy had a hole in his side, where one horn had gored him, while the thick felt saddlecloth was cut through by the other. This very narrow escape had no effect on Dandy's nerves." Indeed, Dandy seemed

to have a catlike knack for survival: he was one of the three horses that the General took along with him on the 1876 campaign but was left behind when his master rode into his last battle. Dandy survived to become the saddle horse of Custer's grieving father and a family pet until his death about 1890. So much was he a part of the happy days of 1869 that Mrs. Custer devoted a chapter to him as a coda to her reminiscences of that period, *Following the Guidon*. See G. Custer to E. Custer, November 22, 1868, in Frost, *General Custer's Libbie*, p. 179; and *Following the Guidon*, pp. 184–185, chap. 22.

17. This corroborates the story told by Miss Talmadge's younger brother and erases the doubt that has been raised about its veracity. He wrote that his sister killed a large buffalo on the second day of the hunt with no assistance save that provided by her officer escort in handing her the loaded revolvers that she used. When she looked around for witnesses to confirm her prowess "no one was in sight but my escort and his orderly, whose testimony never would do. So later in the day I killed another when everybody could see." This jibes with Custer's account, though one of the noncommissioned officers who was along on the hunt remembered that Miss Talmadge's second kill was actually a coup de grace: "We shot a number of buffalo, and finally we crippled one so that he sat on his haunches, almost dead. The young lady then rode up and shot him with her pistol." See Talmadge, "Buffalo Hunting with Custer," quoted in Frost, *General Custer's Libbie*, p. 187, n. 27; and John Ryan (1909), quoted in Millbrook, "Big Game Hunting with the Custers," p. 440, n. 34.

18. Artemus Ward was the comic persona of Charles F. Browne (1834–1867), a widely quoted American humorist whose columns and lectures caught the fancy of his countrymen in the 1860's. In a little piece, "On 'Forts,'" Artemus argued that "every man has got a Fort. It's sum men's

fort to do one thing, and some other men's fort to do another, while there is numeris shiftliss critters goin round loose whose fort is not to do nothin." Experience had taught him that "fitin" and "playin hoss" wasn't his "Fort." See *Artemus Ward: His Works, Complete* (New York: G. W. Carleton, 1875), pp. 26–28.

19. On this subject, Theodore Davis remarked: "For an old buffalo hunter there is no better sport than to go out with a number of tyros and witness their first hunt. To be sure the shots from their carbines and revolvers sometimes come hurtling past you. Will Comstock used to remark at such a time that the safest place was nearest the buffalo . . ." Custer endorsed Davis' observations but in light of his own early misadventures was not about to be disdainful of the beginners' efforts. Nor could he join in Davis' parting shot: "A hunter who is unused to the sport, and becomes excited during the run, will frequently shoot his horse—how, I never could quite comprehend; but the revolver goes off, and the horse has the bullet. The rider loses his mount, gets no sympathy, but learns how to bear jokes of all descriptions. He may learn, if he will, 'that there is no particular demand for horse-robes just at present, though they may come in style if he remains on the Range for any length of time'" (Davis, "The Buffalo Range," pp. 155–156).

20. K. C. Barker had given Custer two staghounds the previous year—Maida and Blucher—and as pups they displayed a tenacity, courage, and speed that captivated the General. On one of their first trips out in the field, they tackled a buffalo and a wolf, and both ran down and killed jackrabbits. But Custer's favorite, Maida, was to fall victim soon after on a buffalo hunt, described in letter #7, that Custer hosted for Barker. See G. Custer to K. C. Barker, undated (1868) extract, and G. Custer to E. Custer, October 18 and November 3, 1868, in *Following the Guidon*, pp. 9–10, 12, 14–15.

21. Mrs. Custer seconded her husband's enthusiasm about their English guests. Both frankly conceded they had awaited their arrival with some trepidation, having had previous experiences with ungrateful or incompetent visitors, but "Lords Paget and Waterpark proved to be charming and unassuming gentlemen, delighted with everything done for them and able to rough it with anyone who had been years out here. They were such good riders (though very awkward in appearance—our own officers appeared to be perfect centaurs beside them) that they killed thirteen. I was of course prepared to dislike them and mentally called them 'snots' before seeing them, but such good breeding and genuine kindheartedness made them many friends. They 'took' to Autie [Custer] as they are so fond of hunting and horses and dogs . . . We have had some other 'highnesses' out here before this party, but they were not to compare with the last." The Englishmen, in turn, were impressed with the hospitality extended them, and while there is no evidence that Lord Paget followed through on the promise of a pure English staghound, he did present the General with a cased Galand & Somerville revolver "as a token of a sincere regard and in remembrance of the very happy time spent at Fort Hayes [sic] while Buffalo hunting in Kansas in Sept. 1869." See E. Custer to Laura Noble, September 19, 1869, quoted in Burkey, *Custer, Come at Once!* pp. 85–86; and John E. Parsons and John S. du Mont, *Firearms in the Custer Battle* (Harrisburg, Pa.: Stackpole, 1953), pp. 20, 22–23.

22. Brigham Young (1801–1877), president of the Church of Jesus Christ of the Latter Day Saints and the guiding spirit behind the epic Mormon trek to the Salt Lake Valley in 1847. For all of Young's accomplishments, it was his advocacy of plural marriages and his own family of who knew how many wives that titillated and alone seemed to interest the vast American public.

23. Nomad's next letter provides the answer to his question. Barker, after receiving repeated invitations, had already decided to come down to Kansas to go buffalo hunting with the Custers. During the hunt, as Custer relates, he would survive a dangerous tumble from his horse. But he would not be so lucky six years later when he and three companions drowned in an accident on the Detroit River that may well have involved the "beautiful yacht" *Coral*. See G. Custer to E. Custer, May 21, 1875, in Frost, *General Custer's Libbie*, p. 216.

Editorial Note: *"The Hunt on the Plains,"* September 24, 1869

1. This picture—an impressive photograph under the circumstances—was actually taken during the hunt Custer mentions as having occurred "but a few days before" the English lords arrived. He credited the small party of officers involved with having bagged "forty-seven fine fat buffalo"; Mrs. Custer, in sending a copy of the picture to a friend, on September 19 wrote: "You see they brought one to bay to have his phiz—in fact his tout ensemble 'tooken.'" A linecut of the photograph illustrated her *Tenting on the Plains*. See E. Custer to Laura Noble, September 19, 1869, quoted in Millbrook, "Big Game Hunting with the Custers," caption to illustration.
2. Custer was something less than a brilliant orator, though his nervousness was compensated for by an intensity and obvious charisma that impressed one reporter who caught an impromptu Custer "speech" at the Soldiers and Sailors Convention in Cleveland in 1866. Just when the convention began to bog down in procedural wrangling, Custer, who was on the platform, "turned the tide by springing forward . . . and calling for three cheers for the Fenians [the Irish activists seeking independence from British rule whose cause had the support of many Irish-American war veterans]. It was a trick of course, but on the instant he stood there, not leading the cheers, but himself a cheer." To repeated calls from the audience for a speech Custer shook his head and retired to the rear of the platform. As the clamor persisted despite the chairman's repeated pleas for quiet, Custer, having collected his thoughts and gathered his resolve, sprang forward again, parting the officials in front of him and, "while his own name yet hung on . . . [the delegates'] lips, united the whole convention in three magnificent cheers for the old flag." It was not exactly a speech, but it was a masterly platform performance. As Elizabeth Custer wrote, "If the General went away to some soldiers' re-union, he tried on his return to give me a lucid account of the ceremonies, and how signally he failed in making a speech, of course, and his subterfuge for hiding his confusion and getting out of the scrape by proposing 'Garryowen' by the band, or three cheers for the old brigade. It was not that he had not enough to say: his heart was full of gratitude to his comrades, but the words came forth with such a rush, there was little chance of arriving at the meaning." Nevertheless, and despite a continuing aversion to public speaking, in January 1876, Custer seriously contemplated going on a lecture tour. His feats in the West and his writings about them assured him of an audience; there was room for one buckskin-clad army officer among Buffalo Bill Cody and the other buckskin-clad plainsmen who were making their mark on the Eastern stage. "For years I have been approached to deliver a series of lectures, throughout the country, but circumstances have prevented," he wrote his brother. "Since my arrival in New York Mr. Pond, manager of the Redpath Agency (in Boston), has come to see me and offer a contract. When I tell you the terms you will open your eyes. Five nights a week for from four to five months, I to receive $200. a night. My expences would amount to about $10. a day. They urged me to com-

mence this spring, but I declined, needing more time for preparation." After his death, Mrs. Custer supplemented her army pension by writing of their life together in the West and she often gave readings from her reminiscences. See Minnie Millbrook, "Custer in Politics," *Little Big Horn Associates Review* 6 (Winter 1972): 80, reprinting a story from a Detroit paper, September 26, 1866; Monaghan, *Custer*, pp. 278–279; Custer, *Tenting on the Plains*, p. 323; and G. Custer to T. W. Custer, January 1876, in Merington, ed., *The Custer Story*, p. 277.

3. Samuel D. Sturgis (1822–1889) was colonel of the Seventh Cavalry from 1869 to 1881 and Custer's immediate superior. His son, Lieutenant James G. Sturgis, died with Custer on the Little Big Horn. He was only twenty-two, and his grief-stricken father gave an interview at his headquarters in St. Louis in which he likened Custer to a thief who was shot while committing a robbery. Neither should be pitied or excused because he had "paid the penalty." "The burglar wanted money, and sacrificed his life to get it," Sturgis stormed; "Custer wanted notoriety, and lost his life in trying to get it." In a more reflective mood the next day Sturgis regretted his intemperate language but not his argument that Custer was no Indian-fighter. "He wrote much upon the subject of Indian warfare, and the people of the country who read his articles naturally supposed he had great experience in savage warfare, but this was not so, his experience was exceedingly limited, and that he was overreached by Indian tactics, and hundreds of valuable lives sacrificed thereby, will astonish those alone who may have read his writings—not those who were best acquainted with him and knew the peculiarities of his character." Such criticisms, coming from Custer's commanding officer, helped set the tone for the great Custer controversy that has resounded through the years. See "Gen. Custer's Death: An In-

terview with Col. Sturgis," *New York Times*, July 17, 1876, p. 7; "Gen. Custer's Death: An Explanatory Note from Gen. Sturgis," ibid., July 18, 1876, p. 5 (reprinting items from the *St. Louis Times*); and, for another statement, "Sturgis on Custer: A Further Expression of His Views," ibid., July 21, 1876, p. 8 (reprinting an item from the *Chicago Tribune*). As a rebuttal to these charges, Frederick Whittaker published a letter that Sturgis wrote in 1869, under less trying circumstances, praising Custer (*Complete Life of Gen. George A. Custer*, p. 475).

4. Custer began rounding up friends in the press and the business world for a grand buffalo hunt as early as August, apparently. His invitation to the editor of the *New York Citizen* has survived and was probably much like that extended to the editor of *Turf, Field and Farm*:

Can you not find time among your many duties to visit "the Plains," and enjoy that rarest of sports, a buffalo hunt? We are encamped within a half mile of Kansas Pacific railroad in the very heart of the buffalo range, and will probably remain here until the 1st of October, when we are to march to Fort Leavenworth for the winter. The latter half of the month is usually the best season for hunting buffalo, and we will have no difficulty in finding them within an hour's ride of the camp.

If you come, bringing as many friends as will join, I promise you something beyond even what is described in "Field Sports." Hon. K. Barker, President of the Audubon Club, Detroit, Mich., with a party of friends proposes visiting me the latter part of September, to participate in a general hunt, and would be most delighted to welcome you among the number. (*Leavenworth Times Conservative*, September 16, 1869, quoted in Burkey, *Custer, Come at Once!* pp. 87–88)

7. November 8, 1869

1. Barker's party arrived October 8 and the caravan proceeded directly to the buffalo range; they spent the next day hunting, and the day following resting, since it was a Sunday; they resumed the hunt on

Monday morning, then continued on to the Seventh's base camp near Fort Hays, where the Custers continued to lavish even more than their usual hospitality on their guests. The fact that they were from Michigan, where Custer grew up and found his bride, and with which his Civil War career was closely identified, had something to do with the warmth of their reception. Custer's Nomad letter, with its lengthy extract from Jefferson Wiley's report in the *Detroit Post*, provides a very complete account of the hunt. Mrs. Custer devoted a chapter to it in *Following the Guidon* (chap. 18), but since she was not along she relied on her husband's description, supplemented with some reminiscences by J. H. Morgan which she solicited for her book. Millbrook, "Big Game Hunting with the Custers," pp. 443–446, and Burkey, *Custer, Come at Once!* p. 88, provide additional information.

2. In Sir Walter Scott's *The Lady of the Lake* (1810), the Saxon, Fitz-James, wandering alone in dangerous territory in search of rebel chieftain Roderick Dhu, met a stranger whom he told, ". . . I am by promise tied / To match me with this man of pride." "Have then thy wish!" the stranger answered and "whistled shrill":

Instant, through copse and heath arose
Bonnets and spears and bended bows;
On right, on left, above, below,
Sprung up at once the lurking foe;
From shingles gray their lances start,
The bracken bush sends forth the dart,
The rushes and the willow-wand
Are bristling into axe and brand,
And every tuft of broom gives life
To plaided warrior arm'd for strife.
That whistle garrison'd the glen
At once with full five hundred men,

. . . .

The Mountaineer cast glance of pride
Along Benledi's living side,
Then fix'd his eye and sable brow
Full on Fitz-James: "How say'st thou now?
These are Clan-Alpine's warriors true;
And, Saxon,—I am Roderick Dhu!" (Fifth Canto, viii–ix)

3. Morgan had an amusing anecdote about an experience that befell the party when it was detained overnight in Ellsworth on its way to Fort Hays. They looked for all the world like the dudes they were, what with one sporting a stovepipe hat, and two of them, as Mrs. Custer put it, "over size . . . [with] the contour which betokens good dinners and convivial life." Since they were full of excitement over the forthcoming hunt and could not keep it to themselves, they became objects for comment among the local citizens, one of whom addressed the corpulent Judge Beckwith:

"You'uns the folks General Custer is expectin'?"

"Yes, stranger," the Judge proudly answered.

"I was at Custer Camp on Sunday and he was awful busy preparin'."

"What was he doing?"

"He had men out all week corralin' buffalo fer you fellows to kill."

It was a nicely calculated affront to a party who, despite their appearances, were sportsmen to the core and, as Custer relates, acquitted themselves creditably when they got the chance. See J. H. Morgan to E. Custer, June 7, 1889, quoted in Millbrook, "Big Game Hunting with the Custers," p. 444. Mrs. Custer, while changing none of the particulars, embroidered Morgan's anecdote in *Following the Guidon*, pp. 172–173.

4. On October 13 the Seventh Cavalry broke camp and set out eastward to its winter quarters at Fort Leavenworth. The Barker party went along as far as Fort Riley before catching the train to Kansas City and Detroit. The whole affair had been a huge success and was warmly remembered by the participants who, through one of their number, acknowledged "the great kindness and untiring attention" of the officers of the Seventh and paid fair tribute to their hosts: "To General Custer and his accomplished lady are primarily due the pleasure and

satisfaction of this novel and delightful trip to the plains, and to them and to all we give our sincerest, heartfelt thanks" (Wiley, in the *Detroit Post*, quoted in Burkey, *Custer, Come at Once!* p. 88).

8. September 24, 1870

1. On August 15, 1870, fifteen years after its incorporation, the Kansas Pacific railroad, as it was then known, became a reality as far as Denver. Actual construction had begun on September 7, 1863, at Wyandotte, Kansas; almost seven years later to the day, Custer and another 125 guests of the railroad's president, John D. Perry, were in Denver to celebrate the opening of the line. Custer had played a part in the Kansas Pacific story. When he arrived in Kansas late in 1866 the line had progressed only as far as Fort Riley, where Custer and the Seventh Cavalry were stationed. The Hancock Expedition of 1867 had been mounted partially to help secure the unmolested passage of the railroad then building west along the Smoky Hill River, while the winter campaign of 1868–69 had served to stabilize the Indian situation and protect the railroad's interests. Completion of the Kansas Pacific in 1870, as a consequence, had few more ardent well-wishers than Custer. To him, railroads were another name for civilization. "Aside from the ordinary [commercial] benefits and purposes which inspire the building of railroads through the unsettled portions of the West," he wrote a few years later, past experience has shown "that no one measure so quickly and effectually frees a country from the horrors and devastations of Indian wars and Indian depredations generally as the building and successful operation of a railroad through the region overrun." But none of this really explains *why* Custer chose to describe the Kansas Pacific excursion in *Turf, Field and Farm.* His letter offers a pleasant but hardly very inspiring account of a trip similar to those many others were making in the same period.

Perhaps his choice of subjects indicates that, after another summer in camp near Fort Hays entertaining a never-ending stream of visitors and engaging in a succession of buffalo hunts, Custer was becoming bored with writing about the sport, if not with the sport itself. Certainly he skims over the hunt he hosted for a few of the excursionists on the return journey. A second explanation for Nomad's presenting what he himself deemed "indifferent matter" is that his letter was intended as a promotional piece for the Kansas Pacific. In exchange for minor favors—free passes, all-expenses-paid excursion trips, a capacious company tent—Custer over the years proved quite willing to put his pen to use on behalf of the railroads. This exchange of small favors did not involve a serious conflict of interest since Custer's advocacy of the railroads was consistent with his personal convictions. He believed in them, benefited from them, and was willing to do all he could for them. However, there are indications that he may also have been involved in other, less innocent business arrangements with railroads, stage lines, land speculators, and manufacturing concerns, and one student of Custer's various financial dealings has concluded that "the Boy General with the golden locks may not have been the chivalric alternative to, but merely another participant in, the sordid drama of the Gilded Age." Though the evidence is still inconclusive, the subject does merit further investigation. See Joseph W. Snell and Robert W. Richmond, "When the Union and Kansas Pacific Built through Kansas," *Kansas Historical Quarterly* 32 (Summer and Autumn 1966): 161–186, 334–352; G. A. Custer, "Battling with the Sioux on the Yellowstone," *The Galaxy* 22 (July 1876): 91; Edgar I. Stewart, ed., *Penny-an-Acre Empire in the West* (Norman: University of Oklahoma Press, 1968), esp. pp. 82–113; and Richard Slotkin, "'. . . & *Then* the Mare Will Go!': An 1875 Black Hills

Scheme by Custer, Holladay and Buford," *Journal of the West* 15 (July 1976): 60–77.

2. William W. Cooke was, apart from Tom Custer, the General's closest associate among his officers. A Canadian, born in May 1846, he had just turned twenty when he received his commission as first lieutenant in the Seventh Cavalry and had just celebrated his thirtieth birthday when he died at the Little Big Horn. Cooke served as regimental adjutant from December 1866 through February 1867 and again from January 1, 1871, until he was killed. Remembered today principally as the author of the last message received from Custer's doomed command, in his time he was known as a fine rider, a good shot, an all-around athlete, and a man of striking appearance with his full whiskers and his imposingly erect martial bearing. Custer was chary of compliments to individuals in his informal writings—a fact that caused some resentment among his officers—but he frequently mentioned Cooke by name, describing him in *My Life on the Plains* as a "leader *par excellence*" and praising his "services and gallantry" while still a mere stripling in the Civil War. If it seems odd that Custer would constantly misspell a good friend's name, this is explained by the fact that Cooke had appeared as "Cook" on the military records since entering the service in 1864 and did not bother petitioning the adjutant general to have the spelling corrected until late in 1872. See Custer, *My Life on the Plains*, p. 141; and William J. McCulloch, "More about Lieut. William W. Cooke," *Little Big Horn Associates Newsletter* 1 (March 1967): 4–5.

3. This is a jocular reference to the Seventh Cavalry's regimental band, at that time under the direction of a Professor Kaufmann, to accept the spelling of a contemporary press account. Created in April 1867 largely at the instigation of Major Alfred Gibbs, who canvassed the officers corps and several of the companies for subscriptions (Custer personal-ly contributed $50 to help offset the cost of instruments and other accessories), the regimental band originally consisted of fifteen men who were assembled at Fort Riley and excused from "the ordinary details for garrison duty" while they practiced. By early November the band was "discoursing sweet music," and one year later it cemented its reputation and became an essential part of the Seventh's esprit de corps when it blasted out the opening strains of "GarryOwen" while the troopers charged down on Black Kettle's village on the Washita. On April 19, 1870, the band's members were dropped from the company rolls and added to the rolls of the regimental field and staff. In the same period, Professor Kaufmann became the band's director. See *Leavenworth Commercial*, April 30, 1870, reprinted in Minnie Dubbs Millbrook, "Fort Leavenworth Races," *Little Big Horn Associates Research Review* 12 (December 1978): 19; John M. Carroll, "The Seventh Cavalry's Band," ibid. 9 (Spring 1975): 16–18; Utley, ed., *Life in Custer's Cavalry*, esp. pp. 44, 52, 103, 120, 150; Chandler, *Of GarryOwen in Glory*, pp. 382, 412. The *Kansas State Record*, September 14, 1870, and the *Rocky Mountain News* (Denver), September 4, 1870, both noted that "Custer's brass band" entertained the excursionists at Hays City, having apparently arrived at Camp Sturgis from points east (thus Custer's reference) earlier the same day. See Millbrook, "Big Game Hunting with the Custers," pp. 447, n. 52, and 448; and Burkey, *Custer, Come at Once!* p. 100. "Wind-jammers" was slang for musicans who played wind instruments, particularly army buglers.

4. The Custers boarded at this stop and continued on to Denver, while the "other ladies and their soldier lords dined with the excursionists and returned to Hays from Buffalo Station" (*Rocky Mountain News* [Denver], September 4, 1870, quoted in Burkey, *Custer, Come at Once!* p.

100). See also J. C. H., "The Kansas Pacific Railroad," *New York Times*, September 12, 1870, p. 2; and Millbrook, "Big Game Hunting with the Custers," pp. 447–448.

5. This practice of taking pot shots from the moving train was also noted by the *New York Times* correspondent who accompanied the excursion: "Our rifles sounded the alarm at sight of every buffalo, no matter how far off, for the sportsmen were eager, and would not miss an opportunity to shoot at the Lords of the Plains, even when there was not the most distant probability of success." This "hunting" could be chalked up to the enthusiasm of Eastern tyros were it not for the fact that Westerners habitually partook in the same activity, much to the distress of Mrs. Custer, who described the unenviable experience of traveling when one's fellow passengers were armed to the teeth and seemed to feel duty bound to shoot at every passing target—prairie dogs would do as well as buffalo. "It was the greatest wonder that more people were not killed, as the wild rush for the windows, and the reckless discharge of rifles and pistols, put every passenger's life in jeopardy," she wrote. ". . . in the struggle to twist round for a good aim out of the narrow window the barrel or muzzle of the fire-arm passed dangerously near the ear of any scared woman who had the temerity to travel in those tempestuous days." See J. C. H., "Kansas Pacific Railroad," p. 2; Custer, *Following the Guidon*, pp. 117–118.

6. The *New York Times'* report from its correspondent was shorter but equally vivid: "Kit Carson, famous for 'Wild Bill' [Hickok] and frontier ruffianism, was our halting place last night. On the previous evening a characteristic entertainment had been offered the citizens, in the killing of two men and mortal wounding of a third, in an affray which grew out of a game of cards. Some regret was expressed by the good (?) citizens, that we were not in season for this carnival. I blush to confess that we did not realize the extent of our misfortune in the matter" (J. C. H., "Kansas Pacific Railroad," p. 2).

7. William Jackson Palmer (1836–1909) earned a brevet rank of brigadier general in the Civil War and afterward proved himself one of the more visionary railroad builders of his day. Treasurer of the Union Pacific, Eastern Division, he surveyed a route to the Pacific for the railroad when it still had transcontinental aspirations and in 1869, as a director of the renamed Kansas Pacific, supervised construction of the "Denver Extension" from Sheridan, Kansas, across Colorado, and then of the Denver Pacific, connecting Denver to Cheyenne, Wyoming, on the Union Pacific line. Subsequently, Palmer devoted his energies to several interrelated projects of his own, notably the Denver and Rio Grande Railroad, which contemplated building south from Denver to El Paso in defiance of the east-west railway wisdom then prevailing. Palmer also proposed to develop a series of towns along the Denver and Rio Grande, the first and most successful of which was Colorado Springs, founded in 1871. Opposition by the Santa Fe line curtailed the Denver and Rio Grande's southern strategy and forced it westward, where existing towns in the railroad's path were browbeaten into raising bonds to offset construction costs with the threat that they would otherwise be bypassed and economically ruined. Thus the Denver and Rio Grande left behind it a residue of bitterness, and its builder a reputation for ruthless self-interest consonant with that of most of the Western railroad entrepreneurs of the age. Palmer did successfully challenge another piece of conventional railroad wisdom by making his line a narrow-gauge to facilitate construction in the mountainous country. See Robert G. Athearn, *Rebel of the Rockies: A History of the Denver and Rio Grande Western Railroad* (New Haven: Yale University Press, 1962); and, for a critical discussion of Palmer's land development schemes, Brit Al-

lan Storey, "William Jackson Palmer, Promoter," *Colorado Magazine* 43 (Winter 1966): 44–55.

8. Since 1867 the future Kansas Pacific had been lobbying for an amendment to its charter to permit it to build and operate the all-important rail link between Denver and Cheyenne. In 1869 it was given a land grant for that purpose and, in conjunction with the Denver-based Denver Pacific Railroad, completed the road in June 1870. Though the Denver Pacific was effectively merged with the Kansas Pacific, it operated under its own name (some contemporaries knew it more descriptively as the Denver & Cheyenne); Custer wanted this anomaly corrected, presumably to establish more clearly the Kansas Pacific's dominion over rail service into Denver from the east.

9. Horace Greeley (1811–1872), founding editor of the *New York Tribune* and one of the most influential American journalists of the nineteenth century, was a consistent advocate of the West as the land of the future and a panacea for the economic ills plaguing young Easterners during times of depression. Greeley is credited with the famous injunction "Go West, young man, go West," and while almost everyone agrees that he never said those precise words they capture the essence of advice he did repeatedly offer, during the Panic of 1837, for example ("Fly—scatter through the country—go to the Great West—anything rather than remain here"), and, more formally: "If any young man is about to commence in the world, with little in his circumstances to prepossess him in favor of one section above another, we say to him publicly and privately, Go to the West; there your capacities are sure to be appreciated and your industry and energy rewarded." There is also an established tradition that Greeley came close to his famous aphorism in remarking, "Go West, young man, go forth into the Country." He finally took his own advice in 1859 and embarked on a cross-country tour that in-

cluded an inspection of the Colorado mining belt, all dutifully reported back to the *Tribune's* readers in letters that the next year were gathered together in *An Overland Journey, from New York to San Francisco in the Summer of 1859* (New York: C. M. Saxton, Barker & Co., 1860). A few months before Custer's visit to Greeley, the Union Colony, with Horace Greeley its secretary-treasurer, planted the erstwhile "Garden City of the West" in an area that, as Greeley himself wrote, "combines remarkable healthfulness with decided fertility and facility of cultivation, an abundance of serviceable timber with water in plenty for irrigation as well as power, beauty of landscape and scenery with exemption from disagreeable neighbors; and a railroad will soon bring it within three days of St. Louis and five from New York." See Horace Greeley in the *New Yorker*, June 3, 1837, quoted in Roy M. Robbins, *Our Landed Heritage: The Public Domain, 1776–1936* (Princeton, N.J.: Princeton University Press, 1942), p. 71; William Harlan Hale, *Horace Greeley: Voice of the People* (New York: Collier Books, 1961 [1950]), p. 205; Ray A. Billington, *America's Frontier Heritage* (New York: Holt, Rinehart and Winston, 1966), p. 31; and Don and Jean Griswold, *Colorado's Century of "Cities"* (N.p., 1958), pp. 286–287.

10. Wyoming Territory was created July 25, 1868, and John A. Campbell of Ohio, a Republican, was appointed governor effective April 3 of the following year, remaining in office until 1875. He had served on General Schofield's staff in the Civil War, while his territorial secretary, Edward M. Lee of Connecticut, had served as a cavalry officer under Custer. As one of their first official duties, the two men attended the ceremonies at Promontory, Utah, marking the completion of the transcontinental railroad in May 1869; the next year Governor Campbell joined in the celebration marking the Kansas Pacific's arrival in Denver, the city Cheyenne hoped to eclipse as a Western

metropolis. From him, Custer learned of Wyoming's most startling legislative innovation. Among the Laws of Wyoming, 1869—about 90 percent of them borrowed, as was the custom, from the statutes of existing states—was one that stood out as being precedent making: "An Act to Grant to the Women of Wyoming Territory the Right of Suffrage, and to Hold Office." It was passed December 10, 1869, and gave women at the age of twenty-one the same voting rights as men. Secretary Lee observed that thus "by a single step" was "the youngest territory on earth" placed "in the vanguard of civilization and progress." When Democrats in the territorial houses passed a bill repealing women's suffrage, Governor Campbell exercised his veto and ended the last serious challenge to women's voting in the territorial period. Upon being admitted to statehood in 1890, Wyoming again set a precedent by granting women the vote—thus, "The Equality State." See T. A. Larson, *History of Wyoming*, rev. ed. (Lincoln: University of Nebraska Press, 1978), chap. 4; and Lewis L. Gould, *Wyoming: A Political History, 1868–1896* (New Haven: Yale University Press, 1968), chap. 2.

11. Edward M. McCook served as governor of Colorado Territory from 1869 to 1873 and again from 1874 to 1875. A general in the Civil War—which might account for Custer's acquaintance with him—McCook was a model post–Civil War entrepreneur, using political clout to advance his financial interests embracing cattle, lands, and railroads. A man of doubtful morality, he operated a little "Indian Ring" of his own in Colorado by obtaining contracts to provide beef and other Indian annuities to the government, often at astronomical profits. He charged up to five times what he paid for his cattle and in one transaction netted $23,000. He was reputed to be the largest landowner in Colorado, and his brother-in-law summed up the moral tone of his administrations when he advised another relative, "If you make yourself useful to him, you can feather your nest." McCook's own career suggests that the rejoinder he should have made to the ruler of San Salvador, in the Caribbean, was that the "particular advantage" of being an American territorial governor had nothing to do with the annual salary. See Howard R. Lamar, *The Far Southwest, 1846–1912: A Territorial History* (New Haven: Yale University Press, 1966), pp. 286–289, 298.

12. Idaho, situated about thirty-five miles west of Denver, began as Jackson's Diggings (after the man who discovered gold at the site in January 1859), was then known as Sacramento City in the hope that California's Midas touch came with the name, then as Idaho City, and finally by the mid-1860's simply as Idaho. As its economic basis shifted and it was less a mining camp and more a health resort, it became better known as Idaho Springs, the name it bore when it was officially incorporated in 1885. Well before Custer's visit the medicinal properties of the area's hot soda springs had attracted tourists, and the result was better-than-average accommodations for the traveler. Custer's party probably stayed at the Beebee House, and his pleasant surroundings prompted the rosy picture he painted of the town's future prospects. Idaho Springs did enjoy steady growth through the nineteenth century, reaching a population of four thousand by 1900. The discovery that the springs were loaded with radium boosted the town's popularity as a health resort, but its decline since the 1930's has destined Idaho Springs to be something less than the "Saratoga of the mountains" Custer pronounced it in 1870. See Griswold, *Colorado's Century of "Cities,"* pp. 75–77; and Sandra Dallas, *No More than Five in a Bed: Colorado Hotels in the Old Days* (Norman: University of Oklahoma Press, 1967), pp. 179–183.

13. Louis T. Wigfall (1815–1874), a hard-drinking Democrat from Texas, sat in the

Senate from December 1859 through March 1861. A caustic orator and long-time states rightist, he spurned all attempts at sectional compromise and agitated ceaselessly for secession and, if need be, war, confidently predicting a Southern victory. He used his position to provide the seceded states with information about the federal government's deliberations through the early spring of 1861, then served the Confederate cause as a brigadier general through the first year of fighting and as a senator for the duration. Ever feisty and opinionated, he was a constant critic of President Jefferson Davis. With the collapse of the Confederacy, Wigfall disappeared from sight. He eventually made his way back to Texas, departing in March 1866 for England, where he lived in straitened circumstances with other Southern expatriates. Casting about for some business opportunity, around 1867 he became involved in promoting a Colorado gold mine. His enthusiasm built to a pitch in 1870–71, but while his biographer mentions that his son visited Colorado in this period, Wigfall himself apparently remained in London until 1872, when he ended his self-imposed exile by rejoining his family in Baltimore. Thus Custer's mention of Wigfall's activities in the Idaho area in 1870 is intriguing, but his information was secondhand and no doubt referred to the old fire-eater's son instead. See Alvy L. King, *Louis T. Wigfall: Southern Fire-eater* (Baton Rouge: Louisiana State University Press, 1970), pp. 230–231.

14. The favorable situation regarding accommodations is not surprising considering that by 1870 Denver was well connected by two railroad lines, and Colorado's spreading reputation as the "Switzerland of America" had already made it a tourist mecca. It followed that the tourist dollar would encourage a flourishing hotel industry—and eventually a spate of luxury resorts. Custer's brief mention of Georgetown ("the most extensive and promising town we found in the mountains") is interesting for what it omits, since the General was attracted by more than the abundance of wild raspberries nearby. Before the year was out he was part owner of a silver mine ten miles from town, and he spent much of the following April in New York City trying to market $100,000 worth of stock in the mine. He personally retained a $35,000 interest in the venture—probably a promoter's share, since there is no evidence that he invested any funds of his own. Though the matter is unclear, he apparently wrote off his holdings in 1875. See Earl Pomeroy, *In Search of the Golden West: The Tourist in Western America* (New York: Alfred A. Knopf, 1957), pp. 20–23, 33–34; Dallas, *No More than Five in a Bed*, passim.; Frost, *General Custer's Libbie*, pp. 191–192, 195, 216–217; and Slotkin, "'. . . & Then the Mare Will Go!,'" pp. 70–71.

15. Gray's Peak, named after distinguished Harvard botanist and early Darwinist Asa Gray, was one of those obligatory side trips for the visitor to Denver. The tour books said it was not to be missed, and most travelers seem to have made the climb. One who did not tendered apologies by advising others "to go by all means to its summit, from which the view must be such as will amply repay . . . the journey." Samuel Bowles was so astounded by what he saw from the top that he invented a new word for the occasion, ranking the view from Gray's Peak with a handful of great natural wonders of the world "in overcomingness." "It was," he said, "not beauty, it was sublimity; it was not power, nor order, nor color, it was majesty; it was not a part, it was the whole; it was not man but God, that was about, before, in us." Given the competition, Custer was probably just as wise in quoting someone else's description of the view, though I have been unable to locate the "late writer" whose words he borrowed. See George W. Pine, *Beyond the West; Containing an Account of Two Years' Travel in*

that *Other Half of Our Great Continent Far Beyond the Old West*, rev. ed. (Utica, N.Y.: T. J. Griffiths, 1871), p. 105; A. W. Hoyt, "Over the Plains to Colorado," *Harper's New Monthly Magazine* 35 (June 1867): 15; Samuel Bowles, *Our New West* (Hartford, Conn.: Hartford Publishing Co., 1869), pp. 131—132. Bowles was enthusiastic but more restrained in "The Pacific Railroad—Open," *Atlantic Monthly* 23 (April 1869): 500.

16. This paragraph is an obvious case of special pleading, in which Custer boldly steps forward as a mouthpiece for the Kansas Pacific Railroad. There was something grating about being known in Denver as "a second highway to the East," and while not much could be done about the matter of primacy (the Union Pacific–Central Pacific had been joined in 1869, while the branch line connecting Denver to the Union Pacific at Cheyenne was finished two months before the Kansas Pacific reached Denver), Custer was still willing to toot the Kansas Pacific's horn and claim the future for it as "the popular line of travel from the eastern states to the Pacific" (*Rocky Mountain News* [Denver], August 16, 1870, quoted in Snell and Richmond, "When the Union and Kansas Pacific Built through Kansas," p. 351).

III. KENTUCKY, 1871–1873

1. See Thodore J. Crackel, "Custer's Kentucky: General George Armstrong Custer and Elizabethtown, Kentucky, 1871–1873," *Filson Club Historical Quarterly* 48 (April 1974): 144–145; William A. McKay, "With the 7th in Kentucky," *Little Big Horn Associates Research Review* 8 (Summer 1974): 1–2; and, for examples of the type of service the Seventh saw in the South, James E. Sefton, *The United States Army and Reconstruction, 1865–1877* (Baton Rouge: Louisiana State University Press, 1967), pp. 219–220, 224–228.

2. G. Custer to E. Custer, [March], Sep-

tember 4, 1871, and E. Custer to Mrs. Sabin, 1871, in Merington, ed., *The Custer Story*, pp. 239–241.

3. Hamilton Busbey, "The Running Turf in America (First Paper)," *Harper's New Monthly Magazine* 41 (June 1870): 94–95, and "(Second Paper)," ibid. 41 (July 1870): 245. Also see Longrigg, *History of Horse Racing*, pp. 222–225, 245–246.

4. Custer, *Tenting on the Plains*, p. 340.

5. Whittaker, *Complete Life of Gen. George A. Custer*, pp. 476–477.

6. "The Turf: Our Review of the Racing Season of 1872 (Second Paper)," *New York Times*, December 14, 1872, p. 4; "(Third Paper)," ibid., December 21, 1872, p. 4; E. Custer to G. Custer, December 15, 1872, cited in Crackel, "Custer's Kentucky," p. 150, n. 17; and, for Bonnie Scotland, Longrigg, *History of Horse Racing*, pp. 226–227.

7. The only detailed study of Custer's sojourn in Kentucky is Crackel, "Custer's Kentucky," pp. 144–155, which offers a useful bibliographic note.

9. November 26, 1871

1. Sanders D. Bruce (1825–1902), a native of Lexington, graduated from Transylvania University in 1846 and operated a crockery store in town until the Civil War. A loyal Unionist, he was elected colonel of the Twentieth Infantry, Kentucky volunteers, saw active service in Kentucky and Tennessee, and attracted the favorable notice of Generals Sherman and Grant. A heart condition forced his resignation in 1864, and he relocated in New York City where the next year he and a brother founded *Turf, Field and Farm*. Bruce, long involved in horse racing, had been irked by the Northern bias in most coverage of the turf, and although his journal was based in New York it cast a knowledgeable eye on developments in Kentucky and the South. A devoted collector of thoroughbred pedigrees, Bruce began publishing his "stud book" in installments in *Turf, Field and Farm*; the first volume appeared in book

form in 1868, the last in 1894. When the Jockey Club adopted Bruce's *American Stud Book* in 1896, it became the official guide. Thus Custer's comments on Bruce's expertise as a judge of horse flesh were well justified. See *The National Cyclopaedia of American Biography*, VI, 321–322; Mott, *History of American Magazines*, III, 215; and Longrigg, *History of Horse Racing*, p. 231.

2. Woodburn Farm, Woodford County, was the "largest breeding estate in the world" at the time of Custer's visit. The Alexander family acquired the property in 1791, but it was Robert S. C. A. Alexander (1819–1867) who made it into a premier stock farm for Shorthorn cattle, Southdown sheep, trotting horses, and thoroughbreds. Kentucky-born, Cambridge-educated Alexander lived for a time in Scotland managing the family estates, including Airdrie, near Glasgow, which provided many of the furnishings —chairs, tables, chandeliers, and the like—that graced Woodburn after his return to America. He plowed much of his fortune into breeding stock, his single greatest coup being the purchase of Lexington in 1856 for the then-unheard of sum of $15,000. Lexington went on to sire a line of winners, and the reputation of Woodburn was established. The estate, which eventually comprised 3,200 acres, has been described as "one of the most beautiful spots in Kentucky, with its sweep of rolling meadows and its trees of infinite variety. The house, with its twenty-six rooms, situated in the midst of a magnificent park, grips one with its spell of grandeur. Large white columns support the porch, and wide doors open into the hall where the massive woodwork is of cherry and mahogany, and a stair leads to the upper floors." No wonder Custer was impressed by his surroundings. See Busbey, "Running Turf in America (Second Paper)," p. 252; and Elizabeth M. Simpson, *Bluegrass Houses and Their Traditions* (Lexington: Transylvania Press, 1932), pp. 171–179.

3. Col. Cook was William W. Cooke (see letter #8, n. 2); Zeb Ward was a Kentucky horseman who fielded winners in both the spring and fall meetings at Lexington in 1872; Mr. Lowell was probably the Richard Lowell mentioned in letter #10 as the proprietor of Mentella Stock Farm.

4. Benjamin Gratz (1792–1884), from a distinguished Jewish family in Philadelphia, graduated from the University of Pennsylvania in 1811 and briefly practiced law before entering the family business. In 1824, five years after he married a Kentucky woman, he purchased the house known as Mount Hope about a mile from Woodburn. See Joseph L. Blau and Salo W. Baron, eds., *The Jews of the United States, 1790–1840: A Documentary History*, 3 vols. (New York: Columbia University Press and The Jewish Publication Society of America, 1963), I, 295, n. 93; and Simpson, *Bluegrass House and Their Traditions*, pp. 387–388.

5. Custer's indelicate reference to "an overgrown fifteenth amendment"—that is, a black domestic—reflects his generally low opinion of the Negro's capabilities. On October 5, 1865, while serving in Texas, he wrote: "I am in favor of elevating the negro to the extent of his capacity and intelligence, and of our doing everything in our power to advance the race morally and mentally as well as physically, also socially. But I am opposed to making this advance by correspondingly debasing any portion of the white race. As to trusting the negro of the Southern States with the most sacred and responsible privilege—the right of suffrage—I should as soon think of elevating an Indian Chief to the Popedom of Rome." Thus, he could hardly welcome the Fifteenth Amendment (ratified March 30, 1870), which provided that "the right of citizens to vote shall not be denied or abridged . . . on account of race, color, or previous condition of servitude." Custer's views, it should be added, placed him in the mainstream of Midwestern opinion in his

time. See G. Custer to D. S. Bacon, October 5, 1865, in Merington, ed., *The Custer Story*, p. 175. While the Custers employed black cooks, and Mrs. Custer wrote warmly of two of them in her memoirs, both simply assumed the *race* to be inferior. See, for example, the revealing anecdote narrated by Mrs. Custer in *Tenting on the Plains*, p. 423.

6. Custer's comments are interesting because Benjamin Gratz has been cited as typical of those Jews "who settled in the interior of the continent in the early nineteenth century [and] realized they were ending their contact with religious Jewish life and were prepared for partial or total assimilation." Both of his wives were non-Jews and his children were raised as Christians, but in matters of diet Gratz still observed Jewish tradition. See Abraham J. Karp, ed., *The Jewish Experience in America: Selected Studies from the Publications of The American Jewish Historical Society*, 5 vols. (New York: KTAV Publishing and the American Jewish Historical Society, 1969), II, 14.

7. Since Robert Alexander was a bachelor, upon his death in 1867 Woodburn passed into the hands of his brother, A. John Alexander, who maintained the stock farm but, as Custer notes, without the same intense personal involvement. Instead, he left its day-to-day supervision to an assistant, and this arrangement endured, judging from the observation made by one visitor in 1896 that A. J. Alexander was "at the head of the farm, but the practical directing mind is Lucas Brodhead . . ." (Hamilton Busbey, "The Evolution of the Trotting Horse [First Paper]," *Scribner's Magazine* 19 [May 1896]: 582).

8. Harry Bassett, sired by Lexington out of Canary Bird in 1868, was one of the outstanding race horses of the early 1870's. He was described as a beautiful chestnut, with "a good clean head, well set on a strong neck, running into powerful and well-inclined shoulders. Although he has plenty of body and long reach, he is com-

pactly built—has fine back and loins—most powerful quarters and thighs, and ribs long and strong." He lost once in four starts in 1870 as a two-year-old, and as a three-year-old he "ran away from every horse who came in competition with him, starting nine times and winning every race with ease." Coming off such a performance, he was naturally a name to conjure with as racing aficionados looked ahead to the 1872 season. Colonel D. McDaniel, his owner, was indeed a "successful turfman." Harry Bassett was the pride of his stable, but it also included two other steady winners in 1872, Tubman and Joe Daniels, and its overall strength was regarded as unequaled at the time. Thus, McDaniel capped the 1872 season by offering to match his stable "three races against any horse or horses in the world, to name at the post, two, three and four mile heats, for $10,000 or $20,000 each race" anytime between July 31 and September 1, 1873. See "The Great Race," *New York Times*, July 3, 1872, p. 5; and "Turf Notes—A Challenge from Col. McDaniel's Stable," *ibid.*, November 16, 1872, p. 4.

9. Lucas Brodhead, of Woodburn Farm, was of the opinion that "the breeding of trotters systematically . . . began with Hambletonian, Mambrino Chief, Pilot, Jr., and Clay. . . . They are the foundation families." Woodford Mambrino was sired by Mambrino Chief, whose blood also ran in Belmont. Belmont's sire, Alexander's Abdallah, was a son of Hambletonian (or Rysdyk's Hambletonian, as he was known, to avoid confusion with other horses of the same name), and, as Custer intimated, Belmont carried a strain of thoroughbred blood. Both Woodford Mambrino and Belmont were thus of distinguished pedigree. Belmont proved himself the superior sire, ranking high, a contemporary wrote, as "a progenitor of speed" with sixty-five descendants that by 1896 had trotted the mile in 2:15 or less. Custer was right, then, in predicting that some of the Belmont

weanlings and yearlings he saw were "certainly destined to become fast ones." See Longrigg, *History of Horse Racing*, pp. 244–245; and Busbey, "Evolution of the Trotting Horse (First Paper)," pp. 569, 582.

10. August Belmont was one of the commanding presences in American thoroughbred racing before the Civil War, and during and after the war he helped revitalize a sagging sport when he and Leonard W. Jerome worked together to promote the American Jockey Club, headquartered as of 1866 at Jerome Park, Fordham, Long Island. Much was expected of Belmont's horse Grey Planet, as the $10,000 price tag implies, but at the July 1872 meeting at Saratoga his best finish was a tie, and he was judged at year's end "a lamentable failure, and a loss to his owner." See Longrigg, *History of Horse Racing*, p. 223; "The Turf: Our Review of the Racing Season of 1872 (Third Paper)," p. 4.

11. Great things were expected of Asteroid. After the race at Louisville in which he defeated Loadstone and ran a marvelous first mile in the second heat of a two-mile race, interest focused on a dream match set for Jerome Park in September 1866 pitting him against his once-defeated half-brother, Kentucky. Anticipation mounted as race day drew near, and track fans from around the country gathered to watch the horses work out. "But one Sunday morning a gloom fell upon all hearts," an observer wrote four years later. "Lip spoke to lip, and the intelligence rapidly spread that Asteroid had broken down in a trial gallop in the mud—had sprung a tendon and his career as a racer was abruptly brought to a close. . . . Asteroid returned to the West to luxuriate in the stud; and the fond dream of seeing him measure stride with Kentucky was at an end" (Busbey, "Running Turf in America [Second Paper]," p. 250).

12. After emerging victorious from a trial match at the Metairie, April 14, 1855,

against his half-brother and greatest rival, Lecomte, the only horse ever to beat him, Lexington retired from racing and began an even more glittering career at stud at Woodburn Farm. Like his sire, Boston, he went totally blind, but during his nineteen years at Woodburn he was champion sire sixteen times, fourteen in a row, and got some 600 foals, 231 of them winners. His first crop included three outstanding colts, Norfolk, Asteroid, and Kentucky, the first two never beaten, the latter beaten only once, by Norfolk. A popular bard of the turf, "Hyder Ali," paid Lexington fair tribute: "Whispers fly about the race-tracks when some mighty deed is done: / 'Tis no more than we expected from the blood of Lexington!'" See Peter Willett, *The Thoroughbred* (London: Weidenfeld & Nicolson, 1970), pp. 156–157; Busbey, "Running Turf in America (Second Paper)," pp. 246–248, 250–251; and Roy King and Burke Davis, *The World of Currier & Ives* (New York: Random House, 1968), p. 78.

13. This was a parochial preference on Custer's part. Australian, an English import and son of the Triple Crown winner in 1853, was dam's sire of Iroquois, who performed impressively in England in the 1880's; was the first American horse to win the Derby; and after his return to the United States himself became champion sire in 1892. Australian also mated with a Lexington mare to produce Spendthrift, who had the distinction of being great-grandsire of Man O' War, "the greatest race horse ever bred in America." Planet's get included Katie Pease, a mare who soundly defeated the California wonder horse Thad Stevens in 1874. See Longrigg, *History of Horse Racing*, pp. 226–228; and Willett, *The Thoroughbred*, pp. 158, 161.

14. In an army filled with heavy drinkers—not to say outright drunkards—Custer was an abstemious exception. Elizabeth Custer, who admired her husband's enormous self-restraint and praised him for it, wrote that in Kentucky, where everyone

drank whiskey, brandy, and wine, the General always toasted with his favorite libation, "a glass of Alderney" (E. Custer to Mary Kendall, 1871, in Merington, ed., *The Custer Story*, p. 241).

15. Daniel Swigert, a thoroughbred breeder and one-time manager of Woodburn, owned Elmendorf, a 544-acre estate nine miles south of Lexington. Swigert's most notable horses included Springbok, who enjoyed success at Saratoga in 1872 and went on to win the Belmont Stakes in 1873 and the Saratoga Cup in 1874, deadheating for the same prize the following year. Springbok was by Australian out of a Lexington mare—the same combination that produced another of Swigert's exceptional horses, Spendthrift. See Simpson, *Bluegrass Houses and Their Traditions*, pp. 63, 65, 123, 125; "Saratoga: The Greatest Contest in American Turf History," *New York Times*, July 17, 1872, p. 5; and Longrigg, *History of Horse Racing*, p. 224.

16. Longfellow was by Leamington, an English horse with a good racing record but a poor record at stud, who was consequently acquired cheaply and imported by Sir Roderick Cameron for his Staten Island stock farm in 1865. Subsequently Leamington went to Pennsylvania where he proved himself at stud, becoming champion sire in the year Lexington died, 1875. Outstanding among Leamington's sons (including Iroquois) was Longfellow. Foaled in 1867, Longfellow eventually reached a height of nearly seventeen hands and was reputed to be the "largest race horse in the country." He first raced as a three-year-old, losing once, then winning his next four outings. As a four-year-old he had four wins in five starts, including a notable victory (that Custer predicted and witnessed) over Kingfisher for the Saratoga Cup. But, as Custer mentions later, Longfellow came off this triumph only to lose a four- mile dash to a lesser horse, Helmbold, that he had beaten the month before in winning the Monmouth Cup at Long Branch. At the time of Custer's visit, then, Longfellow had a solid reputation for speed but his stamina was in doubt. See Longrigg, *History of Horse Racing*, pp. 225–226; G. Custer to E. Custer, [July], 1871, in Merington, ed., *The Custer Story*, p. 238; and "The Great Race," p. 5.

17. Edward Troye (1808–1874), the most highly regarded American animal painter in the nineteenth century, was actually born in Switzerland and raised in England, emigrating in 1828 to Jamaica where he lived for two years before moving on to Philadelphia. Sketching trips took him through the South, and he soon established himself as a gifted delineator of thoroughbreds and fine cattle. He spent the next forty years improving upon his reputation, living with many of the rich Southern planters who owned the storied horses of the age. While Troye also worked in Virginia and South Carolina, he naturally concentrated on Kentucky, making his home there the center from which he embarked on his wanderings in search of commissions. The Civil War drove him to Europe for a few years, but he was back in Kentucky before it ended and spent his remaining years there, periodically interrupting his Southern peregrinations with trips to New York. He was vividly characterized in 1870:

Mr. Troye, though advanced in years, is still alive, and devoted to art. . . . His face and figure are striking. Tall, well-proportioned, and no stoop in his shoulders, notwithstanding he verges on fourscore years. He wears his hair long, and it falls in gray masses down his back. He is eccentric, both in dress and manner, and has a contempt for that portion of mankind having no sympathy with aristocratic institutions. The wealthiest and most cultivated men of the last decade were his warm personal friends; and, if you talk with him long, he is very apt to remind you of the fact. His speech is affected, inclining to a drawl. Those who know him well admire his genius, while smiling at his eccentricities; and they often ask themselves why the gifted should be peculiar.

When Troye died in 1874, he left behind an encyclopediac pictorial record of the most celebrated thoroughbreds in the United States, virtually all painted from life. See Busbey, "Running Turf in America (Second Paper)," p. 253; J. Winston Coleman, Jr., "Edward Troye: Kentucky Animal Painter," *Filson Club History Quarterly* 33 (January 1959): 32–45; and *Sport and the Horse* (Richmond: The Virginia Museum of Fine Arts, 1960), p. 23 and the plates for five Troye oils.

18. The much-anticipated match—"the great racing event of 1872"—came off on July 2 at Monmouth Park, Long Branch, New Jersey. Longfellow had warmed up by winning dashes of a mile and a half and three miles at Lexington in May, while Harry Bassett had shown his form in defeating John Harper's other fine horse, Lyttleton, at Jerome Park in June. Thus, interest was running high when Longfellow and Harry Bassett finally met, though the race proved anticlimactic, Longfellow winning easily in an undistinguished time. Later that month, on July 16, Harry Bassett got his revenge, beating a badly faltering Longfellow by three-quarters of a length to win the Saratoga Cup in record time. During the race, Longfellow was either injured by a broken horseshoe or else re-injured an already-weakened leg. Racing fans could take their choice. The first explanation exonerated John Harper, who was described in the *New York Times* after the Monmouth Cup victory as a much-beloved figure in turf circles since he never bet but raced for the pure enjoyment of the sport and thus represented its "best element"; the second explanation, whereby Harper was blamed for racing Longfellow on a damaged leg, condemned him in the same *New York Times* as a "sordid old man." Though Harper is said to have "wept unconsolably" over his horse's misfortune, Longfellow went on to new laurels as champion sire in 1891. See "The Great Race," p. 5; "Saratoga," p. 5; "The Turf:

Our Review of the Racing Season of 1872 (Third Paper)," p. 4; and Longrigg, *History of Horse Racing*, p. 225.

19. H. Price McGrath, "Irish gambler and turfman," holds the distinction of having owned Aristides, first winner of the Kentucky Derby at Churchill Downs, Louisville, in 1875. A colorful character, McGrath was rumored to keep his fortune hidden in a hollow tree, beneath a hedge, or inside a wall—anywhere but in a bank. His 416-acre estate three miles outside Lexington, McGrathiana, was sold in 1882 after his death and its name changed to Coldstream, though a poet did not forget its tradition:

McGrathiana!
Such a friendly sounding name,
Like a sort of merry game,
Sure, from Emerald Isle it came,
McGrathiana!
Brimming with Kentucky lore,
Still it's Irish to the core,
Seems a pity there's no more—
McGrathiana!

Robinson and Morgan together owned several winning horses in this period, while one of the premier trotters in the early 1870's, credited unofficially with a record 2:15.5 mile, was named Joe Elliott after the *Herald* scribe. See Simpson, *Bluegrass Houses and Their Traditions*, pp. 141–143, 148; and Hamilton Busbey, "The Trotting Horse in America," *Harper's New Monthly Magazine* 47 (September 1873): 612–613.

20. The issue of allowing yearlings to trot was a contentious one in 1871, and Custer disapproved of the practice, as he makes clear in letter #12. But it won adherents, and in answer to his question, "What may we not expect?" the yearling record stood at 2:23 for the mile before the century was out. See Hamilton Busbey, "The Evolution of the Trotting-horse (Second Paper)," *Scribner's Magazine* 19 (June 1896): 704.

21. This confident assertion was very much

a matter of opinion and one certainly open to challenge. Dexter, foaled in 1857 in New York state, was the premier trotting horse in the United States from 1864 until he was retired from competition at the end of the 1867 season when he was bought by a gentleman horse fancier for $35,000. He was the top miler in 1865–67, setting a time of 2:17.25 in harness against the clock in his last public appearance, on August 14, 1867. He had met Lady Thorne periodically since 1865, losing occasionally, winning more often. Dexter's best time in a two-mile race—4:51—was made against Lady Thorne shortly before his retirement. Precisely why Custer thought Lady Thorne, whose fastest mile, 2:18.25, was recorded in October 1869, would "undoubtedly" have beaten Dexter's record is unclear. One expert—indeed, an editor of *Turf, Field and Farm*—argued in 1873 that it was "manifest" to all serious students of the subject that Dexter retired from competition before he reached "his highest development" and would have been quite capable of reducing his time for the mile to 2:12 or so. Custer's reference to Ericsson as Woodford Mambrino's superior as a sire seems to have been wishful thinking based more on loyalty to the horse's owner, K. C. Barker, than on the record. See John Elderkin, "The Turf and the Trotting Horse in America," *Atlantic Monthly* 21 (May 1868): 526–531; and Busbey, "Trotting Horse in America," pp. 609–610, and "Evolution of the Trotting Horse (First Paper)," pp. 580–581.

10. [August 1872]

1. The meeting at Lexington actually took place over six days—September 16–21—so that the schedule Custer outlined was inaccurate. The two horses he mentions, Planetarium and Bazaine, turned in respectable performances in the spring meeting. Planetarium won two victories early on and looked like a "world-beater" but then faded; Bazaine, having run second to Planetarium in the three-year-old

sweepstakes, came on to win the Clay Stakes (mile heats for three-year-olds) but did not live up to promise in the summer's racing in the East. Neither horse ran in the Kentucky Association's fall meeting. See "The Turf: Review of the Racing Season of 1872 (Second Paper)," p. 4, and "(Third Paper)," p. 4.

2. American thoroughbred racing before the Civil War retained elements of a gentleman's sport in which wagers were made in the spirit of determining who owned the fastest horse. After Appomattox it became a business, attracting a large public eager to bet at the races. The American Jockey Club strove to make the turf respectable, and the *New York Times* in 1866 gave the newly completed Jerome Park course a clean bill of health, noting that "there is no bribing of jockeys, no 'dosing' of horses with laudanum." The Jockey Club hoped to police racing throughout the country to ensure uniform high standards on all tracks and encourage the public interest that between 1867 and 1875 saw the three races that make up the American Triple Crown—the Belmont Stakes at Elmont, New York, the Preakness Stakes at Pimlico, Maryland, and the Kentucky Derby at Louisville—get their start. They also confirmed the revolution in American racing that had taken place since 1860 as the four-mile heats that were once the supreme test of a horse's speed and endurance gave way to "sprints" or "dashes" of a mile and a quarter or a mile and a half (speed, traditionalists lamented, at the expense of bottom). The age of the contending horses underwent a corresponding reduction as the more mature champions of the past were replaced by two- and three-year-olds in the public's esteem. Custer's comments would suggest that he was out of sympathy with the commercialization of what had been a gentleman's sport and was unpersuaded that the Jockey Club's own high standards of conduct pertained on the average race course in the United States. See Willett, *The Thoroughbred,*

p. 159; and Longrigg, *History of Horse Racing*, pp. 223–225. For two contemporary viewpoints on the issue of speed versus bottom—or dash races versus heats over longer distances—compare Busbey, "Running Turf in America (First Paper)," pp. 96–97, to "The Turf: Review of the Racing Season of 1872 (First Number)," *New York Times*, November 29, 1872, p. 2, which labeled the fears of concerned horsemen "sheer nonsense."

3. Trotting, like thoroughbred racing, was in a state of flux after the Civil War. It was under assault for the abuses associated with it even as it was enjoying rising and widespread popularity. In 1868 a writer predicted the decline of racing as an important consideration in trotting circles since the best trotters were being bought up by wealthy gentlemen for their private use. (This development seemed especially pronounced in light of the great Dexter's abrupt retirement from competition the previous year.) The writer thought the kind of trotting whereby gentlemen engaged in friendly trials or "brushes" with other drivers on the open roads was a healthy recreation, furnishing "the great corrective of American life" by providing a release from urban and business pressures. But the amateur spirit was in fact losing ground. Roger Longrigg notes that the 1,095 trotting races of 1869 had increased to 3,304 by 1875. In the same period, the moral tone of the trotting track underwent a transformation. By the end of the 1860's trotting had become a major vehicle for gambling, and respectable society—at least the female half of it—shunned the races. "There was little or no system in the management of the trotting turf," a contemporary wrote, "and consequently it was difficult to put a stop to rascality. There was no positive way to punish fraud. A driver might be ruled off one course, but he cared little for this, since the punishment did not extend to other courses." Thus, in February 1870 several local trotting associations came together to form the National Associa-

tion for the Promotion of the Interests of the American Trotting Turf. Its primary goal was the promulgation of a code of standards, to be enforced by a Board of Appeals on all participating tracks. So great were the board's discretionary powers that a rival organization, the Trainers and Drivers Protective Association, sprang up in 1873. Ultimately the two groups fused into the National Trotting Association, and the desired reform in the sport's image followed as careful policing forced the criminal element from the trotting circuit. All that was needed to make trotting simon-pure was the elimination of gambling on the track. "The revolution is sure to come," Hamilton Busbey wrote in 1873, "and after the revolution thousands will pass through the gates of our trotting parks who now stand aloof." In this and the following letter, then, Custer was speaking out of the same sense of concern manifested by other friends of the turf in the early 1870's, though it is noteworthy that he was not opposed to gambling per se and indeed urged the elimination of racing abuses so that those with "great interests at stake" could count on an honest result. See Elderkin, "The Turf and the Trotting Horse in America," pp. 532–533; Busbey, "Evolution of the Trotting-horse (Second Paper)," p. 699; Longrigg, *History of Horse Racing*, pp. 245–246; and Busbey, "Trotting Horse in America," pp. 611–612.

4. Lord Dundreary was the dull-witted but self-confident and pompous representative of English aristocracy in *Our American Cousin* (1858), the comedy by Tom Taylor that President Abraham Lincoln was watching the night he was assassinated. Taylor, a British playwright and satirist, edited *Punch* magazine for several years and had some seventy plays on the London stage to his credit. *Our American Cousin* had its debut in New York City, and Dundreary entered into the language to characterize any empty-headed swell. It also gave name to a fashion, the so-

called Dundreary whiskers (long and split into two distinct points) associated with Lieutenant Cooke of the Seventh Cavalry, among others.

5. Kentucky boasted three distinctions: its bourbon, its horses, and its beautiful women. Custer conceded all three but then chose to challenge the third as it applied to Louisville. This was hardly in keeping with his customary chivalry, and it remains a mystery what prompted his outburst. Always a flirt and a ladies' man (despite his devotion to Libbie) and worldly enough to jest about *The Black Crook* and New York's marriage mores, Custer could hardly censure the women of Louisville for aspiring to look like Lydia Thompson. An established English music hall performer, plump yet winsomely girlish in keeping with the tastes of the time, Thompson (1836–1908) and the rest of The British Blondes took America by storm in 1868, and Custer was one of her rapt admirers. He watched the troupe perform in Chicago in 1869 and reported back to Libbie that one of the papers "informed the public that I was pursuing blondes instead of the dusky maidens of the Plains." He professed to be scandalized by the suggestion, but the next spring jotted in a young lady's autograph book that his favorite style of beauty was "Blonde (a la Lydia Thompson)." Nevertheless, Custer came down hard on the ladies of Louisville for wanting to emulate the star. A later observer was kinder, writing: "The women of Kentucky have long had reputation for beauty. An average type is a refinement on the English blonde—greater delicacy of form, feature, and color. A beautiful Kentucky woman is apt to be exceedingly beautiful. Her voice is low and soft; her hands and feet delicately formed; her skin pure and beautiful in tint and shading; her eyes blue or brown, and hair nut brown or golden brown; to all which is added a certain unapproachable refinement." See Young, *Famous Actors and Actresses on the American Stage*, II, 1075–1079; G. Custer

to E. Custer, December 2, 1869, in Merington, ed., *The Custer Story*, pp. 229–230; Gordon L. Olson, "A Bit of Custer Humor," *Chronicle, the Magazine of the Historical Society of Michigan* 13 (Winter 1977–78): 27; and James Lane Allen, *The Blue-Grass Region of Kentucky, and Other Kentucky Articles* (New York: Macmillan, 1900), pp. 40–41. Lydia Thompson had become quite the celebrity in the United States by the beginning of the 1870's, and her name continued to pop up in the Custer story. On February 5, 1872, for example, Elizabeth Custer recorded in her diary that Grand Duke Alexis of Russia, whom the Custers accompanied on a portion of his American tour, was concerned "only with the pretty girls" and music— "he sings magnificently, and has already learned Lydia Thompson's music hall ditty—which he renders 'If efer I cease to luf . . .'" (Merington, ed., *The Custer Story*, p. 247); while a journalist a year later wrote that Custer was a "chivalric young soldier . . . whose hair flies around in a fight like Lydia Thompson's in a breakdown, but whose mind is at anchor all the while, like a countryman's eyes fastened on said Lydia" (George Alfred Townsend, in the *Cincinnati Commercial*, June 30, 1873, reprinted in the *Little Big Horn Associates Research Review* 6 [Summer 1972]: 30).

11. [October 1872]
1. In the years before the Civil War, Alexander Keene Richards bred horses at his Kentucky estate, Blue Grass Park, near Georgetown, where he experimented with the improvement of American blood lines by importing Arabian stock. He made his initial trip to the Middle East for this purpose in 1851–1853, and returned in 1855–1857, taking along with him the artist Edward Troye, who was to make portraits of Arabian stallions and paint whatever else captured his fancy. Richards remained Troye's most steadfast patron and, along with Robert A. Alexander of Woodburn Farm, hosted the

artist's family through much of the Civil War. Afterward, with his fortune depleted, Richards continued to provide Troye with quarters so that he could still make a living as an artist in an impoverished South. Troye died at Richards' home in 1874. As a man who had dedicated his life to horse breeding, Richards spoke as a formidable authority on the subject of Jim Irving's pedigree. See Coleman, "Edward Troye," pp. 37–44.

12. [November 1872]

1. Custer was here modifying the stance taken by highly respected trotting horse trainer and driver Hiram Woodruff, who in 1845 inherited Harlem Park, in northern Manhattan, and operated "America's most famous trotting stables." In a book published in 1867, *The Trotting Horse of America*, Woodruff argued that trotters, unlike thoroughbreds, had to be brought along slowly and would attain their prime at seven or eight. Before the 1870's ended, this conventional wisdom was demolished by the successful trials conducted by Leland Stanford in California, who demonstrated that trotters, like thoroughbreds, could perform handsomely as two-year-olds and, despite Custer's reservations, yearlings. At Stanford's Palo Alto Farm "the track education of colts began as soon as they were weaned," and he maintained that "if the exercise is judicious the colt takes no harm from it. I do not remember a single instance where an animal of mine was injured by early work." The fruit of this changing philosophy in the 1870's was a boom in races matching young trotters—a development very much in the interest of the breeders who wished to establish the quality of their stock as soon as possible. See Longrigg, *History of Horse Racing*, pp. 239, 242–243, 246; and Busbey, "Evolution of the Trotting-horse (Second Paper)," pp. 702, 704.

2. There was some justification for the *Turf, Field and Farm*'s position. Before the Civil War only one horse—Flora Temple—trotted the mile in less than 2:20; in the years after, the record dropped steadily, and by 1873 eight horses had trotted below 2:20 and another seventeen below 2:23. Thus, while horses that could trot in the low 2:20's were hardly a dime a dozen, they were no longer rare. See Elderkin, "The Turf and the Trotting Horse in America," p. 532; and Busbey, "Trotting Horse in America," p. 612. A century after Custer wrote, the one-mile trotting record stood at 1:54.8.

3. The month before, on October 15, 1872, Prospero trotted the mile in 2:33.5, a time regarded as "wonderful, considering the age of the performer." While Custer stressed the fact that Prospero brought $20,000 despite his being a gelding, it is worth remembering that the same was true of the great Dexter, and the buyer in both cases was obviously willing to forego future rewards for present gratification. See Busbey, "Trotting Horse in America," p. 613.

4. Custer's position on prices for trotting horses seems reasonable. He, like most of his contemporaries, was naturally impressed by the enormous sums commanded by exceptional performers. In 1868, John Elderkin estimated that the price increase for trotters had been "about one hundred per cent every ten years," adding that "it is now no unusual thing for fast trotting horses, and fine stock horses of the best trotting blood, to sell for amounts varying from ten to twenty thousand dollars." Five years later Hamilton Busbey noted that "a horse of first-class speed commands from $20,000 to $35,000." And, as Custer pointed out, average trotting horses had also substantially appreciated in value, to the real and long-term benefit of the breeders. See Elderkin, "The Turf and the Trotting Horse in America," p. 532; and Busbey, "Trotting Horse in America," p. 612.

13. [January 1873]

1. The outbreak of epizootic, an equine influenza, in New Orleans was so severe

that at the time it was assumed the Louisiana Jockey Club would simply cancel its December meeting. See "The Turf: Racing Statistics of 1872," *New York Times*, December 13, 1872, p. 2.

2. This was in sharp contrast to the Louisiana Jockey Club's inaugural meeting in April 1872, which was pronounced "a great success both in a racing and financial point of view." A crowd of eight thousand attended on the opening day. See "The Turf: Review of the Racing Season of 1872 (First Number)," p. 2.

3. In 1872, Ulysses Grant was running for a second term as president. The South was still in the throes of Reconstruction, and the political situation, complicated everywhere by the strong third-party movement of Liberal Republicans challenging Grant's renomination and then re-election, was especially byzantine in the former Confederate states where various Republican and Democratic factions vied for the vote. Louisiana's politics in 1872, according to Joe Gray Taylor, "in complexity of shifting alliances might be compared to the Italian peninsula during the Renaissance or China during the 1920s and 1930s." But as the election neared, party lines sorted themselves out, with the regular Republicans opposing the Fusion ticket combining two Democratic factions and the Liberal Republicans on a platform marked by its racial conservatism. The election's prelude and the election itself were "so shot through with fraud that no one ever had any idea who had actually won," Taylor writes. "There is no question that the vote, as reported, elected the Fusionist ticket, but it is impossible to determine how closely the vote reported corresponded with the vote cast. . . . The election was dishonest, the count was dishonest, and there was no honest way in which the result could be decided." The Returning Board established to decide the question was under the governor, Henry Clay Warmoth, himself a prominent Fusionist, but this advantage was offset by the fact that

Grant's easy re-election put pressure on the Liberal Republicans in the Fusion to return to the regular party and, by their support, regain the ground lost by their defection and earn what preferment was to be had. Eventually *two* Returning Boards were seeking legal recognition, and when a Republican-appointed judge gave the nod to the board favoring his party, Warmoth resorted to a last maneuver whereby both boards were abolished, to be replaced by an elected board. Since the state senate was to do the electing, and since the legislature was not in session, the power devolved upon the governor to *appoint* the board. This Warmoth did on December 3, and the next day it certified the Fusionist victory. But the original pro-Republican board had not given up and on its own accord announced the same day that the Republicans had carried Louisiana. Next it prevailed upon a federal circuit judge to order the legislature closed to illegal assembly—that is, to the assembly of those individuals declared elected by Warmoth's board. Grant's administration was involved in this ploy and had previously arranged to back the judge's order with a show of force. Since the judge issued his order on the evening of December 5, and two companies of federal troops moved in by 2:00 A.M. on the sixth, Custer naturally saw the Republicans carrying out their nefarious deed at the midnight hour "as if shunning the light of open day." Under the circumstances, the final election results were unsurprising: the Republicans were declared the winners with substantial majorities in both houses of the state legislature. The issue did not end there, but the character of the whole episode—perfectly consistent with that of Louisiana politics generally after the Civil War—suggests that there was no clear right or wrong, and that Custer in his remarks was simply speaking as a Democrat long opposed to the Republican Party and to its leader and his eventual nemesis, President Grant. See Joe

Gray Taylor's careful untangling of the affair in *Louisiana Reconstructed, 1863–1877* (Baton Rouge: Louisiana State University Press, 1974), pp. 227–246.

4. Gambling was the ultimate barrier to racing's attaining respectability, especially in the blatant form Custer encountered it at New Orleans. The test that all who wished to improve the image of the track automatically applied was acceptance of the sport by the opposite sex. "Where pure-browed woman goes, order and gentility reign," Hamilton Busbey asserted in 1873. What is interesting here and in Custer's comments is the objection, not to gambling, but to its detrimental effects on the moral and social climate of the sport. Indeed, Custer himself gambled at poker and the races and waged a gallant war against what was one of his few remaining vices, since he long ago had given up drinking and (so the story goes) swearing and had never used tobacco. His New Year's resolution for 1870, solemnly offered in writing to his wife, promised: "From the 1st of January, and forever, I cease, so long as I am a married man, to play cards or any other game of chance for money or its equivalent." A visit to a luxurious New York gambling casino the following year failed to shake his resolve: ". . . would my girl believe it? I remained nearly two hours without the slightest desire to succumb to my old foe." And in 1873 he was able to boast, "I have told Satan to get behind me so far as poker is concerned. Notwithstanding the pleasure and excitement I used to find in it, it no longer possesses the slightest power over me, and I never feel tempted to take a hand. You often said I could never give it up. But I have always said I could give up anything—except you." The repeated references suggest that Custer's struggle with gambling was not a one-sided contest and that the ground gained after one bout was sometimes surrendered up in the next. We have Custer's own testimony on this point when he wrote the inspector general of the army from Elizabethtown,

December 30, 1872, in response to the charge that some of his officers were "addicted to gambling": "Exactly what meaning is intended to apply to the word 'gambling' which is construed differently by different persons I am at a loss to understand. If by gambling the act of betting money or risking it on games of chance or contests of speed between horses and if among games of chance are included that usually known as poker, and similar games my answer is that so far as my knowledge and belief extends none of the officers of this command are 'addicted to gambling' except the Commanding Officer and he is addicted to it only so far as it neither interfere with his duties, violate any rule of propriety nor meddle with other peoples business." (See Busbey, "Trotting Horse in America," p. 612; G. Custer to E. Custer, December, 1869, 1871, June 26, 1873, in Merington, ed., *The Custer Story*, pp. 231, 237, 250; and G. Custer to D. B. Sackett, December 30, 1872, quoted in Crackel, "Custer's Kentucky," p. 150.) Though Custer did apparently break his gambling habit and stick to his resolution, the impression has persisted that he was an avid gambler and encouraged his officers to participate in poker and high-stake horse races. See, for example, the materials in John M. Carroll, comp., *Custer in Texas: An Interrupted Narrative* (New York: Sol Lewis/Liveright, 1975), pp. 97, 138, 140, 162–163, 266–267; the Frederick W. Benteen letters in John M. Carroll, ed., *The Benteen-Goldin Letters on Custer and His Last Battle* (New York: Liveright, 1974), pp. 248, 254–256, 258, 262; Wagner, *Old Neutriment*, pp. 92–96; and, for an objective assessment, Edward S. Godfrey's views in Minnie D. Millbrook, "Godfrey on Custer," *Little Big Horn Associates Research Review* 6 (Winter 1972): 79.

5. Dr. Elisha Warfield, Jr., was the eldest son of a Maryland family that moved to Kentucky in 1790. Nineteen at the time, Warfield went on to earn a medical degree, but after teaching at Transylvania

University in Lexington in 1809, he abandoned medicine and prospered as a merchant. In 1831 the Warfields moved to an estate known as The Meadows and the doctor became one of Kentucky's leading horse breeders. In 1836 he bred the filly that fourteen years later gave birth to the immortal Lexington. The point of Custer's story, of course, is that because of an outburst of temper—quite out of character, according to his reputation as "gentle, genial and eminently just"—Warfield came perilously close to nipping Lexington's unrivaled career at stud in the bud. See Simpson, *Bluegrass Houses and Their Traditions*, pp. 105–109.

6. John Gilpin's wonderful ride was the subject of William Cowper's humorous poem, first published in 1782, "The Diverting History of John Gilpin; Showing How He Went Further than He Intended, and Came Safe Home Again." The picture Custer meant to conjure up was of Gilpin astride his bolting horse:

Away went Gilpin, neck or naught;
  Away went hat and wig;
He little dreamt, when he set out,
  Of running such a rig.

The wind did blow, the cloak did fly,
  Like streamer long and gay,
Till loop and button failing both,
  At last it flew away.

. . . .

The dogs did bark, the children scream'd,
  Up flew the windows all;
And every soul he cried out, Well done!
  As loud as he could bawl.

See *Poems, by the Late William Cowper, Esq., of the Inner-Temple*, 2 vols. (London: W. H. Reid, 1820), I, 367.

IV. DAKOTA TERRITORY, 1873–1875

1. Custer, *"Boots and Saddles,"* p. 11.
2. G. Custer to E. Custer, August 15, 1874, in Merington, ed., *The Custer Story*, p. 275. In the version of the letter printed in"*Boots and Saddles,*" p. 304, Cus-

ter mentions the other members of the hunting party but still takes credit for killing the grizzly. It is a small matter, but typical of Custer historiography, that there is dispute over the General's claim. Journalists along with the expedition reported the kill; two were noncommittal about who was most responsible (*Bismarck Tribune*, September 2, 1874, and *St. Paul Pioneer*, August 25, 1874), while one, reporting in the *New York Tribune* for August 29, 1874, gave Custer almost all the credit (see Krause and Olson, *Prelude to Glory*, pp. 28, 69–70, 223). Luther North, who in other respects was critical of Custer's marksmanship, assigned him the honor of killing the grizzly (see Danker, ed., *Man of the Plains*, p. 187; Grinnell, *Two Great Scouts and Their Pawnee Battalion*, p. 242; and Robert Bruce, *The Fighting Norths and Pawnee Scouts: Narratives and Reminiscences of Military Service on the Old Frontier* [New York: Robert Bruce, 1932], p. 20); but Custer's own brother-in-law and acting assistant adjutant general on the expedition, Lieutenant James Calhoun, recorded in his diary for August 7, 1874, that four persons shot the bear, including Custer (see Lawrence A. Frost, ed., *With Custer in '74: James Calhoun's Diary of the Black Hills Expedition* [Provo, Utah: Brigham Young University Press, 1979], pp. 70–71). Private Theodore Ewert, who was never lacking for an opinion and was unimpressed by his commanding officer, pooh-poohed the whole affair and insisted that the bear was a cinnamon, not a grizzly, but he abandoned the subject when he saw "the sour looks and angry frown" his remark occasioned (see John M. Carroll and Lawrence A. Frost, eds., *Private Theodore Ewert's Diary of the Black Hills Expedition of 1874* [Piscataway, N.J.: CRI Books, 1976], pp. 58–59). Donald Jackson, in the standard history of the Black Hills Expedition, *Custer's Gold: The United States Cavalry Expedition of 1874* (New Haven: Yale University Press, 1966), p. 94, offers an appropriate summation of the grizzly controversy: "Nobody asked whether or nor Custer's bullet had been the fatal one. It was Custer's bear the way it was Custer's expedition." There is an extensive literature on the Black Hills Expedition; besides Jackson's *Custer's Gold* the reader should also consult the more recent, well-documented discussion by James D. McLaird and Lesta V. Turchen, "Exploring the Black Hills, 1855–1875: Reports of the Government Expeditions (Colonel William Ludlow and the Custer Expedition, 1874)," *South Dakota History* 4 (Summer 1974): 281–319.

3. Since the Sioux Expedition of 1876 is at the heart of the ongoing Custer myth, its bibliography is simply enormous. Of the bibliographical guides available, Tal Luther's *Custer High Spots* (Ft. Collins, Colo.: Old Army Press, 1972) is the one to begin with. Edgar I. Stewart, *Custer's Luck* (Norman: University of Oklahoma Press, 1955), has been the standard treatment since its publication; but several recent monographs have offered good overviews of the Sioux Expedition, notably John S. Gray, *Centennial Campaign: The Sioux War of 1876* (Ft. Collins, Colo.: Old Army Press, 1976).

14. [October 1873]

1. Custer was riding Vic, a thoroughbred (sire Uncle Vic, grandsire Lexington) acquired in Kentucky. In letter #15 he relates an anecdote about this horse—his mount the day he died and the subject of speculation that he was captured by the Indians and survived his master's Last Stand.

2. Custer's jocular reference to a race with the Sioux, rendered in the idiom of the turf, refers to the narrowest escape he ever had in action against Indians. A restless sort, Custer was rarely content to plod along with the main column when in the field. When he was not off chasing game, he was habitually far out in front of the column scouting the route and locating a suitable camp for the night. Such

was his preferred role in the Yellowstone Expedition, particularly after he and General Stanley had a contretemps soon after taking the field. Thus, on the morning of August 4, 1873, Custer, with a squadron of ninety men, was well in advance of the main column when, a little before noon, they dismounted by the Yellowstone to await the others. Since the spot chosen would be the expeditions's campsite, the soldiers proceeded to unsaddle their horses and make themselves comfortable. Custer remembered that "after selecting a most inviting spot for my noonday nap, then arranging my saddle and buckskin coat in the form of a comfortable pillow, I removed my boots, untied my cravat, and opened my collar, prepared to enjoy to the fullest extent the delights of an outdoor siesta." But there was to be no rest that day. A party of six Sioux rode boldly up to stampede the grazing horses. Driven off by rifle fire, the Sioux lingered long enough to be sure they had attracted the attention of the cavalry, then began a measured retreat in front of the troops. It was the old decoy trick—the one that had worked so well against Captain William Judd Fetterman and his eighty men near Fort Phil Kearny in December 1866 and had resulted in a slaughter in which "not one escaped or was spared to tell the tale." Since Custer penned these words as part of a full description of the Fetterman battle just the year before, he should have been well aware of the Indian ploy. But it was vintage stuff, and since the Indians were always so elusive the chance to engage them in a fight was too much to resist. So with some twenty troopers under the command of his brother-in-law, Lieutenant James Calhoun, and his brother, Lieutenant Thomas W. Custer, the general set off in pursuit of the Sioux. When he found that his detachment was not gaining ground, he ordered a halt and approached the Indians himself escorted by either one or two orderlies. The details are not entirely clear since Custer's accounts of the episode varied, but the self-portrait he painted is a revealing one. Halting "a few hundred yards" from the rest of his men, he sent the orderly (orderlies?) back with a message, leaving himself entirely on his own. Like a rocket fired into space jettisoning its successive stages, he had extricated himself from the main command, then from his squadron, then from his detachment, and then finally from his escort, placing himself in gravest peril as became instantly apparent when the Indian decoys, realizing that the game was up, turned to charge on Custer—and were joined by 300–400 warriors who at the same moment burst out of a nearby woods where they had been waiting in ambush. So began the race for life that Custer alludes to in this letter and fleshed out fully, as he said he would, in an article in *The Galaxy* a few years later:

To understand our relative positions the reader has only to imagine a triangle whose sides are almost equal: their length in this particular instance being from three to four hundred yards, the three angles being occupied by Colonel [Tom] Custer and his detachment, the Indians, and myself. Whatever advantage there was in length of sides fell to my lot, and I lost no time in availing myself of it. Wheeling my horse suddenly around, and driving the spurs into his sides, I rode as only a man rides whose life is the prize, to reach Colonel Custer and his men, not only in advance of the Indians, but before any of them could cut me off. . . .
Swiftly over the grassy plain leaped my noble steed, each bound bearing me nearer to both friends and foes. Had the race been confined to the Indians and myself the closeness of the result would have satisfied an admirer even of the Derby. Nearer and nearer our paths approached each other, making it appear almost as if I were one of the line of warriors, as the latter bore down to accomplish the destruction of the little group of troopers in front. Swifter seem to fly our mettled steeds, the one to save, the other to destroy, until the common goal has almost been reached—a few more bounds, and friends and foes will be united—will form one contending mass.

The climax to this dramatic account was provided by a stout resistance by the troopers in Custer's detachment who were progressively augmented by the separate elements sloughed off during the day, until the whole command was reunited around 3:00 P.M. and the last of the Indians melted away. At the time, Elizabeth Custer was moved to reflection on her husband's close call and the whole pattern of his life. "Swept along as I am in the current of your eventful life I can still stop to realize that your history is simply marvelous," she wrote. "Every event seems to fit into every other event like the blocks in a child's puzzle. Does it not seem strange to you?" But even she could not have imagined the coincidence that three years later would have her reading the General's account of his brush with the Sioux in *The Galaxy* only a few days before he died on the Little Big Horn. *The Galaxy* had been publishing Custer's Civil War memoirs since January of that year. But perhaps because the latest installments had not been received from the field, or more probably because Custer had left the manuscript of his 1873 fight with the editors before departing for the West to join the Sioux Expedition, *The Galaxy* interrupted the Civil War memoirs to carry Custer's more topical essay, "Battling with the Sioux on the Yellowstone," in its July issue. Whatever *The Galaxy's* reasons for its scheduling, Mrs. Custer had the melancholy fortune of reading her husband's account of his race for life against the Sioux exactly four days before he lost the rematch. "It is the hottest day of the season, yet cold chills are running down my back at your description of the Yellowstone fight," she confessed to him in a letter he would never receive and that, returned, would remain unopened among her papers until her sunset years. See Custer, *My Life on the Plains*, pp. 83–85 (his whole account of the Fetterman battle eerily foreshadows the reactions to his own Last Stand in tone and language); Custer, "Battling with the Sioux on the Yellowstone," pp. 91–102; G. A. Custer, "Official Report of the Engagements with Indians on the 4th and 11th ultimo" (August 15, 1873), reprinted in Custer, *"Boots and Saddles,"* pp. 280–284; E. Custer to G. Custer, quoted in Frost, *General Custer's Libbie*, p. 205; and E. Custer to G. Custer, June [21], 1876, in Merington, ed., *The Custer Story*, pp. 303–304.

3. The years had brought wisdom—or at least discretion—since Custer's first patrol in Indian country back in 1867 when, as he was quite willing to admit, he exhibited more than a little imprudence in chasing off with his hounds after antelope and a lone buffalo (letter #1). He had learned from that experience and, especially, from the anxiety that his behavior caused his wife. Thus, on all his expeditions into Sioux country he reined himself in. "I remember your wishes and ride at the head of the column, keeping inside our lines all the time, although it is a great deprivation to me not to go outside and hunt," he reassured Elizabeth during the Black Hills Expedition of 1874. "I feel exactly like some young lady extremely fond of dancing, who, having a cold, has been forbidden by her anxious mamma to do more than look on at some elegant party" (G. Custer to E. Custer, July 15, 1874, in *"Boots and Saddles,"* p. 301).

4. Custer's fondness, indeed mania, for animals of every stripe is discussed in all three volumes of Mrs. Custer's memoirs. Long suffering and patient as she was about her ever-boyish Boy General's "animal kingdom," she admitted to drawing the line at the wild cat and provided the sequel to his story:

As the soldiers and citizens all knew the general's love of pets, we had constant presents. Many of them I would have gladly declined, but notwithstanding a badger, por-

cupine, raccoon, prairie-dog, and wild turkey, all served their brief time as members of our family. They were comparatively harmless, and I had only the inconvenience to encounter. When a ferocious wild-cat was brought in, with a triumphant air, by the donor, and presented with a great flourish, I was inclined to mutiny. [It was Custer who acquired the animal while on the expedition, forewarning her by letter.] My husband made allowance for my dread of the untamed creature, and decided to send him into the States, as a present to one of the zoological gardens; for in its way it was a treasure. While it remained with us it was kept in the cellar. Mary [their black domestic] used to make many retreats, tumbling up the stairs, when the cat flew at her the length of its chain. She was startled so often that at last she joined with me in requesting its removal as soon as convenient. The general regretted giving it up, but . . . [a soldier] was called to chloroform and box it for the journey. Colonel Tom [Custer] printed some facetious words on the slate of the cover—something like "Do not fondle." They were somewhat superfluous, for no one could approach the box, after the effects of the chloroform had passed away, without encountering the fiery-red eyes and such scratchings and spittings and mad plunges as suggested the propriety of keeping one's distance.

En route, Mrs. Custer recalled, the animal broke its box and gave the freight agent responsible "a wretched day." But the journey was finally completed, and "when we received a letter of thanks from the Scientific Board for so splendid a specimen, I was relieved to know that the wild-cat was at last where it could no longer create a reign of terror." See *"Boots and Saddles,"* pp. 244–245 and p. 298 for G. Custer to E. Custer, September 28, 1873.

5. During the Yellowstone Expedition, Custer formed a new enthusiasm, taxidermy. The taxidermist who was a member of the expedition's scientific corps taught Custer the art, and by early September he could "preserve animals for all practical purposes." He practiced his new hobby long into the night, to the despair

of the two soldiers who assisted him and who, after an all-day march, had every reason to be disgruntled. Custer preserved five heads, a grizzly bear skin, and the "*ne plus ultra* of all," the "King of the Forest." "I have succeeded in preserving him entire—antlers, head, neck, body, legs, and hoofs—in fine condition, so that he can be mounted and look *exactly as in life.* . . . The scientists informed me that there were but few specimens on this continent of elk preserved entire, and none so fine as mine." Custer had originally intended to mount only the head, neck, and antlers and present the trophy to Elizabeth, but since he had gone all the way with it and it now required a room of its own, he decided to present it to the Audubon Club in Detroit instead. See G. Custer to E. Custer, September 6, 1873, in *"Boots and Saddles,"* pp. 292–293.

6. A slip of the pen, providing another, albeit inadvertent, tribute to Maida, whose death Custer had mourned in letter #7. He meant either Blucher, one of the two staghounds whose tenacious work he goes on to describe and, according to his wife, his favorite dog at this time, or Tuck, his choice judging from a letter he sent Elizabeth on July 19, 1873, though he fails to mention Tuck by name in the account that follows. See *"Boots and Saddles,"* pp. 109, 278.

7. Custer did not mention the work of the dogs in his letter to his wife describing his "good fortune" in killing the elk, but he did pay them their due in a letter to a friend, likely K. C. Barker, that was quoted in Mrs. Custer's *Following the Guidon*, pp. 216–217.

8. Sir Edwin Landseer (1802–1873), the preeminent nineteenth-century English painter of animals, was especially known for his renderings of dogs and deer. Custer has reference to one of Landseer's most famous canvases, *The Stag at Bay*, showing a noble stag knee-deep in water turning from one hound he has vanquished to meet the grim attack of a second. A dramatic—even melodramatic—scene, it captured the imagination of the English public and, through the good offices of Currier & Ives, the American public as well. Edward Troye, the painter mentioned in letter #9, was known, "emphatically," as "the Landseer of America." See Campbell Lennie, *Landseer: The Victorian Paragon* (London: Hamish Hamilton, 1976), pp. 95, 144; Busbey, "Running Turf in America (Second Paper)," p. 253; and Coleman, "Edward Troye," p. 36.

9. The photographer with the Yellowstone Expedition, William R. Pywell of Washington, D.C., has sunk into obscurity because none of the three government agencies involved in commissioning, paying, and supplying him secured a set of prints from his negatives, and the originals have long since been lost. The one notable exception is the picture of Custer with his trophy elk. He was so proud of the exploit it recorded that he must have ordered copies from Pywell directly, making it the solitary photograph from the Yellowstone Expedition to have received recognition and exposure. See John S. Gray, "Itinerant Frontier Photographers and Images Lost, Strayed or Stolen," *Montana, the Magazine of Western History* 28 (Spring 1978): 4–5; G. Custer to E. Custer, September 6, 1873, in *"Boots and Saddles,"* p. 292; and Custer to Barker (?), *Following the Guidon*, p. 217. Gray reports that a few other prints from the Pywell negatives have recently turned up.

10. Six days after the Yellowstone Expedition departed Fort Rice, Custer wrote Elizabeth to tell her that he "never saw such fine hunting as we have constantly had . . . I have done some of the best shooting I ever did . . ." So impressive was his total score for the three months the expedition was out that, besides itemizing it for the readers of *Turf, Field and Farm*, he passed it on to his wife and to Remington & Sons, the manufacturer of his hunting rifle, which reproduced his endorsement in its 1875 firearms catalog. See G. Custer to E. Custer, June 26, Sep-

tember 28, 1873, in *"Boots and Saddles,"* pp. 271, 298; and Parsons and du Mont, *Firearms in the Custer Battle,* p. 21.

15. August 23, 1875

1. It was Custer's boast in letter #13 that he owned "probably the finest pack of Scotch staghounds in this country," and his love for hunting dogs runs through his letters to wife, friends, and *Turf, Field and Farm.* He developed the interest during his stay in Texas when he was invited to go hunting by local planters. "I remember the General's delight at his first sight of the different packs—thirty-seven dogs in all—and his enthusiasm at finding that every dog responded to his master's horn," Mrs. Custer wrote. "He thereupon purchased a horn, and practiced in camp until he nearly split his cheeks in twain, not to mention the spasms into which we were driven; for his five hounds, presents from the farmers, ranged themselves in an admiring and sympathetic semicircle, accompanying all his practicing by tuning their voices until they reached the same key." Thereafter Custer was rarely without his dogs. They accompanied him on hunts and on campaigns; they ranged themselves at his feet, rested their heads on his lap, shared his bed and his food, got under foot, made nuisances of themselves, but never lost their special place in his affection. They were like people to him, and more than one critic has suggested that he treated them better than he did his soldiers. They were, as Mrs. Custer noted, his "chosen friends," and he naturally believed they were the best around. See Custer, *Tenting on the Plains,* pp. 161–162, 251.

2. Hunting remained one of Custer's principal recreations during his quiet stay in Kentucky, and he frequently rode with his hounds after deer in the hill country around Elizabethtown. Like other thoroughbred breeders, Price McGrath had obviously diversified if the two foxhounds he gave Custer were raised on his stock farm.

3. At the time Custer was writing, Jules Levy (ca. 1840–1903) was a cornet soloist with Patrick S. Gilmore's renowned Twenty-second Regiment Band of New York City. A man of monumental conceit, Levy was, in his own considered judgment, "the world's greatest cornet player, ALL THE TIME." Interestingly, his contemporaries tended to agree, and Gilmore billed him as "Jules Levy—The greatest cornet player living." A modern assessment notes:

> Levy's forte was fireworks. He loved to play a simple air or a few bars and then repeat it endlessly with all sorts of intricate and showy variations, finally closing with a flourish of runs and trills and ending on an altissimo note of prodigious volume and length. His execution was phenomenal. He played the impossible with the greatest of ease and artistry . . . He cultivated mannerisms calculated to impress and fill his hearers with awe and wonder. He refused to wear the uniform of the 22nd Regiment and always appeared in a dress suit, with medals adorning his breast and a monocle stuck in his eye.

No wonder Custer, renowned for his own flamboyant style, was so impressed! See H. W. Schwartz, *Bands of America* (Garden City, N.Y.: Doubleday, 1957), pp. 90–114; also Richard F. Goldman, *The Wind Band: Its Literature and Technique* (Westport, Conn.: Greenwood, 1975 [1962]), p. 59.

4. Elizabeth Custer remembered that during their Dakota years the General's pack of hounds numbered "about forty: the stag-hounds that run by sight, and are on the whole the fleetest and most enduring dogs in the world, and the fox-hounds that follow the trail with their noses close to the ground. The first rarely bark, but the latter are very noisy. The general and I used to listen with amusement to their attempts to strike the key-note of the bugler when he sounded the calls summoning the men to guard mount, stables, or retreat." Though Custer preferred his dogs pure, he believed that, if they were to be crossed, the best results would be obtained

by breeding fox- and staghounds. But one eyewitness to a trial between Custer's pack and that belonging to General Stanley and some of his officers in 1873 disagreed. Stanley's pack consisted mostly of pure-bred English greyhounds but also included "fighting greyhounds" with bloodhound, bulldog, or Scotch staghound blood in them. Far from being short on stamina, these mongrels had "much more endurance" than the English greyhounds and were "good fighters." In the trial that followed, the packs lit out after two jack rabbits and Custer's hounds were outdistanced both times by their rivals. "During the straight chase our slowest dog kept constantly ahead of General Custer's dogs," the eyewitness wrote, though it might be kept in mind that he was the son of Captain J. B. Irvine of the Twenty-second Infantry, one of Stanley's officers and a dog fancier himself, and thus not an entirely neutral observer. See Custer, *"Boots and Saddles,"* pp. 106–107; and J. B. Irvine, Jr., "A Hunt with General Custer," *Outdoor Life*, May, 1923, reprinted in John M. Carroll, ed., *A Seventh Cavalry Scrapbook #5* (Bryan, Tex.: privately printed, [1979]), pp. 8–10.

Treasured as they were, with his death Custer's dogs became just one more burden to be borne by his widow, and a short item in the *New York Herald* for July 22, 1876, is of poignant interest:

GENERAL CUSTER'S HOUNDS.

[From the Spirit of the Times, July 22]

We are in receipt of the following letter from a gentleman of St. Paul, Minn.:—

ST. PAUL, Minn., July 14, 1876.

DEAR SPIRIT:—I am to-day in receipt of a letter from Mrs. Custer, widow of General Custer, asking me if I could provide homes for a pack of stag hounds and a pack of fox hounds. Our State laws forbid the running of deer with dogs; besides, the Indians shoot them, so that hounds are no use here; but I have written Mrs. Custer to ship them all to me at once, as she wishes to leave the fort [Abraham Lincoln] as soon as possible. Can you, to oblige Mrs. Custer, send me the names of some gentlemen who would like the dogs, and pay the express charges on them to New York, and provide them with a good home? I will ship the dogs, on your recommend, to any gentlemen you may suggest, provided they are not disposed of before I hear from you. Yours respectfully,

C. W. McINTYRE.

We trust that we will at once receive a response to this letter from some party who can conveniently take care of such packs of hounds. The animals could be used in New Jersey when the fox-hunting season opens, and any person who takes the dogs can feel that he is doing a genuine service to the widow of the dead hero.

INDEX

Abdallah (horse), 78, 150 n.9
Adams' Express, 106
Alabama, 73
Alexander, A. John, 76–78, 80–81,
 150 n.7
Alexander, Robert S. C. A., 149 n.2,
 150 n.7, 156 n.1
Alexis, Grand Duke, 134 n.1, 156 n.5
American Jockey Club, 154 n.2
Amherstburg, Ontario, 56
Apache Indians, 21
Arapaho Indians, 118 n.4
Arkansas River, 4, 8, 20–21, 35, 70
Army officers: chivalric ideal of, x,
 113 n.3; diversions and pastimes of, x,
 113 n.2; modern image of, ix–x; status-
 consciousness of, 136 n.13
Asteroid (horse), 79, 151 nn.11–12
Audubon Club (Detroit), 62, 107,
 164 n.5
Australian (horse), 79, 151 n.13

Bakersville, Col., 69
Balaclava, battle of, 45, 134 n.5
Baltimore, Md., 65, 70, 147 n.13
Barker, Kirkland C., 10, 50, 52, 55–57,
 59–63, 83, 107, 120 n.11, 134 n.1,
 138 n.20, 139 n.23, 140 nn.4 and 1,

141 n.4, 154 n.21, 164 n.7
Barnitz, Albert, 122 n.3, 126 nn.4–5;
 quoted, 4
Barras, Charles M., 117 n.1
Bazaine (horse), 84, 154 n.1
Beckwith, W. G., 55, 57, 61–62, 141 n.3
Belmont (horse), 78, 80, 150 n.9
Belmont, August, 78, 80, 151 n.10
Belmont Stakes (Elmont, N.Y.), 154 n.2
Bennett, L. P., 68
Benteen, Frederick W., x, xvi, 114 n.5
Big Timber Creek, 58
Bismarck, D.T., 106
Black Crook, The (Barras), 7–8, 117 n.1
Black Hills, D.T., xiii
Black Hills Expedition, xiii, 104, 160 n.2
Black Kettle, 42, 143 n.3
Blackwood (horse), 76, 87
Blair Athol (horse), 80
Blucher (hound), 107, 138 n.20, 164 n.6
Blue Grass country (Ky.), 74, 76–77,
 86–87, 89, 93, 95, 105
Blue River, 70
Bogen, Mr., 68
Bonaparte, Napoleon, xi
Bonnie Scotland (horse), 74–75
Boston (horse), 151 n.12
Boston, Mass., 65